Corporate Response to Declining Rates of Growth

Corporate Response to Declining Rates of Growth

Katherine Hughes

LexingtonBooks
D.C. Heath and Company
Lexington, Massachusetts
Toronto

Library of Congress Cataloging in Publication Data

Hughes, Katherine.
  Corporate response to declining rates of growth.

  Includes index.
  1. Industrial management—United States. 2. Industry and state—
United States. 3. United States—Economic conditions—1971-
4. Stagnation (Economics) I. Title.
HD70.U5H8   658.4'062   81-47623
ISBN 0–669–04698–1   AACR2

Published simultaneously in Canada

Printed in the United States of America

International Standard Book Number: 0–669–04698–1

Library of Congress Catalog Card Number: 81–47623

Contents

List of Tables

Corporate
Response
to Declining Rates
of Growth

Part I
Economic Decline

This section of the book considers the decline of growth dynamism in the U.S. economy during the 1970s. In chapter 1 the debate surrounding the issue of slow growth is surveyed. Factors contributing to the phenomenon as well as proposals to ameliorate it are summarized. Questions surrounding the response of major American industrial corporations to declining rates of national output and to their own contracting revenues are considered in chapter 2. All avenues to the analysis of declining growth dynamism examined in this section of the book point to the need for a fundamental reevaluation of traditional approaches to management of the economy including private sector control of the capital allocation process.

1 The Growth Debate

After decades of enjoying the world's highest standard of living, Americans have been slow to come to terms with their faltering economy, an economy beset by rampant inflation, unemployment, towering debt, productive over-capacity, persistent underemployment, and negative international trade balances. They appear even more hesitant to grapple with the complexities of an increasingly interdependent global economy, one that reflects an international infrastructure no longer wholly dominated by the United States and the American dollar. Simultaneously, the realization is beginning to take hold that slower economic growth not only erodes material living standards but also diminishes our ability to sustain the social progress of recent decades. Rosy predictions of widely shared affluence and economic opportunity that seemed plausible during the growth decades that followed the Great Depression and World War II today sound naively optimistic as we note our overburdened public policymaking process and progressively deteriorating economy.

Economist Kenneth E. Boulding has recently predicted that facing up to slower economic growth will demand fundamental changes in our ways of thinking, in our habits and standards of decision making, and in our institutions.[1] Other observers of the contemporary American scene note that there is no way of knowing whether we face a permanent end to the steady increase in output of goods and services we have come to take for granted and to which the rest of mankind ostensibly aspires. Some argue that declining growth rates are temporary and merely reflect the "corrective" or "downward" side of various growth cycles such as the short-term inventory or business cycle, the mid-term investment cycle related to the utilization rate of existing productive capacity, or the longer-term cycles thought to be related to the diffusion of new technologies and demographic or socio-political change. Still others identify declining economic growth as a structural rather than cyclical phenomenon related to our transition from an industrial to a postindustrial economy. Finally, there are those who maintain that declining rates of growth reflect the shrinking investment opportunities afforded by advanced market capitalism.

The primary statistical indicator of well-being for a national economy is the *gross national product* (GNP), a measure of the total output of goods and services valued at market prices in constant dollars. Although the United States continues to produce the largest GNP in the world, per capita GNP now ranks behind that of nine other nations.[2] The following table suggests the extent of the recent decline in GNP growth rates for the U.S. economy relative to our major industrial competitors. Each of these nations reported reduced output after 1974, the year oil prices nearly quadrupled, moving from $3 to $11 per barrel. That price tripled once again, reaching an average price of $36 per barrel during 1980. Accelerating oil prices have reinforced the economic stagflation experienced by industrial nations during the last decade, but they do not tell the whole story. In the United States, oil imports from the Organization of Petroleum Exporting Countries (OPEC) took only 4 percent of GNP in 1980, up from 1 percent in 1970.[3]

Table 1-1 indicates declining rates of growth after 1974 and absolute decline in output for the United States, Canada, and the United Kingdom during 1980. This was not, to be sure, the first instance of contraction in the U.S. economy. During the postwar period of general economic expansion, rates of change in national output were negative during the years 1945–1947, 1954, 1957, 1970, and 1974–1975 as well.[4] Yet, in spite of previous experience with flat or negative growth, the intractable nature of the 1974–1980 slow-growth experience has motivated a legion of experts to explain the factors contributing to what the Council of Economic Advisers describes as the "pronounced decline in growth dynamism of the industrial world." With major econometric forecasters predicting continued sluggish growth for the U.S. economy throughout the 1980s, the search for a remedy has gone beyond the confines of conventional stabilization policies. That search now focuses on the infrastructure of our political economy. Produc-

Table 1-1
Growth Rates in Real Gross National Product

	1960–1973 (Annual Average %)	1974–1980 (Annual Average %)	1979–1980 (Annual Growth Rate %)
United States	4.2	2.4	− .2
Canada	5.4	2.6	− .5
Japan	10.5	4.2	5.0
France	5.7	2.9	1.8
West Germany	4.8	2.3	1.8
Italy	5.2	2.8	3.8
United Kingdom	3.2	.9	− 2.3

Source: Extracted from Council of Economic Advisers, *The Economic Report of the President 1981,* no. B-107, p. 353.

tivity, innovation, investment rationality, worker motivation, and the overall competitive strength of U.S. industry are becoming the concerns of a widening audience.[5]

The continuing integration of the global economy has also contributed to declining growth rates among industrial nations. From 1953 through 1974 world trade grew twice as fast as domestic output in Western industrial countries. In conjunction with trade expansion, labor specialization has increased with each nation intent on turning out those products best suited to its resources. As specialization and total world output have increased, U.S. industry has lost overall market share. Despite the 40 percent depreciation in the value of the dollar that made U.S. exports cheaper during the 1970s, the share of the world market claimed by U.S. manufactured goods fell 23 percent, compared to a 16 percent decline during the 1960s. A second indicator of the changing world economy is that imports and exports now constitute 24 percent of GNP in the United States, up from 14 percent in 1970. It has been estimated that the decline in the U.S. position during the 1970s alone amounted to $125 billion in lost production and the disappearance of two million manufacturing jobs.[6]

Other indicators of economic slowdown include labor productivity measures that began to exhibit decline as early as 1965. While U.S. productivity increased at an annual rate of 0.8 percent between 1973 and 1979, Japanese productivity grew at a 7 percent rate and West German productivity at a 4 percent rate.[7] Industrial research and development outlays as a percentage of GNP also began to decline during the mid-1960s. In addition, between 1960 and 1979 the private sector cut basic research funding in half, that is, from 8 to 4 percent of total research and development expenditures.[8] The rate of investment in U.S. plant and equipment as a percentage of GNP remained stable during the 1970s, although the pattern of investment throughout the economy was not aimed specifically at high-productivity operations. As productivity, innovation, and investment rates declined or flattened, even growth industries like aerospace, chemicals, plastics, drugs, telecommunications, and farm machinery lost world market share to formidable foreign competition. Other industries such as steel, textiles, footwear, consumer electronics, and auto manufacturing have been severely eroded—many firms within these industries are no longer viable outside protected domestic markets.[9]

As the performance of U.S. industry has deteriorated, we have failed to address squarely the question of how to deal with those corporations whose ability to attract capital is limited and which therefore may continue to face difficulties in the marketplace. We have developed no national policy concerning declining industries that for national security or employment reasons we cannot afford to see dismantled by foreign competition. We have no widely accepted criteria by which to judge the claims put forth by workers or corporate executives seeking government protection, subsidy, or regulation when their interests are threatened by changing economic conditions. When claimants succeed with their requests, aggregate growth suffers as the economy becomes locked into low-productivity or noncompetitive operations longer than circumstances warrant. The lack of a national industrial policy also puts the United States at a relative disadvantage. Our major industrial competitors do have national policies that direct economic resources toward high-productivity operations that can effectively compete in international markets. In the United States, however, most investment decisions are left to the private sector, where rate of return necessarily prevails over all else as the controlling decision criterion.

In addition to creating concern about the performance of U.S. industry, economic contraction is challenging our historical belief in economic growth as a panacea capable of diverting the social discontents of market capitalism. The difficult and divisive question of what constitutes a just distribution of economic resources in our society has been diffused by rapid economic expansion. The perhaps exaggerated claims or presumptions of entitlement that evolved during the postwar decades of abundance now conflict directly with the stringent economic tradeoffs and often overwhelming sense of apprehension that accompany a period of slow economic growth.

While some Americans seem determined to use credit or debt financing to prolong patterns of consumption conditioned by previously increasing levels of real disposable income, others feel entitled to the continuation of government social programs designed to lessen economic disparities between citizens. Still others feel entitled to deregulation, tax relief, and additional economic incentives for personal investment despite economic losses imposed on others. But it is also becoming possible to discern a developing sense of limits. This can be seen in the desire to contain the size of the federal bureaucracy and in the acknowledgement that the United States cannot afford both guns and butter forever. As we face up to slower economic growth, the recognition that an arms race on the postwar scale can be pursued only by making inroads into public services, social programs, and real disposable income cannot be avoided. Defense spending is a form of consumption and when the economy is forced to produce civilian and military goods simultaneously, the resulting higher prices and inflation ultimately undercut the standard of living for all citizens.[10] The income distribution issue is far from resolved and few parties seem willing to accept direct economic losses. But the notion that it would be in everyone's interest to try to reverse the current slow-growth trend by making basic changes in the way the economy operates, from our economic priorities, to the tax system, to an overhaul of our institutional infrastructure, is beginning to receive the level of attention required to stimulate a national debate.

Coping with slower economic growth need not result in pervasive pessimism or a nostalgic sense of loss. The most demanding requirement for dealing effectively with the socio-economic problems associated with slower growth is the development of a sense of limits, a notion of restraint, and an ability to make equitable economic tradeoffs. A fundamental transformation in the assumptions of the industrial era's growth paradigm is needed as we approach the problems related to slower rates of economic growth in a democratic society. The shared beliefs, assumptions, and values of those actively involved in shaping and managing our society must be reexamined. The assumptions of unending growth and material progress, the traditions of pragmatic self-interest and privileged access to the economic maximization game must be tempered by the exigencies of global interdependence and the need to develop broad based public understanding and support for the economic policies demanded by a changing world economy. As Karl Polanyi concluded in *The Great Transformation* (1944), economic values such as efficiency, productivity, and growth are purely instrumental means for shaping a political economy, not ends in themselves.[11]

Factors Contributing to Economic Decline

Prior to an examination of specific proposals for ameliorating economic contraction and industrial decline, we must identify the basic contributing factors. No single factor fully explains slower economic growth rates or the present extent of industrial decline. To a considerable degree, contributing factors are related to one another in inconclusive ways and often interact with each other in an unpredictable manner. The relationship between the demographic characteristics of the labor force and productivity rates is an example. It is reasonable to assume, however, that each of the factors dealt with below, from changing cultural values to government regulation, has had some bearing on the loss of growth dynamism in the U.S. economy during the last decade. A review of the slow-growth literature reveals that experts attribute causation to a broad spectrum of interacting factors, and, that with an increase in the ideological content of their various arguments, blame tends to be more closely specified and villains more readily identified.

Changing Values and Expectations

The literature of comparative economic development recognizes that basic cultural attitudes, values, and priorities are central to an understanding of patterns of economic growth in different societies. The cultural shift in values and priorities that accompanied the remarkable industrial development of the Western world was first identified by Max Weber in *The Protestant Ethic and the Spirit of Capitalism* (1904–1905). Originating in the teachings of early Protestant religious groups, rigid self-control and rejection of the sacred became the dominant elements of the Protestant ethic. These and related ethical maxims of a puritanical nature profoundly affected western European culture during the industrial era. Far more than mere doctrine or religious asceticism, the secularized Protestant ethic encouraged and supported new views of the purpose of work, the virtue of material progress, and the nature of man. According to Weber, the consequent emphasis on the individual's ability to reason and improve his own material condition provided the driving force of market capitalism. Weber also believed that the rational habit of mind encouraged by the Protestant ethos would instigate cultural forces powerful enough to transform the Western society from its traditional to a modern form.[12]

In recent years, the now conventional values associated with the Protestant ethic have been challenged and in some cases rejected. Many observers of contemporary American culture conclude that we are undergoing another fundamental shift in widely held values, beliefs, and attitudes. There is considerable apprehension that the erosion of Protestant values such as hard work, self-discipline, delayed gratification, and moderation will in effect undermine the capital formation process that is so critical to economic growth under market capitalism.

Like Weber and Marx before him, a concern with the questions of how economic systems generate forces that will eventually transform them led Harvard economist Joseph R. Schumpeter to contend that the rational habit of mind and the pragmatism it engenders would eventually lead to the demise of capitalism as an economic system. "The capitalist process," he wrote, "rationalizes behavior and ideas and by so doing chases from our minds, along with metaphysical belief, mystic and romantic ideas of all sorts."[13]

To Schumpeter's mind, although pragmatic rationality provided the dynamism that fueled the industrial era and shaped the modern world, the logical extension of the rational mode would also eventually transform the institutional infrastructure of capitalism. He saw that the very success of the entrepreneurial class, the catalysts of industrial expansion, would result in large, complex industrial organizations that would require specialized managers, bureaucratic controls, and stable operating environments to maintain acceptable profit levels. He predicted that the risk-taking, innovative entrepreneurial role would become obsolete, to be replaced by a *rationalization* process (the pragmatic manipulation of means to achieve a hierarchy of given ends, including price stability, investment security, and environmental predictability) as the primary industrial dynamic of advanced capitalism.

Schumpeter wrote that rationalism as a cultural value, conditioned by the affluence of a productive economy, simultaneously would begin to undermine loyalty to the concepts of private property, freedom of contract, and the commercial values needed to sustain business-class privilege. He argued that affluence and democratic political values would eventually stimulate popular discontent with the income and opportunity inequities of market capitalism. He predicted that both the structure and the ethos of market capitalism would be significantly altered as commercial values receded and the need for rationalization in the industrial sector progressed.

Schumpeter predicted that the federal government increasingly would assume responsibility for management of the economy both in response to demands for equity and in order to provide the economic stability needed to support rational modes of industrial organization. He wrote that the tug and pull exerted on the federal budget by politically influential special-interest groups would create an inflation spiral for the most part immune to downward adjustment. Finally, he suggested that the upward rigidity of interest group expectations would fuel a permanent inflation that would undermine the rate of economic growth. Completed in 1942, Schumpeter's insightful analysis of the simultaneous interaction of economic institutions with evolving cultural values set the parameters and the direction for the literature on the social limits to growth that followed.

Sociologist Daniel Bell (1976) has more recently evaluated changing values in affluent America and found what he describes as a "disjunction" between the values of our techno-economic and cultural realms. According to Bell, the different realms now have different norms, rhythms of change, and regulatory principles. The axial principle of the techno-economic realm is functional rationality, the axial mode is economizing and the axial value is utility. Bell suggests that the cultural realm previously mirrored and supported the techno-economic realm. But now he finds the fundamental *assumption of modernity,* the belief in the individual as the basic social unit, to be the axial principle of the cultural realm. He believes that cultural concerns are focused on the self, on individual authenticity and freedom from the "contrivances of institutions and conventions, the masks and hypocrises, the distortions of the self by society." Modernism, according to Bell, is characterized by an unyielding rage against the official order. Gone is any sense of *civitas,* the willingness to make sacrifices for the public good.[14]

Bell goes on to argue that because of the disjunction of realms, American capitalism is losing its traditional source of legitimacy as a moral system of reward rooted in the Protestant sanctification of work. He echoes Schumpeter with his conclusion that changing values will intrude on the polity and encourage a revolution of rising entitlements that will result in inflationary pressure on the economy. But where Schumpeter predicted a structural evolution toward a form of socialism, Bell argues for a return to the previous status quo. He complains that rising social expectations will make capital accumulation problematic and weaken the ability of the techno-economic realm to sustain growth. Although somewhat reactionary Bell's argument points to important questions about the governability of democratic institutions during periods of economic decline.[15]

Bell's analysis lends support to positions such as the one taken by the Trilateral Commission, an association of American, European, and Japanese businessmen and scholars launched in 1972 by David Rockefeller. In a recent study of the changing values and rising entitlements issue, Trilateral representatives argue that the increasing level of political partici-pation granted to previously "marginal" individuals and interest groups now poses a threat to the governability of Western democracies. They con-tend that the overload of demands presented by these marginal groups has exceeded the ability of government to respond effectively. They fear that resulting citizen disillusionment will lead to the "delegitimization of established institutions, challenges to authority, and increasing derogation of political leadership."[16]

Other recent observers discussing the relationship between affluence, value change, and economic growth suggest that individuals who have attained an affluent standard of living, especially those who have known no other, tend to be more willing than the less affluent to trade off high-paying or high-status work for more leisure, autonomy, or more satisfying work roles. Willis Harman (1976, 1977) of the Stanford Research Institute has described this shift in priorities as one in which individuals reject material achievements, status goals, and conspicuous consumption as the central activities that give meaning to life. Harman sees the economic-growth issue as inextricably tied to other social problems such as energy and raw mater-ials supply, environmental pollution, the lack of wholesome employ-ment, distributional inequities, and the decision-stalemate issue. He argues that because of the interconnectedness of this complex of issues, politicians and their technical advisers lack the assurance to tackle any one problem. They fear the tendency for second-order effects to negate the intended out-comes of national policies. Politicians also are hesitant to tackle the dif-ficulties of integrating such incommensurables as economic growth, ethical choice, and quality of life. Harman predicts that economic growth will con-tinue to decline because our society has become so complex that its manage-ment is a nearly overwhelming task.[17]

Other experts concerned with the impact of changing values are less troubled by the specter of slower economic growth. Economists such as Herman E. Daly (1973) have argued that the United States will soon reach a point where the unwanted side effects of production and the costs of further growth in gross national product will outweigh the benefits. Daly has devel-oped a model for a steady-state economy. He defines the *steady state* as an economy in which the total population and the total stock of physical wealth are maintained constant at some desired level by a minimal rate of maintenance "throughout," by birth and death rates that are equal at the lowest feasible level, and by physical production and consumption rates that are equal at the lowest feasible level. He argues that once steady state is attained at some level of population and wealth, we are not frozen at that level forever. As values and technology evolve, Daly contends, the level of throughput can be adjusted. He believes that we must change the present momentum of growth in population and capital that has pushed our technological and moral development in directions rarely clear at the outset. In Daly's steady-state model, technological and moral evolution precede and direct growth. Growth phases are temporary passages from one steady state to another.[18]

The British economist E.J. Mishan (1977) was the first to question seriously whether an increasing material standard of living is synonymous with an improvement in the quality of life. He wondered whether continued economic growth in the industrial world would be likely to improve the human condition or whether it would detract from it. His studies suggest that beyond supplying basic food and shelter needs, the social and human consequences of the technological revolution have been mostly negative. In a complementary argument, Fred Hirsch (1978) has argued that economies developed beyond the stage of satisfying basic material needs acquire an increasingly significant positional component. With basic wants satisfied, status becomes relative; people come more and more to covet goods that are inherently scarce. Further economic growth, therefore, is either futile (because status peers maintain parity), or it increases inequities and thus adds to dissatisfaction. Hirsch asserted that continuing economic growth can act as a destabilizing factor in a society based on norms of equity.[19]

The argument that changing values and social forces far more than resource scarcity will constrain the rate of economic growth over the next quarter century is now widely supported. A recent United Nations study of the future of the world economy directed by Wassily Leontief (1977) concludes that the principal limits to sustained economic growth are political, social, and institutional in character.[20] That finding is repeated in a summary report (1978) prepared for the Joint Economic Committee of the Congress on the economic-growth issue. It concludes with the advice: "It would be well for us to close the book on the growth-limits debate and to start exploring the more difficult but more relevant terrain of social adaption to changing consumption preferences and changing attitudes toward employment and job satisfactions."[21]

Structural Shifts

Economic development in the United States has been characterized by the steady evolution from an agricultural to an industrial to a service-dominated economy. Since the 1950s, U.S. workers have relied increasingly on the service-information sector (including the communications, transportation, wholesale and retail trade, finance, insurance, real estate, health care, advertising, entertainment, government, and educational services industries) to provide new jobs. During 1980, the information-handling sector of the U.S. economy employed approximately 47 percent of the U.S. labor force, the service sector employed 25 percent (for a combined total of 72 percent), the industrial sector 26 percent, and the agricultural sector employed approximately 3 percent. This represents a significant change from thirty years ago when 49 percent of the labor force was employed in the service-information sector, 36 percent in the industrial sector, and 15 percent in agriculture. Given the velocity of this transition, soon only 20 percent of the labor force will produce all of the industrial and agricultural goods for the nation. The extent of this restructuring of the economy has resulted in a postindustrial society where the major part of the economy revolves around nonindustrial activities.[22]

Economist William J. Baumol (1967) and sociologist Daniel Bell (1973), among others, have predicted that the structural shift from a production to a service economy may well result in economic entropy. They have argued that the machine-based technologies that so profoundly increased productivity in farming and manufacturing during the last hundred years are only marginally applicable to the activities that characterize the service and knowledge industries.

Bell maintains that the service-information sector is not only intrinsically less productive as men can be displaced by machines more readily in goods production than in services, but it is one of the major sources of inflation in the economy. He asserts that wages rise in the industrial sector in response to productivity increases. In contrast, service-information workers' wages rise as a secondary response to the cost-push inflation factor of rising industrial wages, but without compensatory increases in productivity. Since service productivity is estimated to be 40 percent below the national average, Bell, along with others, argues that the structural shift toward more employment in the service and information industries will reduce average productivity, create a major inflationary force, and ultimately result in a lowered material standard of living for the entire population.[23]

Baumol argues that much of our urban dislocation and the financial problems of our hard-pressed cities can be traced to this differential in productivity. He suggests that if households increase consumption of both services and manufactured goods by about the same proportion, the percentage of total hours worked in industries with slowly rising output per man-hour will then have to increase to meet demand. This will cause the overall average growth rate for total output per man-hour to decline, since a larger share of the total labor force will be employed in industries with low productivity.[24]

Critics of the differential-productivity view maintain that the application of emerging technologies and modern management techniques can and will substantially improve productivity in government, personal services, construction, trade, finance, insurance, and real estate. They point to the downward trend in the birth rate and note that gradually the demand for state and local government services, including education, should decrease along with the number of service-information workers required. Some critics conclude that the measure of productivity itself is in need of revision. Such a revision, they argue, should account for the growing role of information workers and the related impact of new knowledge and information on the economy. Whereas an industrial society is organized primarily around energy and the use of energy in producing goods, a service-information economy is organized around information and the utilization of information. A productivity measure that accounts for the unique characteristics of information resources that are not reduced or depleted by wide distribution and use is needed.[25]

Another group of observers concerned with structural shifts in the economy reason that the slowdown of economic growth in all the industrial economies of the West can be traced to multinational conglomerates whose activities erode the potency of national stabilization policies. They argue that economic growth is a function of a national government's ability to utilize monetary and fiscal policy to overcome the effects of simultaneous inflation, unemployment, balance-of-trade deficits, and international monetary uncertainty. Ronald E. Müller (1977) has concluded that stabilization policies are no longer adequate, primarily because they are based on an obsolete view of the economy. According to Müller, the U.S. economy underwent a structural transformation, completed during the mid-1960s, that fundamentally altered modes of economic interaction and hence patterns of response to national stabilization policies. This structural shift, characterized by the transformation of major institutions of production and finance, into multinational and multi-industry conglomerates, took place as global interdependence rose to unprecedented levels. Müller argues that given their large size and vast resources, these multinational conglomerates were then able to operate as global oligopolies as they rationalized and stabilized their operations at home and abroad. In a recent study sponsored by the Joint Economic Committee of the Congress, Müller estimates that more than 70 percent of total private activity in the United States is now accounted for by manufacturing and financial conglomerates with access to international financial and money markets. These conglomerates can optimize price and resource allocation decisions across their entire worldwide, multiindustry operations. Their decisions are rarely restrained by competitors, and almost never by national markets, national interests, or national policies designed to control either supply or demand factors.[26]

Müller argues that the residual private sector forms a regulated but primarily market-based national economy. Units in this two-tiered economic system, the multinationals and the residual private sector, react quite differently to fiscal and monetary policies, which most often assume that economic units will behave as single-industry, price-competitive national firms. Müller contends that balanced long-run economic growth cannot occur until public policymakers recognize the duality of the U.S. economy and develop different means of dealing with multinational conglomerates with international financial resources and price-competitive, single-industry national firms. Other critics charge that in addition to undercutting national stabilization policies, the foreign investments of multinationals displace U.S. exports and their licensing of new technologies to foreign competitors hastens the extinction of U.S. firms with higher labor costs.[27]

Productivity and Capital Investment

According to John W. Kendrick (1976) of George Washington University, an expert in productivity analysis, when cyclical fluctuations are smoothed, U.S. productivity growth moved in a generally rising trajectory for nearly two hundred years before turning downward in the late 1960s. Kendrick's data indicate that output per worker increased at an annual rate of 0.5 percent a year from 1800 to 1855, 1.1 percent from 1855 to 1890, 2.0 percent from 1890 to 1919, and 2.4 percent from 1919 to 1948, despite the dislocations suffered during the 1930s. From 1948 to 1965 the annual average rate increased at 3.2 percent, then declined to 2.4 percent between 1965 and 1973.[28] Recent data indicate a 0.8 percent annual average increase between 1973 and 1979. Because declining productivity translates into higher prices and makes it increasingly difficult for U.S. industry to compete, it is perhaps more important to note that labor productivity growth has been negative from the fourth quarter of 1978 through the fourth quarter of 1980.[29] These figures apply to the private business sector only. Productivity growth rates for the entire economy would be somewhat lower. The recent decline in productivity cannot be charged against recalcitrant labor since past improvements have largely resulted from nonlabor factors such as technology, capital formation, and the rate of capacity utilization. The changing composition of the labor force, the structural shift toward the service sector, declining research and development expenditures, government regulation, declining capital-labor ratios, and an anemic economic growth rate are generally included on lists of factors contributing to the productivity decline. There is, however, considerable disagreement as to which factors have had the greatest impact in the past and which will be most important in the future.[30]

During the 1965–1973 period of initial productivity decline, the postwar baby-boom populaton surged into the labor market significantly decreasing the overall skill, experience, and education level of the labor force. In addition, a great number of married women have entered the labor force during the last two decades with little or no previous job experience. As these groups gain skill and experience, their negative impact on the average skill level of the labor force is expected to lessen. But, according to experts, the large number of unskilled workers now in the labor force has exerted a downward pull on overall productivity rates.

A second factor affecting recent productivity declines relates to the shift of workers from more productive to less productive sectors of the economy. The shift of workers from the agricultural to the more productive manufacturing sector contributed to annual productivity increases up until the 1960s. In the same vein, the shift from manufacturing to the relatively less productive service-information sector has exerted a negative pull on potential output gains. The economist Lester Thurow (1980) attributes as much as 40 percent of the recent decline in productivity to the shift in employment toward low-productivity industries. Thurow maintains that there is no evidence of a slowdown in productivity in the manufacturing sector once a correction for idle capacity is computed. However, critics of this argument point out that much of the growth is service employment since the mid-1960s has come in industries with relatively high levels of productivity such as finance, communications, and wholesale trade.[31]

A third commonly suggested contributing factor is the drop in research and development expenditures during the 1970s. Research and development expenditures declined from 3 percent of gross national product at the beginning of the 1970s to slightly more than 2 percent at the end of the decade. As some lag time must be assumed, this decline may mean trouble for productivity growth during the 1980s, but it cannot really explain productivity declines that began in the mid-1960s during a period when expenditures were growing on an annual basis. It is likely that a concentration on applied rather than basic research, and on product rather than process innovation is the cause of any research-related negative impact on productivity growth during the 1970s.[32]

In addition to the drag on final output exerted by the costs associated with health, safety, and environmental regulations mandated during the 1970s, the slow-growth economy itself is considered to have had a negative effect on productivity gains. It seems that strong productivity growth tends to push gross national product growth, and strong gross national product growth feeds productivity. An expanding economy opens up opportunities for investment, stimulates innovation and the diffusion of technology, and encourages economies of scale as output rises toward capacity. All these factors tend to increase productivity. Thurow has suggested that the United States adopt public policies that will encourage investment in high-productivity activities and help the private sector to disinvest as quickly as possible from low-productivity activities. "Eliminating a low-productivity plant," asserts Thurow, "raises productivity just as much as opening a high-productivity plant."[33]

Within each industry there is typically a productivity range across different plant sites. New plants or new processes can be as much as four times more efficient than old plants or processes. Productivity growth increases when more economic activities are concentrated toward the high-productivity end of the spectrum rather than the low-productivity end. Thurow has argued that real productivity growth is a function of the pace at which new technology becomes feasible for use by industry and the rate at which the economy is discarding low-productivity activities. He suggests that the main failure of U.S. economic policy has been in the area of disinvestment. Policymakers have been reluctant to let the efficient drive out the inefficient because of the economic and social dislocations that often accompany disinvestment. Special interest groups representing dying or troubled industries have effectively appealed to government for protection in the form of regulation, subsidies, and quotas. The end result has been a slowing of the disinvestment process and, consequently, of the productivity growth rate.[34]

The final factor considered to have had a negative effect on productivity growth is the stock of investment capital per worker, or the *capital-labor ratio*. This ratio did not change appreciably during the entire 1948–1973 period, but it did decline after 1973 as a result of the increase in the number of new workers—another reflection of the postwar birth surge. It is estimated that $50,000 worth of plant and equipment was needed for each new worker added to the employed labor force during the 1970s. Although investment in plant and equipment was maintained at approximately 10 percent of the gross national product during the 1948–1978 period, investment has not increased fast enough to accommodate the number of new workers.[35] But then as Robert B. Reich (1980), former director of Policy and Planning at the Federal Trade Commission, has pointed out, the trend toward a declining overall level of industrial investment may be appropriate for an economy where future growth is dependent on knowledge-intensive rather than capital-intensive industries. Emerging industries such as biotechnology, lasers, and semiconductors require far less capital per worker than the heavy industries that previously dominated the economy.[36]

It does not do much good, however, to argue about what the capital-labor ratio should be as long as government, in an effort to combat inflation, deliberately holds the demand for goods and services below what the economy could produce. Historical patterns of productivity growth are associated with periods of full employment and high capacity utilization. Conversely, growth in productivity slows as the economy moves away from the full utilization of men and capital equipment. Thurow has attributed as much as 30 percent of the current productivity slowdown to idle capacity. Regardless of the benefits of restrained-demand policies in fighting inflation, it is clear that one of the costs is a slower rate of growth in productivity.[37]

As for the related but broader argument that declining investment levels are the cause of slower economic growth, investment in plant and equipment averaged 9.5 percent of gross national product between 1948 and 1965. From 1966 through 1978 that annual average rose to 10.2 percent. These figures reflect stable personal savings rates that averaged 6.8 percent of personal income during the 1950s, 6.6 percent during the 1960s, and 7.1 percent during the 1970s.[38] Investment levels have not declined but remained remarkably stable during the postwar decades. The capital investment issue is central to solving our slow-growth problems, but again, it is the rationality and velocity of capital mobility rather than the overall level of investment that most affect productivity and consequent economic growth.

Management Failure

The relationship between economic decline and *corporate contraction* (an absolute decline in sales revenue) is highly interactive and characterized by a great many intervening variables. *Corporate strategy* (management's long-range plan for profit maximization) is a major intervening variable. With the exception of periods of transition when revenues contract because of the divestiture of operating units or subsidiaries so that resources can be redeployed more profitably elsewhere, contracting revenues threaten not only the viability of the individual firm, but also the firm's creditors, shareholders, workers, suppliers, and customers.

Critics charge that corporate executives deserve a great deal of the blame for the marked deterioration of U.S. competitive vigor. They point out that as late as 1968, when a Yankelovich survey asked whether business strikes a fair balance between profits and the public interest, 70 percent of respondents answered yes. Ten years later the yes vote was a mere 19 percent.[39] Critics argue that management has failed to balance the competitive claims and divergent interests of creditors, shareholders, consumers, and workers. They accuse corporate executives of being unwilling to invest in and modernize American industry without profit guarantees in the form of government subsidies and tax breaks. They maintain that productivity, innovation, and the consideration of other long-term goals have been sacrificed in the pursuit of short-term profitability.

According to management experts Robert H. Hayes and William J. Abernathy (1980) of the Harvard Business School, gradual changes in the emphasis of American management theory and technique over the last thirty years have resulted in a preoccupation with near-term results. They argue that an unfortunate by-product of the trend toward decentralized structuring of large firms has been the development of performance evaluation techniques that rely on quantifiable short-term criteria. As independent profit centers or strategic business units have increasingly become the primary units of managerial responsibility, top-level executives have tended to give up "hands-on" management for an overview approach supplemented by continuous financial reports designed to measure performance-to-date against quarterly or year-end goals. As a result, performance appraisal and management incentive programs have become depersonalized. Year-end bonuses are nowadays routinely tied to divisional or profit-center performance and reflect general economic conditions for the firm and internal transfer pricing techniques more than personal performance.[40]

The most negative impact of depersonalized management, or "management by numbers," has been the development of corporate environments that penalize risk taking and discourage innovative activities. According to Hayes and Abernathy, reliance on objectively quantifiable short-term criteria tends to penalize failure or even a quarterly dip in profits unduly. When failure carries too high a price, innovative activities suffer. Hence executives have tended to become risk averse, hesitant to invest in new ideas, processes, or high-risk programs that do not offer a payoff in the near term. Formularized approaches to investment decision making (internal rate of return or discounted cash flow techniques for instance) have replaced educated instincts despite the innate difficulty of quantifying the unknown aspects of future technologies or new marketing concepts. At present, top executives are rarely presented with investment alternatives unless the project indicates a near-guaranteed 15 to 20 percent return. The fact that middle-level managers are aware that failure to provide a specified return on a project will penalize their entire management team also acts to restrain innovative activity.[41]

Other critics, like Thomas H. Naylor (1981) of Duke University, maintain that this short-term emphasis has led to the neglect of strategic long-term planning in many large corporations. Naylor blames this on the rise to power of financially oriented executives who feel comfortable with the complexities of detailed budgets and quantitative approaches to decision making. He argues that although accounting may be a useful language for evaluating historical performance, it is not the most effective language for planning, which is a forward-looking task.

In most large firms there is considerable conflict between the needs and priorities of the budget, commonly controlled by the chief financial officer, and long-term planning, usually headed by a director or vice-president who reports to the chief executive officer. The budget official is concerned with next years's operating results, the planning official with the long run. If the budget director has more political clout than the planning official, which is normally the case according to Naylor, the chief executive tends to side with the budget official in disputes over resource allocation. Also contributing to this short-term preference is the fact that most chief executives take over the corporate reins with the knowledge that they have only five or six years to make their imprint on the firm. It is difficult for the typical chief executive, who is nearly sixty years old, to make decisions that may depress current earnings but will be lucrative for successors. Naylor suggests that the major danger in budget-driven planning is that, to meet short-term financial targets, zealous managers will give inadequate attention to research, replacement of plant, and investment in new products.[42]

In their own defense, corporate executives attribute some of their short-term perspective to the pressures exerted on them by equity markets and their own boards to increase earnings each quarter by cutting back on investments. Stock analysts tend to research the numbers and give less attention to management depth and long-term growth potential when they make recommendations for purchase. Creditors tend to gauge terms to market performance. Large institutional investors want quarterly results, not explanations of potential future growth. The fear of outside takeovers also motivates executives to keep quarterly earnings and dividend payouts high, so that stock will not become undervalued by the market.[43]

An example of these combined pressures can be found in the dividend policies of the two major American steel firms. These firms have taken huge writeoffs and increased their debt levels by nearly 100 percent since 1970. Nevertheless, they have been unwilling to let the impact hit investors too hard. From 1975 through 1979, dividend payouts averaged 72 percent of U.S. Steel's earnings and 83 percent of Bethlehem Steel's earnings.[44] In order to provide for continued payouts, U.S. Steel directed 37 percent of its investment during the same period into nonsteel businesses and closed down major steel-making operations in the state of Ohio that were unable to produce the required rate of return.[45] During the late 1970s, the U.S. share of total world steel production fell to 16 percent, down from 55 percent in the 1950s when the domestic steel industry was a symbol of America's advanced industrial economy.[46]

Professors Hayes and Abernathy go on to charge that American corporations have lost their leadership position in both mature and high technology industries because of their preoccupation with immediate results. They argue that a strong competitive position can be maintained only through in-house technical superiority, which is by nature a long, arduous, and often unglamorous task. Their research indicates that the short-term perspective predisposes managers of American firms to increase profits by developing products for existing markets. American managers, they argue, tend to opt for customer satisfaction and lower risk in the short run at the expense of superior products in the future. This imitative approach to product design and marketing strategy is guided by consumer analysis and formal market survey techniques geared to achieve maximum predictability. Truly new products not only tend to make obsolete existing investments in marketing and manufacturing organizations, but they also represent a choice of considerable uncertainty in terms of acceptance, timing, and economic return.

Short-term rewards have also encouraged managers to integrate backward in order to control sources of supply. Backward integration can offer rather substantial cost benefits by eliminating certain purchasing and marketing functions. It can offer other efficiencies, depending on the firm involved. Hayes and Abernathy point out that great efficiencies have been achieved by firms producing commodity-like products, but the backward-integration strategy can become highly problematic in industries exposed to technological advances that require flexible patterns of resource deployment. They describe American managers as reluctant to invest heavily in the development of new manufacturing processes, particularly in mature industries, because there is no short-term payoff. They assert that American managers tend to restrict investments in *process development* (new technologies to manufacture established products more efficiently) to only those items likely to reduce costs in the short run. In contrast, they found European managers, even in high technology industries, committed to increasing market share through internal development of advanced process technology.[47]

Based on his own studies of European industries, Bruce R. Scott (1973) of Harvard has pointed out that our European competitors have emphasized process innovation because their major investment decisions are geared to maintaining world market share over the long run.[48] Process innovation has also been the major strength of Japanese competitors in steel, autos, and consumer electronics. Japanese industrial planners are geared to export markets where they seek to optimize long-term market position. Japanese industry routinely plans ahead in fifteen- to twenty-year increments for research, factory construction, and service networks, while few American firms seriously plan ahead by more than five years.[49]

Other critics, including Reich, have noted that corporate managers have contributed to the industrial decline problem by frittering away much of the available investment capital on nonproductive uses such as rearranging the ownership of industrial assets through mergers, acquisitions, and selloffs. Reich estimates that between 1977 and 1980, some $100 billion of corporate cash resources were used to acquire existing corporate assets through tender offers. Despite the claims about the synergy that such combinations produce, there is little evidence to suggest that the average merger has enhanced the basic profitability or productivity of the merging firms. Reich also points out that the speculative investments now so popular among money managers, such as foreign currency contracts, commodities, financial futures, and real estate, create profits but do not necessarily enhance productive capability. The rearrangement or redeployment of corporate assets is currently very much in vogue. The justification, of course, is short-term profitability. American management increasingly is prone to sell off a division or subsidiary that does not consistently meet minimum investment return requirements. The long-term consequences of this trend are difficult to assess. This flurry of selloff and acquisition activity may leave American industry more efficient in the long-term, as some have predicted, or it may act as camouflage to hide the further contraction of U.S. productive capacity in patterns contrary to national interests.[50]

At a more abstract level, but complementary to arguments that the short-term perspective of many corporate executives has contributed to the slower growth phenomenon, is evidence that increased levels of technological complexity, the large size, and increasing degree of interdependence among and between economic units and institutions in the economy have exerted a negative pull on economic growth. Discussions of the impact of these forces on society generally assume that inefficiencies at the organizational level are aggregated at the macroeconomic level.

Technological Complexity, Size, and Interdependence

Generations of optimistic Americans have sought comfort in the belief that science and its application as technology would eventually solve all economic problems, especially those related to production and resource scarcity. The American experience with industrialization offered proof after proof that technology, in principle, was capable of unlimited extension and improvement. The continual innovation of technique and the efficiency of mass production have encouraged confidence in the possibility of ever-increasing levels of productivity, consumption, and wealth. During the last several decades, however, many have come to realize that technical progress has also meant the proliferation of technological complexity and specialization. Technical progress has increased economic efficiency at the cost of a tremendously escalated level of interdependence among organizations, production processes, and distribution networks. This interdependence has increased the cost and the difficulty of management and coordination functions both for the corporation and for the government in its role as regulator of the economy.

Industry now operates under numerous technologically complex constraints aimed at environmental protection, worker safety, and product liability. Previously unrecognized technological considerations (second, third, and fourth-order effects) have inundated government decision makers who must regulate the use of new technology in a rapidly changing and unpredictable environment. The overload of demands frequently exceeds the capacity to respond. From both the corporate and the regulatory viewpoint, it often appears that the time available between the perception of a problem and its becoming critical has shortened as the time required to solve the problem has lengthened. This overall complexity leads to arguments that red tape, or the cost of regulation to business and government, acts as a force to slow down economic growth.[51]

Largely as a result of past experience with technological progress, we remain hesitant to issue restraints or deny ourselves the benefits of new technologies. But economists such as E.J. Mishan (1977) and Jay Forrester (1976) argue that the trend toward economic density and the dangerous side effects of technology will eventually require an increase in governmental authority inconsistent with the ideals of a free society. In addition to the costs associated with managing increasingly complex technologies, there is also the ethical issue of ultimate use. The contradictions of a technological society have been exposed in recent public debates over the end use of developments in genetic biology and nuclear power. Serious discussion of the intrinsic limits to technological process are now reaching beyond the halls of academe. It is evident that we can no longer rely wholly on technological progress to solve economic problems—clearly long-term costs can outweigh benefits.[52]

A feature of growing importance in the evolution of the U.S. economy is the sheer size of our institutions and the necessary complexity of their internal operating systems. As society has become more populous, interactive, and urbanized, we have tended to aggregate what were once comprehensible smaller organizational systems into larger, often incomprehensible supersystems. Frequently the actual level of interactive complexity of such systems is poorly understood. Overall goal setting and planning activities are often neglected as subsystem crises absorb all attention. Size and complexity also frequently correlate with a high level of system inertia that acts to constrain innovation, flexibility, and adjustment to changing environmental conditions. Broadening interdependence heightens the demand for regulation and frequently increases the rigidity of interactive systems because a change in one element of the system means change for all interrelated elements. These factors contribute to a tendency toward low performance, which can be exacerbated by bureaucratic approaches to decision making.

In addition, the large scale, technical specialization, and interdependence of many productive organizations leave incorporated systems highly susceptible to shutdown. The failure of one component can bring down an entire system. Interdependence increases vulnerability to accidental or deliberate disruption. The limits of the human capacity to design and effectively manage large, complex interdependent systems are realized whenever terrorist groups threaten sabotage. But even in systems well buffered from external political pressures, it is no longer uncommon to find that complex, interdependent systems of organization actually diminish rather than enhance the ability to solve difficult problems.[53]

Government Regulation

There is little disagreement that costs related to the new wave of government regulation mandated during the 1960s and early 1970s have been substantial. While regulations promulgated to provide safer working conditions, consumer protection, and the reduction of environmental pollutants have tended to enhance the quality of life, they have also forced businesses to absorb costs previously externalized to the society as a whole. Increased costs passed on to the consumer contribute to inflation and can undercut competitive strength. The broader argument that excessive regulation of corporate activity, including antitrust, tax, and trade law, has worked to undermine industrial vigor and trade competitiveness now finds wide support among businessmen, academics, members of Congress, and federal regulatory officials. Administrative and compliance costs related to federal regulation have been calculated to run as high as $100 billion annually.[54]

While it is estimated that the United States has fewer regulations than most other industrialized countries, those regulations are imposed in an advisory legal system that makes the regulatory process costly and implementation difficult. More and more, legislation forged in the Congress tends to reflect the continuing conflicts of interested parties rather than a workable compromise on the policy issue at hand. Means are often left unspecified and ends stated in vague, even contradictory, terminology in the legislative documents that become the law of the land. Thereafter, congressional intent and agency promulgated regulations are scrutinized in the courts as interested parties seek judicial interpretation of exact requirements for specific cases. The delays and uncertainties created during the advisory legal process add significantly to the costs of implementation. The unwieldy nature of the public policy decision process is further complicated by the interdependent nature of our integrated economy; integration means that regulation in one sector will often lead to regulation in another. When government moves to protect the steel industry from foreign competition in domestic markets with subsidies or import quotas, it raises the price of steel to domestic manufacturers. It raises the cost of building cars in the United States, which in turn contributes to the loss of competitiveness of the U.S. auto industry. Thus a regulation designed to protect one interest can damage another group and generate a second set of protective regulations.[55]

How have we arrived at the point where government in its modern regulatory role can be blamed for undermining the growth potential of the economy? What has happened to the long-held belief that *competitive* private enterprise would ensure economic growth? Many observers, both here and abroad, blame business more than government. They see over-regulation as a self-inflicted malady. Even conservative economist Milton Friedman has characterized the businessman as

> the most insidious and effective enem[y] of free enterprise. He is all in favor of free enterprise and free markets. But when it comes down to practice, it turns out he's in favor of free enterprise and free markets for everybody else but not for himself. Oh, no. He's a special case. His business requires special government protection.[56]

In U.S. economic history, two strains of thought have always existed side by side on the regulation issue. One is the rhetoric of free enterprise and the other is the desire for orderly market conditions. Demands for protection through regulation have grown in response both to rampant competition and to increasing levels of economic interdependence; there have been no strong political forces demanding regulation for the sake of regulation.

The economic historian Douglass C. North (1978) has described the rise of regulatory government as a consequence of the political clout developed by the *economic losers* of nineteenth-century America. These relative losers were the farmers, shippers, railroad companies, and manufacturers whose previously established economic positions were undermined by the rigors of competition in free markets. Each group sought government protection in the form of regulated markets. Despite negligible private gains, the fight for regulated markets succeeded in harnessing widespread popular resentment against the primacy of unfettered property rights and the politically powerful big-business interests. Deep-seated convictions that the degree of income inequity under nineteenth-century capitalism was unjust fed a political reform movement that ultimately legitimized a regulatory and redistributive role for government. Subsequently, particularly in conjunction with the second burst of regulatory activity during the 1930s and the third burst during the 1960s and early 1970s, broad-based political reform movements have legitimized a larger interventionist role for government. As North indicates, conditions now prevail where,

> Markets still dominate the allocation of resources in the society, but entry into the market, the characteristics of product, the price of the factors of

production, employment conditions, and the price of the product are all influenced or specified by government fiat.[57]

Putting aside ideological arguments and the search for villains, most
critics of the current regulatory scene would agree that some level of government regulation of the economy is necessary, that economic interests will
continue to act to hold protective regulation in place, and that while a few
industries currently require less regulation, solving growth problems will inevitably include a regulatory role for government.

The New Players. Under democratic capitalism, special interest groups are
actively encouraged to solicit the protection of government on behalf of
their economic interests. But, as economist Mancur Olson points out in his
studies of public goods and common-interest organizations (1965, 1976),
organized interests "weave webs of constraints" that slow economic
growth. Olson argues that the barriers erected to protect special interests
curtail the growth of productivity, and thus income, by preventing the flow
of resources to best use, which reduces the output of society as a whole.
Members of common interest blocs, he explains, get most or all of the gains
and bear few or none of the costs of the protective public policies they
seek.[58]

In the United States, organized business interests have long maintained
a privileged position in the public policymaking process that results in
regulation of the marketplace. Their position derives from a tacit understanding between business and government officials of the conditions under
which business can profitably operate and contribute to a politically acceptable level of economic growth. While the public policymaking process is one
of compromise between interested parties, it is also a highly competitive
game where organized interests seek to maximize economic gains. Different
segments of the business community as well as representatives from different regulatory bodies frequently find themselves adversaries rather than
cooperative partners. Yet, in the final analysis, differences are mitigated on
behalf of a common interest in economic growth.

As Charles E. Lindblom (1977) of Yale University has pointed out, the
unspoken possibility of adversity for business has operated as an all-
pervasive constraint on government authority over the conditions of the
marketplace. Even implicit threats of poor performance activate government concern for business conditions. Elected officials are particularly vulnerable to the consequences of poor performance and, therefore, generally
are eager to meet business demands. Business interests are privileged not
only with respect to the consideration given their needs, but also because
they participate directly in the policy deliberations of government. No other
special interest group is regularly accorded this privilege because no other
group can so directly affect general economic conditions and hence the elec-

torate. Lindblom argues that government officials do not have to be bribed, duped, or pressured to grant businessmen a privileged position relative to other interests. To government officials, businessmen appear not simply as representatives of special interests, as other interest group representatives do, but as functionaries performing tasks indispensable to government.[59]

Until recently economic policy and the regulation of the marketplace have been in the hands of government and business leaders who have collaborated to make the economy work. But, beginning in the mid-1960s, broad-based social concern with the issues of economic security and the externalities associated with the productive process has resulted in congressional mandates that restrain business interests to an extent heretofore unknown. Mandates involving health, safety, environmental protection, equal employment opportunity, social security, public jobs, and urban renewal have forced government officials to view the national interest in terms broader than growth and stability. Access to government officials in a position to make decisions that result in gains or losses for organized interests is increasingly widespread.

New interest groups representing environmentalists, consumers, workers, and the economically disenfranchised now influence the public policymaking process through direct lobbying efforts. They constitute new players in the economic maximization game. The new interest groups are denied the privileged status of business executives in the deliberations of government, but they can exert influence through the media or the courts if they are excluded or their interests ignored. Despite broad resistance in the American business community, the new interest groups have revived the notion that the public interest does not automatically equate with the needs of business.

Interest Group Rigidity and Decision Stalemate. The past conviction that economic growth would provide for all citizens as the size of the distributional pie increased has encouraged competing interest blocs to reach compromise positions on public policy issues. The promise of economic growth and the reality of rising living standards has helped U.S. policymakers avoid the divisive issue of income distribution. However, when the size of the resource pie contracts and it becomes clear that gains for any one group will necessitate losses for others, distribution issues will demand attention. In addition, as interest blocs become sensitized to second, third, and fourth-order effects of any change in the status quo, the ability to make economic decisions is likely to collapse into lengthy adversary procedures and decision stalemate with ever more frequency.

We have already reached the point where all economic decisions are also political decisions and where each decision impinges on nearly all other decisions, even when ramifications are less than perfectly understood. In addition, contemporary economic losers appear less willing than in previous eras to accept further losses. Recent economic losers such as the consumer electronics industry, which has actively sought protected domestic markets, or groups such as racial minorities and women who, as full-time workers, continue to earn far less than their white male counterparts, are examples.[60] Although these particular interest blocs may not be influential enough to redirect public policy, they are capable of utilizing the courts to affect costly delays (another form of stalemate) in the implementation of programs and projects that further impinge on their interests. Litigation not only introduces a costly level of uncertainty for all parties involved, but adversary procedures require the services of intermediaries such as lawyers, lobbyists, public relations specialists, and specialized journalists whose own interests are served by extending regulatory confrontation. As the public policymaking process becomes increasingly combative, effective compromise becomes a less likely outcome.[61]

Given interest group rigidity, expectations of increasing economic parity, and slower rates of economic growth, instances of decision stalemate may well accelerate despite our need to more effectively manage the complex, interdependent, industrialized social system we inhabit. As Thurow has pointed out in his book *The Zero-Sum Society* (1980), distributional issues are highly contentious and precisely the kind of issues that democracies find the most difficult to solve. Economist Robert Heilbroner goes on to predict that the antagonism between interest groups over the distribution of income in a slow-growth economy will result in the incremental contraction of private property rights. Heilbroner believes that capitalism as a system of privilege and concentrated economic power based on private property will not survive that antagonism. He echoes Schumpeter when he suggests that as the political apparatus of government usurps functions formerly delegated to the economic realm in response to interest group demands, the U.S. economy will evolve into a postcapitalist phase.[62]

In the near term, what are the public policy alternatives for dealing with the slow-growth issue? Conservative observers argue for a return to the economic relationships of the past maintaining that the influence gained by the new players over corporate decisions has grievously impaired efficiency. Others argue that growth problems of the 1980s should be addressed with a comprehensive industrial policy that concentrates on how government can obtain the most productive pattern of investment throughout the economy. As a group they do not see the new players as posing a threat, but rather believe their inclusion is a necessary factor in developing broad-based support for any national policy. A third group contends that the real issue is one of capital formation. For this group, any workable industrial policy must address the fundamental question of who will control capital and for what purposes. Representatives argue that a greater level of democratic participation must inform economic affairs at every level of the process that leads to public policy.

National Industrial Policy

The term *industrial policy* has been used in various ways. It is sometimes used interchangeably with trade policy; it sometimes refers to policies directed toward a particular industry; and at other times it denotes comprehensive measures designed to influence patterns of economic activity throughout the economy. The suggested parameters for industrial policy, or industrial strategy, differ markedly with political point of view. Industrial policy has been described as a means to encourage the growth of supply-side factors of the economy, to end faltering trade competitiveness, to rationalize excess capacity in world industry, or to help workers adjust to the dislocations of disinvestment. Strict usage would suggest that the word *policy* be confined to deliberate and systematic actions that are consistent in purpose. In the United States, industrial policy has evolved in an ad hoc, piecemeal fashion, the total of the parts falling considerably short of a coherent, pragmatic policy.

Government shapes industrial policy to a significant degree through procurement and research and development expenditures. It also affects the pattern of investment in the economy with tariffs, quotas, subsidies, ordered marketing agreements, tax laws, loan guarantees, public lands management, and publicly financed insurance. In 1980 alone, tax benefits to particular industries reached an estimated $70 billion, and the federal government issued $221.6 billion in loan guarantees, $60 billion in direct loans, and $2 trillion worth of outstanding insurance. Actual expenditures amount to 13.9 percent of the gross national product according to Reich's estimates.[63] Reich goes on to note that none of these expenditures have been evaluated in terms of impact on U.S. competitiveness, nor have they been viewed as a part of a coherent industrial policy. Rather, each aid program, whether formulated by the courts, federal agencies, or congressional subcommittees, has developed in response to specific problems and particular interest group demands. In the past, the government has agreed to bail out Penn Central, Lockheed, and Chrysler with loan guarantees, but denied aid to firms in the steel and consumer electronics industries. As steelworkers fought unsuccessfully to keep plants operating in Ohio, the government provided a $12 million loan guarantee for a new steel plant in New Jersey.[64] According to Reich, the government now spends five times as much for commercial fisheries research as it does for steel-related research. It gives $455 million in tax breaks to the timber industry but none to the semiconductor industry. More than $6 billion in loans and loan guarantees go to the shipbuilding industry compared with $940 million to the troubled U.S. auto industry.[65] In order to understand the parameters of U.S. industrial policy, consideration must be given to any government intervention in the marketplace whether aimed at defending the status quo, or adapting to, even initiating, structural change in the economy. Interventions must be judged by effect rather than intent as their initiation may have been in response to a myriad of economic problems.[66]

Historically, declining industries and their workers have had to make their own adjustments to structural change in the economy. No systematic approach or objective criteria have been established to determine when a particular firm should receive government aid or protection and when its fate should be left to the rigors of the market. Government protection is now meted out in a piecemeal fashion, for the most part according to political rather than economic considerations. Unlike the marginal farmers of the 1930s, who were encouraged to leave their farms by agricultural policies designed to support the large-scale specialized farm, industrial interests are organized and politically powerful. It is unlikely that the government would be able to pursue for long an unarticulated national policy of encouraging the marginal industrial unit to fail. The current economic transition is more likely to entail heavy grants of protection unless a broadly supported, carefully specified industrial policy can be developed and implemented.

Clearly, if we are unable to forge a national policy, we will be left with protection for the most politically powerful firms and industries. As a case in point, several major oil and steel companies have actively lobbied for a national strategic minerals policy as they diversify their assets into minerals and other energy resources. Because the mining industry suffers from excess world refinery capacity and soft markets due to Third World production, lobbyists are requesting an easing of U.S. antitrust and air- and water-quality regulations, guaranteed government purchases, and guaranteed minimum prices for certain metals. Without a coherent national industrial policy there is no systematic way to weigh this request for special protection against any other. Without decision criteria, political clout will remain the basis for determination.[67]

During the final year of the Carter administration, government officials began to develop plans for a more systematic approach to industrial policy with the objective of reversing the erosion of American industry. President Carter established an Economic Revitalization Board cochaired by DuPont chairman and Business Roundtable spokesman Irving Shapiro and AFL-CIO president Lane Kirkland. The board was charged with the responsibility of advising the president on the mobilization of public and private resources to help "revitalize" American industry. The board was also asked to make recommendations on the desirability of creating an investment development authority. These objectives derived from the work of a special White House task force that had been contemplating for some time the political difficulties associated with stepped-up economic planning and increased government control over the capital allocation process. Given the apprehension that has come to characterize discussions of our international competitors' ability to adapt to rapidly changing economic conditions, it is not surprising that the task force delved directly into the details of the industrial advisory boards and national planning models developed in Japan, West Germany, France, and Great Britain.[68]

In Japan, now the world's most successful industrial society, government coordinates business strategies along a fast-growth track by means of a pervasive industrial plan. The strategy of Japan's Ministry of International Trade and Industry has been to identify, promote, and protect during early phases of market development those domestic industries capable of developing new technologies and exploiting world-market opportunities. West Germany has also set national industrial priorities, though it has relied more heavily than Japan on market forces to channel resources toward firms and industries with high export potential. All political parties in West Germany, however, support government efforts to retrain and relocate workers displaced by industrial transitions. Workers are encouraged to retrain for jobs in new technologies under government programs that compensate workers at previous wage levels. France began national planning in 1947. Goals have changed and the government's power to direct business activities has waned as the economy and business have strengthened, but *indicative planning* is still used to point out where the national economy needs expansion and strengthening. In contrast, after two decades of trying to reshape the economy through a network of government-business-labor councils and approximately $130 billion in government grants, subsidies, and equity investments aimed at revitalizing specific domestic industries and export-oriented firms, Britain has failed to accomplish a turnaround in its declining economy.[69] As many observers have pointed out, what Japan and West Germany have, and what Great Britain and to a lesser extent France lack, is a broad national consensus among socio-economic groups on basic economic priorities.

The task force concluded that a national planning effort seemed inappropriate not only because the United States lacked such a broad consensus, but because Europeans and even the Japanese were beginning to voice second thoughts about their *picking the winners* strategies. Task force members representing the Treasury and Commerce Departments, the Office of Management and Budget, and the Council of Economic Advisers were skeptical about the government's ability to identify those industries with the most growth potential. Only Environmental Protection Agency and Labor Department representatives favored allocating capital for specific purposes such as retooling the steel industry or the development of industrial robots.[70]

The task force failed to provide guidance for the task of defining a national industrial policy vis-à-vis world markets. Are national interests best served by leaving the capital allocation process in the private sector governed by the rate-of-return criterion? Should U.S. policy continue to encourage private firms active in the textile, apparel, footwear, rubber, and consumer electronics industries to disinvest because they have lost the competitive edge in world markets? Does it make a difference if divestiture is also taking place in industries like steel and chemicals? Is it in the national interest to maintain a basic domestic steel industry? Without intervention, will contracting steel interests necessarily shrink to the most efficient units? Can U.S. firms compete with state-owned or state-supported firms based in countries where international competitiveness is an explicit national policy goal, and where subsidies, loans, and special tax advantages are routinely granted to growth industries? The task force had nothing to recommend here but the continuation of current ad hoc approaches.

On the question of whether to create a national development bank to aid companies with credible economic potential in capital-short industries, the task force again backed down. A new development bank was resisted because of fears that it would become an institution that bailed out the losers of capitalism. The task force concluded that industrial bailouts would ultimately undermine the market system of capital allocation. In the end, they rejected the opportunity for a rational reorganization of current industrial aid programs and agreed with Charles Schultz, then chairman of the Council of Economic Advisers, that the government does not have the ability to pick winners or aim programs at precise targets. Schultz maintained that of the twenty products and industries that grew fastest during the 1970s, only five (various plastics, oil and gas drilling equipment, semiconductors, small cars) looked predictable in retrospect. The other fifteen, including utility vehicles, vacuum cleaners, construction glass, cheese, tufted carpets, and poultry rearing, did not.[71] The task force did, however, recommend relocation assistance efforts designed to link workers with economic opportunity. Finally, instead of resuscitating old industrial cities, they advised that the government in effect give "large segments of the urban lower classes" bus tickets to the Sun Belt.[72]

As the White House task force was dismissing a redevelopment bank and Carter's Economic Revitalization Board disbanded without formal recommendations, political pressure to create an investment development authority continued. Senator Edward Kennedy, Lane Kirkland, and liberal factions of the business press continued to back the concept. Felix Rohatyn, an investment banker and chairman of New York City's Municipal Assistance Corporation, continued to advocate the creation of a new Reconstruction Finance Corporation funded at the $5 billion level.[73] Management experts and economists throughout the country have also continued the debate in the general press as well as the academic journals. Though we are far from a policy consensus about how American industry can improve its competitive performance in world markets, the knowledge that U.S. firms will increasingly have to face foreign competitors backed by the national equivalent of a corporate finance committee energizes the debate. It is recognized that a national industrial policy must go beyond ad hoc adjustments made in response to the needs of the strongest and most entrenched interest groups. And, it is now generally acknowledged that a basic philosophy of industrial development needs to be established; one that can guide future decision making and the design of investment, trade, taxation, manpower, and technological development strategies. It must be capable of gaining broad-based support throughout the economy. The view that formulation of a national industrial policy should be explicit and public, involving small businesses, emerging industries, nonunion workers, consumers, and environmentalists as well as organized labor, entrenched business interests, and government officials is also gaining support. Three basic philosophies of intent have surfaced in the national-policy debate with substantially different implications for future programs. A brief review of each follows.[74]

Conservative Proposals

Liberating the free enterprise system is the major emphasis of conservative proposals for revitalizing American industry. Program scenarios generally call for the reduction of social expenditures, a restructuring of the tax system to encourage savings and investment, and the elimination of government regulations that do not help business, particularly environmental, antitrust, consumer protection, and worker safety laws. A representative conservative proposal has been set forth by Amitai Etzioni (1980), director of the Center for Policy Research in Washington and former senior adviser to the Carter White House. Etzioni coined the term *reindustrialization* to describe his national industrial policy proposal. He asserts that a consumer society with a deteriorating industrial base must make the fundamental choice between continued expenditures to enhance the quality of life and an increasing economic growth rate. According to Etzioni, since the 1890s America's core project has been the development of an industrial plant capable of mass production. This capacity was used to generate affluent life-styles, then social justice, and then a quality-of-life society. Affluence encouraged the tendency to place social progress above economic progress. Etzioni believes that decades of overconsumption and underinvestment must be rectified with a renewed commitment to production. If America fails to rebuild its industrial base, he argues, it will have to accept a lower material standard of living on a permanent basis. As a means of shoring up our productive capacity, Etzioni proposes a ten-year period of belt tightening, including reduced social expenditures and consumer spending, accelerated depreciation plus larger research and development writeoffs for business, and lower capital-gains taxes for investors. He adamantly recommends against national planning or any further government regulation of the marketplace. He believes that the capital allocation function should be left unfettered and squarely within the private sector.[75]

Etzioni's analysis characterizes a point of view maintained by a group of former liberals, now calling themselves neoconservatives, who have become disillusioned with the ability of public policy and regulatory government to solve basic social problems. Neoconservatives as a group have also been fundamentally concerned with what they interpret as a deep erosion of traditional American values such as deference, self-discipline, moderation, restraint, and hard work. They not only mourn the loss of nineteenth-century values that were so well-suited to capitalism and economic growth but also claim contemporary values reflect primary concerns with immediate gratification and the pursuit of hedonistic life-styles. As a group the neoconservatives agree with Daniel Bell's charge that this value change has led to a loss of civitas and a consequent revolution of rising entitlements. In effect, they believe that special interest groups have overtaxed the public policymaking system in their efforts to protect the interests of their constituents.

In a review of the neoconservative movement, Michael Walzer (1979) has characterized their concerns as an essential fear of equality. He writes that the neoconservatives have mistakenly equated moderation and civility with the past. It is not hedonism but the inclusion of economic losers and others with divergent interests that has radically changed the public policy-making process, according to Walzer. This new inclusiveness makes public policy outcomes much less predictable and ultimately threatening to established interests. Citing Thorstein Veblen, Walzer comments that it is not so much that we have suddenly become inveterate consumers, as that equality of access to the maximization game has increased concerns about relative standards of material well-being. The quality-of-life issue has become ubiquitous; it is no longer identified solely with the upper class.[76]

An agenda for national industrial policy that bears many similarities to Etzioni's has been proposed by the Trilateral Commission. The influential commission has called for a U.S. industrial policy that will recognize the private sector as the prime mover in the economy and maintain premises that market forces and entrepreneurship are the foundation of an efficient economy. The Trilateral Commission study includes proposals that member governments act not only to promote innovation and research within the private sector but also support declining industries for limited periods with protective policies, while bringing their capacity into line with demand. The National Association of Manufacturers and the AFL-CIO have endorsed comparable plans.[77]

The Trilateral Commission study calls for the protection of declining industries while it supports the concept of open international markets and free trade. This contradiction is not new. From the turn of the century, the American business community has been divided on the issue of international economic policy. Banks, manufacturers, mining companies, and agribusinesses with overseas interests have supported free trade and open access to the underdeveloped world. Other business groups have been content with the world's largest domestic market and have acted to protect that market from low-cost foreign imports. Since World War II, U.S. policy-makers have been committed primarily to an open international market, although protectionists have not been without political influence. Protectionist acquiescence to free-trade policies has been contingent on economic growth and expanding domestic markets.

In response to recent declining rates of economic growth, however, a stream of literature warning of the threat of rising foreign imports has begun to emanate from business-lobby groups. These groups include not only the Chamber of Commerce and the National Federation of Independent Business lobbyists, but also the Chase Manhattan Bank, the Business Roundtable (representing the 200 largest U.S. corporations), the American Business Conference (formed to represent the interests of medium-sized growth companies), and the Emergency Committee for American Trade (a group representing sixty-five of America's largest multinational corporations that average half their assets and profits abroad). It is in their common interest to use the threat of foreign imports as an argument to obtain deregulation, which they believe will leave American business more competitive in world markets. They particularly advocate the relaxation of environmental protection and antitrust laws and currently support new legislation that would ameliorate the international application of antitrust laws to allow banks and other corporations to form export trading companies.[78]

Beyond the deregulation issue, however, business groups with overseas interests and those with mostly domestic interests have little in common when it comes to proposals for national industrial policy. Because the international banks and multinational corporations have been in the vanguard of the shift in production from industrialized to developing nations, where wages and costs are lower and profits higher, their fear of the rising tide of protectionism throughout the world is deep and abiding. From the multinational viewpoint, calls for protectionism from U.S. auto and steel makers are an aberration in the "structural readjustment" or "industrial redeployment" process they believe will gradually leave the industrialized economies competing in world markets in high-technology capital goods areas and the less-developed countries competing with low-technology, labor-intensive products. As this structural readjustment reduces jobs and living standards in the major developed countries of the world, spokesmen for the multinational view foresee economic austerity in the coming decades. But their major fear is that this *necessary* structural transition will be undermined by successful pleas for protection from declining industries plagued by import competition. In opposition, organized labor has joined those business groups oriented toward the domestic market in an uneasy alliance to gain support for *necessary* import restrictions and prevent the further "demolition of our industrial base."[79]

Once firmly allied with the provincial interests clamoring for protectionism but now beholden to Wall Street and the international business community whose support he needs to govern effectively, President Reagan has introduced a supply-side proposal for national industrial policy. His program for economic recovery reduces taxes (corporate and personal) to encourage savings and investment. He proposes to reduce regulations to encourage business expansion as well as government expenditures for Social Security, health, welfare, education, and job-training programs to offset increased military expenditures. A full statement of the supply-side philosophy can be found in a recent study of the U.S. economy compiled at the Hoover Institution of Stanford University (1980). Contributors include Milton Friedman, Murray Weidenbaum (current chairman of the Council of Economic Advisers), and Martin Anderson (current member of Reagan's White House staff).[80]

The Hoover group emphasize themes of unfettered capitalism, blame past administrations and public expectations for current economic problems, and call for austerity while suggesting that all Americans will have to become more "puritanical." Rather than a national plan for industrial revitalization, the Hoover group prefers to rely on the private actions of businessmen to allocate capital and rededicate the nation to profits and prosperity. They believe that industry's ability to compete must be fortified with economic growth rather than old-style protectionism. The massive Hoover study does not address the issue of governability or the social and political tensions that can strain democratic institutions when a population, particularly that portion at the bottom of the income-security hierarchy, is forced into austerity and deprived of social services as well as full employment. The authors have faith that a return to the business-government relationship enjoyed twenty-five years ago will lead to economic revitalization and ultimately greater social cohesion. But as economists Michael Best and Jane Humphries have argued (1981), supply-side political philosophy attributes failures of economic performance to the power of government to tax, spend, print, and borrow money. Such a philosophy obscures the fact that the government has become the scapegoat for the dislocations rooted in the lack of democratic accountability that characterizes the market as a social form. The Best-Humphreys argument suggests less optimism in terms of our ability to maintain social cohesion under supply-side economic policies.[81]

Liberal Approaches

While the ethos of capitalism is systematic inequality, the political principles of democracy support universally distributed rights and privileges that proclaim the equality of all citizens. The marketplace efficiently allocates resources and incomes, but it also generates substantial disparities among citizens in living standards and material welfare. Democratic societies with capitalistic economic institutions must continually address the tradeoff between economic principles of efficiency and political principles of equality in the formulation of public policy. The liberal tradition in America has consistently viewed government regulation as the instrumental means of establishing somewhat more equity among citizens than market forces alone would provide. For the most part, those who hold the liberal economic world view have been willing to give up some economic efficiency for the goals of marginal income redistribution and political stability. An interventionist role for government in the capital allocation process is the basic premise that distinguishes liberal approaches to the national industrial policy issue. However, liberals and conservatives share a commitment to economic growth as a first priority. Representative figures include Reich and Thurow who have persuasively argued against the efficacy of conservative revitalization proposals on the grounds that such policies call for measures to raise the level of investment in the economy, while no evidence exists that can show a direct link between capital investment and output. They assert that it is not the level of investment in the economy but the pattern of investment that directly determines our national competitiveness. They further argue that conservative proposals do not address the significant problem areas of excess capacity, increasing interdependence, and distributional politics. They believe that an investment surge, void of specified targets, will fail to achieve desired outcomes and that any policy where the most entrenched and politically active firms might gain control over policy objectives will result in the channeling of capital to economic losers.[82]

Reich suggests that the emerging debate between supply-siders and other proponents of industrial policy has been more ideological than pragmatic. It has been framed in terms of the ideal relationship between governments and markets rather than the hard realities of international competition. As a practical matter, he asserts that a rational industrial policy will provide a far more efficient means to enlarge national wealth than will the random approach of supply-side economics where allocation decisions will be made by corporate executives outside of public view. He is also critical of proposals for tripartite boards, composed of government, business, and labor representatives, intended to hash out an industrial policy for each major industry. He suggests that such boards should be made more representative and involve consumers, small businesses, emerging industries, and nonunion workers as well as organized labor and big business. Reich maintains that industrial policymaking should be made both explicit and public; it should seek to achieve a broad public consensus about how American business can improve its competitive performance in world markets.

Thurow's analysis of the need for a rational industrial policy is similar to Reich's in that he feels the process of picking and supporting winners in the economy has to be a community enterprise, not one left strictly to business and government representatives. Although he asserts that businessmen have a great deal to contribute to the public policymaking process, both in terms of identifying growth areas in the economy and planning expertise, he believes that the major investment decisions of the economy have become far too important to be left to the profit constraints of the marketplace. Thurow argues for the establishment of a national investment bank that would work independently or through private banks, as in Japan. Such a bank would direct funds toward areas of major national interest— energy development would be an obvious starting point. His major fear is that without an explicit industrial policy, recovery efforts will continue for longer periods of time than circumstances warrant and will focus on aid to low-productivity "sunset" industries that have political clout. He suggests that the United States disinvest from low-productivity industries as quickly as possible rather than continue to encourage firms in declining industries with accelerated depreciation schedules and tax subsidies or credits. In addition to minimal support for failing firms, he also suggests that recovery programs be directed toward individuals (retraining, relocation), not firms or regions of the country. This, of course, means devising guidelines for determining when economic losers should suffer income losses and when they should be compensated. Thurow does not underestimate the difficulties involved in getting interest groups to accept losses. But he is surely correct when he argues that Americans must learn to make, impose, and defend distributional (or equity) decisions if we are going to sovle our economic problems.[83]

Other recent proposals within the liberal camp include modest proposals such as the one put forth by Arnold J. Packer (1980), a former assistant labor secretary for policy evaluation and research. He suggests a continuing forum in which interest groups would examine industrial problems and make policy recommendations to the president and Congress. He recommends that government support be marshalled for what he designates as "early certain markets." These are markets with high-growth potential in which the United States now has a significant technological advantage. Packer lists energy-saving and energy-producing equipment, agricultural equipment, medical technology and services, and education/training as appropriate first targets.[84] A somewhat less modest proposal has been out-

lined by Ronald E. Müller in his *Revitalizing America* (1980). Müller calls
for the development of quasi-public national industrial development boards
along with a more forceful role for government in economic matters. He,
too, asserts the need for a working consensus within the country that can
ultimately provide the support needed to implement the changes required if
industrial capitalism is to continue to expand. He suggests that the tradeoffs
between equity, efficiency, and participation will remain dominant issues in
the new public debate over private versus social goods and productive versus nonproductive wealth.[85]

Müller goes on to argue that the fundamental source of difficulty facing the advanced industrial economies lies in the improved bargaining position of the Third World governments vis-á-vis the multinationals and governments based in the West. He argues that as Third World countries have
developed industries such as shipbuilding, petrochemicals, autos, steel, textiles, clothing, shoes, and consumer electronics, those industries have experienced a relative decline in western Europe and the United States. To
counteract strong protectionist responses from workers and corporations
faced with import competition, Müller suggests that the U.S. government
take the lead in promoting international development by establishing a
global Marshall Plan to help channel capital from OPEC and the West into
the industrializing world. The purpose of the plan would be to stimulate
demand for western technology and consumer goods and provide investment opportunities for western capital seeking high rates of return.

Müller's plan may seem utopian and without constituent support, yet
he convincingly demonstrates that nothing has been so destructive of the
economic development in the Third World as the slowdown of growth in the
West that took place during the 1970s. Müller's strongest suit lies in his
recognition of the interdependent features of the slow-growth issue and in
his enthusiasm for an integrated approach to the search for solutions.[86]

Finally, in a special report in *Business Week* on the reindustrialization
issue, the editors led the rest of the business press in urging the development
of a "consensus-forming framework" and a "new social contract" under
which government, business, labor, and other major interest groups can
reach agreement on a system of tradeoffs that would strengthen the
economy. Signatories to this new social contract are asked to scale down
income expectations and shift their priorities from consumption to investment. The *Business Week* editors further suggest that each interest group be
rewarded in terms of its contribution to the economic revitalization effort:
"Each group's income must be related firmly to its economic achieve-
ment." They suggest, for example, that corporate executives be rewarded
according to how well they manage growth measured in terms of their ability to increase productivity, risk-taking activity, and long-range planning.[87]

In response to the general acclaim that greeted the *Business Week*

special report, William E. Connolly (1981) of the University of Massachusetts has pointed out that the reindustrialist search for a more productive
economy (including an expanded military establishment) is approximately,
what, for decades, a prominent group of neo-Marxists have prophesized
would emerge as the new imperatives of advanced capitalism. Connolly's
critique of the reindustrialist position emphasizes that related proposals,
liberal or otherwise, bear a commitment to growth as the first priority. This,
he stresses, is necessarily a commitment to the intensification of discipline
and selective austerity that will result in diminishing levels of equity among
citizens.[88]

Radical Critiques

Critiques from the left share a central concern with the impact of disinvestment on individual workers and communities. Radical proposals for industrial policy, such as those posed by Martin Carnoy and Derek Shearer in
their *Economic Democracy* (1980), can be characterized by their emphasis
on the need for democratic control of the crucial areas of economic decision
making, including investment, organization of the work place, plant location, distribution of goods, choice of technology, and employment strategy.
As another example, Michael Harrington argues in *Decade of Decision*
(1980) that democratization of the investment function is the key to a long
overdue structural transformation of corporate power in America. He
asserts that private corporate domination of the capital allocation process,
with its short-term profit maximization imperative, has been the major
cause of economic decline or stagflation.[89]

Most observers on the left warn that the reindustrialization debate has
been framed in the terms of and according to the agenda of corporate interests, to the detriment of labor and society as a whole. In fact, the revitalization proposals associated with the Carter and Reagan administrations have
shared the assumptions that business needs more capital; that business can
best judge how to allocate capital; that government should regulate business
activity less; and, that representatives of labor, consumer, and environmentalist interest groups should have less influence over corporate decisions. In
addition, those proposals have urged the sacrifice of public services and
worker income in order to support the capital formation effort thought to
be necessary to fuel future growth.

David Moberg (1980), an editor of *In These Times,* represents the radical economic world view when he argues that main-line industrial policy proposals would act to increase corporate power at the same time they excuse
corporate management from any responsibility for industrial decline.

Moberg argues that nothing in the conservative approaches would direct managers to focus on long-term investment at the expense of short-term profitability. Nothing in the conservative proposals would necessarily act to revitalize U.S. industry or to redirect the flow of capital from the Sunbelt region of the country, or from more profitable foreign investment, back into basic domestic industries. Moberg finds it remarkable that the remedy for the faltering corporate economy is more corporate control over investment priorities. He believes that the reindustrialization issue should trigger an intensely political national debate, which squarely addresses the equity, efficiency, and participation tradeoffs involved. Instead, he fears that the debate will continue to be characterized by patriotic urgency that effectively neutralizes the issues.[90]

Moberg has urged the political left to organize around the vision of democratic control over capital investment and to demand that if a needy industry or individual corporation is to receive public support, the public should receive something tangible in return. Board representation or partial public ownership are possibilities that would achieve greater public control over capital. Ralph Nader represented this view when he opposed the bailout plan for the Chrysler Corporation during 1980 on the grounds that the plan actually rewarded incompetent managers. Nader argued that as major beneficiaries of federal loan guarantees, Chrysler's stockholders and dealers should contribute money to the bail-out, not just Chrysler workers who contributed in the form of lower wages. Nader also argued that if Chrysler was to be rescued by the taxpayers some quid pro quos would be in order. He proposed that Chrysler be required to manufacture one of the safety cars designed for the Department of Transportation—initially for government procurement and then for the American market.[91]

Moberg has also argued that the political agenda for the left should include advocating the strict regulation of plant closings and the export of capital so that revitalization aid is not used to camouflage corporate strategies intended to move old technologies to new locations simply to take advantage of cheaper labor. In addition, he calls for a reduction in military spending and the conversion of military to civilian production in an effort to avoid the sustained inflation that will predictably result from an accelerated commitment to military production.

Other critics of main-line proposals include Gar Alperovitz and Jeff Faux (1980), codirectors of the National Center for Economic Alternatives, who argue that the goal of a national industrial policy should be full utilization of productive resources and avoidance of the waste that results from massive dislocation in dependent communities when production facilities are closed. They favor conversion planning, skill retraining, and economic development assistance for areas suffering from major shut downs. They stress that revitalization should lead to reemployment not just high productivity. At the firm level, Alperovitz and Faux propose the reorganization of troubled firms in order to take advantage of productivity gains associated with worker participation and employee ownership. They maintain that the first goals of any reindustrialization policy should be to revitalize useful production and keep people working at productive jobs in economically healthy communities. The policy should provide mechanisms that will assure that capital is invested in both an efficient and a socially responsible manner. And, it should reflect a comprehensive strategy, one that treats the economy as a whole. Alperovitz and Faux conclude that if the political left is to become influential in shaping industrial policy, its representatives must move beyond critique and develop specific proposals for the deployment of investment capital.[92]

Other radical critiques of the reindustrialization issue concentrate on the impact of declining industries on labor. Some labor experts predict that the inability to bargain for real wage increases because of declining corporate revenues or public policy restraints will cause organized labor to adopt new stances toward corporate management. There are predictions that white-collar workers will organize in response to the tighter management controls provoked by falling profits. Some experts believe that the politically conservative, procapitalistic U.S. labor movement may well move to the left during the next decade, toward a commitment to the democratization of capital. Following trends in western Europe, organized labor may seek to gain a voice in decisions on plant closings, pension fund investment, and major capital allocation strategies. When the AFL-CIO rejoined the international union advisory council set up under the Organization for Economic Cooperation and Development (OECD) in 1978, that move linked the AFL-CIO back into the European trade union movement. The reunion has been interpreted by the left as being in the best interest of American workers because it reactivates the principle of labor participation in macroeconomic policymaking. Within that framework, matters related to trade policy and the regulation of multinational corporations are of fundamental interest because of their impact on worldwide employment trends.[93]

Labor lawyer Staughton Lynd (1981) argues that the American labor movement must unite and support the citizen's right to a job and government's responsibility to protect communities from the short-term profit perspective of private corporations. Lynd represented the steel workers of Youngstown, Ohio, in their unsuccessful efforts to maintain jobs and community in the face of major steel company disinvestment during the late 1970s. He suggests an examination of the Swedish experience with overcapacity and low profitability in their steel industry. In Sweden business and government worked together to develop a plan to modernize and rationalize production while they retrained and relocated excess workers. The communities survived, the plants regained profitability, and the unemployment rate in Sweden average 2.1 percent between 1971 and 1979.[94]

Not all radical critics of the status quo believe that reindustrialization is necessary or even desirable. Some critics, such as Connolly, argue that "the hegemony of growth reflected in the obesiance both major political parties give to it," is sustained by the "infrastructure of consumption;" not by a popular belief in a shared future.[95] Tom Hayden rather wistfully writes of the new American frontier wherein the affluent who have become dissatisfied with their pursuit of higher income and consumption will urge the government to deemphasize economic productivity and growth in order to concentrate on quality-of-life issues.[96] On the whole, however, the radical view is much more prone to warn of the increasing social and political tensions that will accompany the unavoidable strains and crises of advanced capitalism. There are warnings that if the United States continues to address the problems of economic decline within an ad hoc and exclusive framework, interest groups denied meaningful participation in the economy, either as workers or consumers, may threaten the public order. Without economic growth to assuage demands for equity on behalf of what has become a permanent underclass in our society, critics argue that it is unclear how long those at the bottom of the income-security hierarchy will be willing to watch rather than share the good life of those at the top. The search for instant remedy may well intensify. While terrorism and crime are regarded as wanton acts that undermine the social order, from the viewpoint of those who seek to change the status quo, they are the desparate but logical response to sustained exclusion.[97]

Notes

1. Public speech, Seattle, Washington, 13 May 1978. Professor Boulding joined Ernest Mandel and Douglass C. North at a University of Washington sponsored seminar to discuss the future of American capitalism.

2. Lester C. Thurow, "Getting Serious About Tax Reform," *Atlantic (Monthly)* (March 1981):68. For more widely available but less current (1979) per capita GNP data, see *World Development Report: 1981* (Washington, D.C.: World Bank, 1981)), p. 135.

3. *Business Week (BW),* 1 June 1981, p. 57; Thurow, "Tax Reform," p. 68.

4. Council of Economic Advisers, *The Economic Report of the President, Gross National Product in 1972 Dollars, 1929-80,* no. B-2 (Washington, D.C.: Government Printing Office (GPO), January 1981), p. 235.

5. Council of Economic Advisers, *The Economic Report of the Presi-*

dent (Washington, D.C.: GPO, January 1979), p. 136. For a survey of recent econometric forecasts, see *BW,* 30 March 1981, pp. 70–77.

6. *BW,* 1 June 1981, p. 57; Robert B. Reich, "The True Road to Industrial Renewal," *The Nation,* 7 March 1981, p. 264; *BW,* 30 June 1980, p. 58. For discussions of evolving global economic interdependence, see Daniel Yergin, "Order and Survival," *Daedalus* (Winter 1978):263–287; W. Arthur Lewis, *The Evolution of the International Economic Order* (Princeton, N.J.: Princeton University Press, 1978); Jagdish N. Bhagwati, ed., *The New International Order* (Cambridge, Mass.: MIT Press, 1977); E.R. Fried and P.H. Trezise, "The United States in the World Economy," *Setting National Priorities* (Washington, D.C.: Brookings Institution, 1976).

7. Council of Economic Advisers, *The Economic Report of the President, Labor Productivity Growth, 1948–80,* no. 8 (Washington, D.C.: GPO, January 1981), p. 69; Thurow, "Tax Reform," p. 68.

8. *BW,* 30 June 1980, p. 61.

9. Lester C. Thurow, *The Zero-Sum Society* (New York: Basic Books, 1980), p. 86; *BW,* 30 June 1980, p. 60.

10. For a discussion of the military expenditures tradeoff, see Seymour Melman, *The Permanent War Economy* (New York: Simon and Schuster, 1974).

11. Karl Polanyi, *The Great Transformation* (New York: Rinehart and Co., 1944).

12. Max Weber, *The Protestant Ethic and the Spirit of Capitalism,* trans. Talcott Parsons (New York: Charles Scribner's Sons, 1958). As a classic American statement of the secularized Protestant ethic, see Benjamin Franklin, *The Autobiography and Other Writings* (New York: New American Library, 1949). For further discussion of the relationship between cultural values and capitalism, see R.H. Tawney, *Religion and the Rise of Capitalism* (New York: Harcourt, Brace and World, 1926); Polanyi, *Great Transformation.*

13. Joseph A. Schumpeter, *Capitalism, Socialism and Democracy,* (New York: Harper and Row, Harper Torchbooks, 1942), p. 127.

14. Daniel Bell, *The Cultural Contradictions of Capitalism* (New York: Basic Books, 1976), p. 19.

15. For a somewhat different treatment of the same theme, see Christopher Lasch, *The Culture of Narcissism* (New York: W.W. Norton, 1978).

16. Michel Crozier, Samuel P. Huntington, and Joji Watanuki, *The Crisis of Democracy* (New York: New York University Press, 1975), pp. 114–115.

17. Willis W. Harman, "Contemporary Social Forces," *The Futurist* (February 1977):68; Willis W. Harmon and Thomas E. Thomas, "The

Challenges of Noneconomic Factors to Economic Growth," *The Factors and Processes Shaping Long-Run Economic Growth,* U.S. Economic Growth from 1976 to 1986: Prospects, Problems, and Patterns, vol. 2, 94th Cong. 2d sess., 1976, p. 42.

18. Herman E. Daly, "The Steady-State Economy: Toward a Political Economy of Biophysical Equilibrium and Moral Growth," *Toward a Steady-State Economy,* ed. H.E. Daly (San Francisco: W.H. Freeman, 1973), pp. 149–174. For a critical discussion of the steady-state concept see, "The No-Growth Society," *Daedalus* (Fall, 1973), entire issue.

19. E.J. Mishan, *The Economic Growth Debate* (London: George Allen and Unwin, 1977); Fred Hirsch, *Social Limits to Growth* (Cambridge, Mass.: Harvard University Press, 1978).

20. Wassily Leontief, et al., *The Future of the World Economy* (New York: Oxford University Press, 1977), pp. 10–11.

21. U.S. Congress, Joint Economic Committee, *A Staff Study, U.S., Long-Term Economic Growth Prospects, Entering a New Era,* 95th Cong., 2d sess., 1978, p. 24. For discussions of the resource scarcity issue see, Harold J. Barnett and Chandler Morse, *Scarcity and Growth* (Baltimore: Johns Hopkins University Press, 1963); Donella H. Meadows, Dennis L. Meadows, Jorgen Randers, and William W. Behrens, *The Limits to Growth* (New York: Universe Books, 1972); Mihajlo Mesarovic and Eduard Pestel, *Mankind at the Turning Point* (New York: E.P. Dutton, 1974).

22. U.S. Congress, Joint Economic Committee, *Staff Study,* p. 16; Daniel Bell, *The Coming of the Post-Industrial Society* (New York: Basic Books, 1973), p. 132.

23. Bell, *Post-Industrial Society,* pp. 154–157; Thurow, *Zero-Sum Society,* p. 88.

24. William J. Baumol, "Macroeconomics of Unbalanced Growth: The Anatomy of Urban Crisis," *American Economic Review* (June 1967):419–420.

25. Theodore Levitt, "Management and the 'Post-Industrial' Society," *The Public Interest* (Summer 1976):69–103; Edward R. Renshaw, "Productivity," *Productivity,* U.S. Economic Growth, vol. 1, 1976, pp. 37–38; U.S., Congress, Joint Economic Committee, *Staff Study,* p. 16.

26. Ronald E. Müller, "National Economic Growth and Stabilization Policy in the Age of Multinational Corporations: The Challenge of our Postmarket Economy," *Economic Growth in the International Context,* U.S. Economic Growth, vol. 12, 1977, pp. 35–79.

27. *BW,* 30 June 1980, p. 112. Raymond Vernon has chronicled the growth, development, and impact of the multinational conglomerate on the nation-state in *Sovereignty at Bay* (New York: Basic Books, 1971); idem, *Storm Over the Multinationals* (Cambridge, Mass.: Harvard University Press, 1977).

28. William Bowen, *Fortune,* 3 December 1979, pp. 68–86.

29. Council of Economic Advisers, *The Economic Report of the President, Labor Productivity Growth, 1948-80,* no. 8 (Washington, D.C.: GPO, 1981), p. 69.

30. For more detail, see John W. Kendrick, "Productivity Trends and Prospects," *Productivity,* U.S. Economic Growth, vol. 1, 1976, pp. 1-19; Renshaw, "Productivity," pp. 21-56; Richard R. Nelson, "Research on Productivity Growth and Productivity Differences: Dead Ends and New Departures," *Journal of Economic Literature (JEL)* (September 1981):1029-1064.

31. Thurow, *Zero-Sum Society,* pp. 85-87.

32. Ibid., pp. 85, 92-102.

33. Ibid., p. 80.

34. Ibid., p. 79.

35. Thurow, "Tax Reform," pp. 68-72.

36. Reich, "Industrial Renewal," pp. 264-267.

37. Thurow, *Zero-Sum Society,* p. 86.

38. Ibid.; Council of Economic Advisers, *The Economic Report of the President, Disposition of Personal Income, 1929-80,* no. B-21 (Washington, D.C.: GPO, 1981), p. 258.

39. *Fortune,* 16 June 1980, p. 126.

40. Robert H. Hayes and William J. Abernathy, "Managing Our Way to Economic Decline," *Harvard Business Review (HBR)* (July/August 1980):70.

41. Ibid.; *BW,* 30 June 1980, pp. 74-82.

42. Thomas H. Naylor, *BW,* 6 April 1981, pp. 14-16; Lawrence R. Jauch, Thomas N. Martin, and Richard N. Osborn, "Top Management Under Fire," *Journal of Business Strategy* (Spring 1981):33-41.

43. Frank A. Weil, *BW,* 3 December 1979, p. 14; Douglas Bauer, "Executives," *The New York Times Magazine,* 8 March 1981, pp. 80-81.

44. *BW,* 30 June 1980, p. 75.

45. Staughton Lynd, "Reindustrialization: Brownfield or Greenfield?," *Democracy* (July 1981):24-25.

46. Paul Blumberg, *Inequality in an Age of Decline* (New York: Oxford University Press, 1980), p. 112.

47. Hayes and Abernathy, "Managing Our Way," pp. 71-74.

48. Bruce R. Scott, "The Industrial State: Old Myths and New Realities," *HBR* (March/April 1973):139-142.

49. *BW* 30 June 1980, p. 138.

50. Reich, "Industrial Renewal," p. 264; *BW,* 24 August 1981, pp. 68-74.

51. Harman and Thomas, *U.S. Economic Growth,* vol. 2 (1976), pp. 41-58.

52. Mishan, *Growth Debate;* Nathaniel J. Mass and Jay W. Forrester, "Understanding the Changing Basis for Economic Growth in the United

States," *Forecasts of Long-Run Economic Growth,* U.S. Economic Growth, vol. 6, 1976, pp. 38–75. For a discussion of the intrinsic limits to progress in the biological sciences, see Gunther S. Stent, *Paradoxes of Progress* (San Francisco: W.H. Freeman, 1978).

53. Kenneth J. Arrow, *The Limits of Organization* (New York: W.W. Norton, 1974); Rufus E. Miles, Jr., *Awakening from the American Dream* (New York: Universe Books, 1976), pp. 179–190. Also, see Mishan, *Growth Debate;* Mass and Forrester, "Changing Basis for Economic Growth," pp. 38–75.

54. *BW,* 30 April 1980, pp. 66–67. For a discussion of the regulation issue, compare Kenneth J. Arrow, "Two Cheers for Government Regulation," *Harper's* (March 1981):18–22 and Murray L. Weidenbaum, *Business, Government, and the Public* (Englewood Cliffs, N.J.: Prentice-Hall, 1977).

55. Thurow, *Zero-Sum Society,* pp. 122–154. Also, see James E. Post, *Corporate Behavior and Social Change* (Reston, Va.: Reston Publishing Co. 1978).

56. The Milton Friedman quote is cited in Ronald E. Müller, *Revitalizing America* (New York: Simon and Schuster, 1980), p. 200. The original quote appeared in Allen Heslop, ed., *Business-Government Relations* (New York: New York University Press, 1976), p. 12.

57. Douglass C. North, "Structure and Performance: The Task of Economic History," *JEL* (September 1978):969.

58. Mancur Olson, *The Logic of Collective Action* (Cambridge, Mass.: Harvard University Press, 1965); idem, "The Political Economy of Comparative Growth Rates," *The Factors and Processes Shaping Long-Run Economic Growth,* U.S. Economic Growth, vol. 2, 1976, pp. 25–40.

59. Charles E. Lindblom, *Politics and Markets* (New York: Basic Books, 1977), pp. 175–178.

60. U.S. Bureau of the Census, *Current Population Reports, Consumer Income 1977,* Series P–60, no. 118 (Washington, D.C.: GPO, March 1979), p. 228.

61. See Robert B. Reich, "Regulation by Confrontation or Negotiation?" *HBR* (May/June 1981):82–93.

62. Thurow, *Zero-Sum Society,* p. 18; Robert L. Heilbroner, *Business Civilization in Decline* (New York: W.W. Norton, 1978). For a discussion of the politicization trend in the economies of Great Britain and western Europe, see Samuel Brittan, *Capitalism and the Permissive Society* (London: Macmillan and Co., 1973); Peter Jay, "Englanditis," *The Future That Doesn't Work,* ed. R. Emmett Tyrrell, Jr. (Garden City, New York: Doubleday, 1977); Michele Salvati and Giorgio Brosio, "The Rise of Market Politics: Industrial Relations in the Seventies," *Daedalus* (Spring 1976):43–71. For a discussion of interdependence and rising entitlements themes as they relate to the private U.S. corporation, see George C. Lodge, *The New American Ideology* (New York: Alfred A. Knopf, 1976).

63. Reich, "Industrial Renewal," p. 265.

64. *U.S. News and World Report (U.S. News),* 22 September 1980, p. 59.

65. Reich, "Industrial Renewal," p. 265.

66. For a recent comparative discussion of the national industrial policy issue, see William Diebold, Jr., *Industrial Policy as an International Issue* (New York: McGraw-Hill, 1980).

67. *BW,* 6 April 1981, pp. 54-6; *Newsweek,* 18 May 1981, pp. 22-23; David Dickson, "Scuttling the Sea-Law Treaty," *Nation,* 30 May 1981, p. 668.

68. *Time,* 14 July 1980, pp. 42-43; *U.S. News,* 11 September 1980, pp. 59-60; President's Commission for a National Agenda for the Eighties, *A National Agenda for the Eighties* (New York: New American Library, 1981).

69. *BW,* 30 June 1980, pp. 138-142.

70. Judith Miller, "The Emperor's New Policy," *Working Papers* (November/December 1980):12-14.

71. James Fallows, "American Industry: What Ails It, How to Save It," *Atlantic,* (September 1980):50.

72. Andrew Hacker, "Up for Grabs," *The New York Review of Books (New York Review),* 30 April 1980, p. 8.

73. *Time,* 14 July 1980, p. 43.

74. For a discussion of the opposing economic world views that underly the national policy debate, see Benjamin Ward, *The Conservative Economic World View, The Liberal Economic World View, The Radical Economic World View,* Ideal Worlds of Economic Series (New York: Basic Books, 1979).

75. Amitai Etzioni, "Choose America Must," *Across the Board* (October 1980):42-49; idem, *BW,* 25 August 1980, p. 16.

76. Michael Walzer, "Nervous Liberals," *New York Review,* 11 October 1979, pp. 5-9. The journals *The Public Interest* and *Public Policy* regularly present neo-conservative views on public policy issues.

77. John Pinder, Takashi Hosomi, and William Diebold, Jr., *Industrial Policy and the International Economy* (New York: The Trilateral Commission, 1979).

78. Jeff Frieden, "The Coming Trade War at Home," *Nation,* 19 April 1981, pp. 464-468; Peter H. Stone, "The New War on Antitrust Laws," *Nation,* 28 March 1981, pp. 364-367.

79. Frieden, "Trade War," p. 466.

80. Peter Duignan and Alvin Rabushka, eds., *The United States in the 1980s* (Stanford, Calif.: Hoover Institution, 1980); Hacker, "Up for Grabs," pp. 8, 10.

81. Michael Best and Jane Humphries, "Thatcherism," *Democracy* (July 1981):48.

82. Reich, "Industrial Renewal," pp. 264-267; Thurow, *Zero-Sum*

Society. For discussion of the liberal world view, see Arthur M. Okun, *Equality and Efficiency* (Washington, D.C.: The Brookings Institution, 1975); Philip Green, *The Pursuit of Inequality* (New York: Pantheon Books, 1981).

83. *U.S. News,* 22 September 1980, pp. 61–62; Thurow, *Zero-Sum Society,* pp. 96, 191–194; Lester C. Thurow, Barry Bluestone, and Harley Shaiden, "Reindustrialization and Jobs," *Working Papers* (November/December 1980):50.

84. Fallows, "American Industry," p. 50.

85. Müller, *Revitalizing America,* p. 236.

86. Ibid., p. 280; David Vogel, "How to Put Humpty Together Again," *New York Review,* 11 June 1981, pp. 29–32.

87. *BW,* 30 June 1980, pp. 86, 88.

88. William E. Connolly, "The Politics of Reindustrialization," *Democracy* (July 1981):14, 18. For neo-Marxists critiques of advanced capitalism see James O'Connor, *The Fiscal Crisis of the State* (New York: St. Martin's Press, 1971); Jürgen Habermas, *Legitimation Crisis* (Boston: Beacon Press, 1973); Ernest Mandel, *Late Capitalism* (London, NLB, 1975).

89. Martin Carnoy and Derek Shearer, *Economic Democracy* (White Plains, N.Y.: M.E. Sharpe, Inc., 1980); Michael Harrington, *Decade of Decision* (New York: Simon & Schuster, 1980), pp. 29, 320.

90. David Moberg, "Retooling the Industrial Debate," *Working Papers* (November/December 1980):32–39.

91. Ibid.

92. Gar Alperovitz and Jeff Faux, "Beyond Bailouts: Notes for Next Time," *Working Papers* (November/December 1980):14–18. Also, see Gar Alperovitz and Jeff Faux, *Rebuilding America* (New York: Simon & Schuster, 1981).

93. *BW,* 28 January 1980, pp. 76–78; *BW,* 17 April 1978, pp. 126–130.

94. Lynd, "Reindustrialization," pp. 22–36.

95. Connolly, "Politics," p. 20.

96. Tom Hayden, *The American Future* (Boston: South End Press, 1980).

97. Hacker, "Up for Grabs," p. 16.

2 Corporate Strategy

This chapter examines the issue of corporate behavior in a slow-growth economy. How do declining growth rates affect corporate decision makers? What corporate strategies are pursued during periods of economic decline? Even within stringent constraints, there are no economic models capable of predicting firm-level outcomes that result from specified changes in the macroeconomic environment. Economic models of firm behavior cannot specify rational strategic responses to changes in interactive macroeconomic variables, such as declining aggregate demand, accelerating interest rates, and the imposition of import quotas. The models are helpful in predicting the direction of rational change in terms of pricing, input, or output levels for large groups of firms, but they cannot specify the magnitude of change for a single firm.[1]

Despite the theoretical gap that exists between macro- and micro-level economic theories and the behavior of the individual firm, casual observation indicates that macroeconomic factors shape the conditions of the marketplace and the corporate decision process. It is also clear that a negative or declining gross national product growth rate does not indicate an across the board pattern of economic contraction. Slow growth does mean, however, that a larger proportion of the economic units in an economic system will undergo contraction in one form or another. As Kenneth E. Boulding explains, at any given time, some economic units in the economy will be expanding while others will be contracting. Under growth conditions, this distribution is weighted toward expanding economic units, and only a few economic units will be experiencing economic contraction. In an economy where growth is slowing, a larger proportion of economic units will be contracting, and, in a stationary economy, roughly half of the economic units will be contracting while the other half will be experiencing growth.[2]

Questions abound regarding the impact of growth constraints on corporate behavior. What are the basic patterns of response to contracting corporate revenues? Are those patterns related to specific causal factors, such as short-term national stabilization policy, management failure, foreign import competition, or diminishing demand for a specific product? We can observe that firms threatened by contracting revenues often adopt corporate strategies that will, over time, effectively redeploy their assets from capital or labor-intensive industries to industries where such requirements are less stringent. Other firms attempt backward integration in order to own fuel supplies or control the cost of basic materials. Some threatened firms acquire existing facilities as a means of checking competition, decreasing overhead, or increasing productivity with new technology or higher volume. Diversified firms often disinvest or exit from unprofitable markets. Some firms develop new export markets. Others request government intervention in the form of loan guarantees, subsidies, or tax relief. Still others seek trade barriers to protect their domestic markets. The goal of these strategies is to *rationalize* (to make stable, predictable, and secure) to the greatest extent possible the firm's external environment by whatever means are available.

We can also observe that firms respond to the threat of economic decline by reorganizing staff and restructuring relationships between organizational work groups. Top management is frequently replaced with a new *turnaround* crew. There are accounts of competitors redoubling their efforts to woo customers and suppliers away from a contracting firm with suggestions that the firm is no longer reliable. There are also reports that contracting firms are besieged by personnel raids while necessary efficiency moves are counteracted by defensive employees seeking to protect their terrain because they realize that further efficiency gains will result in more layoffs. Organizational theorists predict that flexible and innovative response patterns will become increasingly difficult to orchestrate in firms confronted with a declining resource base.[3]

As general observation makes evident, there are many questions that must be answered before a systematic approach to the issues surrounding corporate strategy under conditions of revenue contraction can be formulated. Clearly, the cause of contraction will vary with each firm depending on its history, structure, technology, markets, strategy, and its susceptibility to changing market conditions. The specific causes of contraction present important distinctions for public policy. In growth industries, ineffective managers can be replaced, corporate strategies can be realigned, and government policies can redirect resource utilization. But contracting firms in declining industries present different policy issues—those of transition rather than revitalization.

Regardless of cause, the issue of corporate response to decline is an important one. To date, relatively little serious consideration has been given to the problems of the contracting firm. For the most part, the firm and the more abstract complex organization have been studied under conditions of expansion with broad theoretical assumptions of unlimited growth potential. In fact, as organizational theorist Jeffrey D. Ford recently noted, growth has been used as a surrogate for organizational effectiveness in much of the economic and organizational research. While there is ample past evidence of American corporations, public agencies, and even entire industries that have expanded and then contracted in size, incidents of contraction have for the most part been considered anomalous in the theoretical literature. The difficulties faced by the managers of decliining organizations have been regarded as outside the mainstream of management thought. There is a small body of literature concerned with corporate failure and turnaround management. But the rater eclectic group of authors involved generally write in a prescriptive mode and commonly assume that growth can and will resume as soon as management is set straight. In recent years, organizational theorists such as Richard M. Cyert, Charles H. Levine, and William G. Scott have addressed the issue of governance in organizational units facing decline and Kathryn R. Harrigan has discussed strategy formulation in response to declining market demand (products made obsolete by technological, cultural, or demographic change).[4] But, there are no major studies that go beyond product-market decline to deal with corporate behavior in terms of the overall pattern of accommodation once corporate contraction has become an unavoidable reality. Nor has any major study of corporate decline focused on the collaborative relationship between the private corporation and government regulators when continuous rates of economic growth can no longer provide a feasible means of problem solution for either or both parties.

Basic Questions

There are many basic questions to be addressed in a study of the corporate response to declining rates of growth. These questions, as they have been posed by various interested parties, reflect opposing assumptions, theories, and models of firm behavior. The perspective brought to bear on the issue results in different types of questions about the contraction process, different terminologies, and different levels of specificity (see table 2-1).

A single study cannot deal extensively with all basic questions, even if rendered comparable in terms of point of view, vocabulary, and variable definition. Many of the questions cannot be answered at all given the public data currently available. Outside of the financial and employment data published quarterly and annually by the business press (*Fortune, Business Week, Forbes*), comparable corporate statistics on individual U.S. firms are difficult to locate. While various federal agencies require a vast number of statistical reports from U.S. corporations, federal policy, which seeks to disguise information from competitors of reporting firms results in the publication of corporate statistics on an industry level only. Consequently there is considerable pressure for the researcher in need of corporate data to shift

Table 2–1
Basic Questions: Corporate Response to Declining Rates of Growth

---

1. To what extent are major U.S. corporations forced to cope with prolonged periods of sales revenue contraction?

2. Is contraction primarily related to:
changing investment patterns?
obsolete technology?
excess productive capacity?
declining research and development expenditures?
increased competition for resources (including energy)?
vigorous foreign competition?
changing consumer tastes/declining markets?
loss of control by management (to creditors, majority shareholders, regulators, the courts)?

3. Does corporate contraction result in:
increased levels of government assistance for the firm? the industry? employees?
increased levels of diversification?
increased levels of international market penetration?
increased centralization of decision authority within the firm? increased decentralization?
increased long-term planning activity?
increased concern with the supply of basic materials?
increased levels of conflict and coalition activity within the firm?
increased willingness of the board of directors to change top management?
increased levels of litigation between the firm and claimant groups?

4. Are highly diversified multinationals or conglomerates immune to contraction?

5. Does contraction tend to encourage merger activity resulting in increased rates of industrial concentration?

6. Does the firm attempt to externalize some of the costs of coping with slower growth through the political process? the market?

7. How are evolving business-government relations perceived under conditions of contraction? Is government assistance requested? Are antiregulatory attitudes maintained?

8. Does intensive special interest lobbying on behalf of the firm in Congress and before regulatory agencies, shareholders, and the public correlate with contraction?

9. What patterns of internal resource utilization emerge for the firm under conditions of contraction in terms of finance, marketing, employee relations, management incentives, and litigation?

10. What happens to shareholders' equity under conditions of contraction? Do management's interests prevail?

11. Which characteristics of the firm contribute to a successful pattern of accommodation?

12. How does decline affect the morale of employees? What types of personnel are attracted to the contracting firm?

13. What are the apologetics of decline? Who gets the blame: politicians? management? government bureaucrats? foreign competitors? What is the vocabulary of explanation? How is contraction explained to shareholders, the investment community, the general public?

14. Which field in the social sciences provides the most appropriate concepts, theories, models, and methods for the further study of the corporate response to contraction and economic decline?

---

the level of analysis from the firm level to the industry level—an instance of means determining ends. Given the questions under consideration here, such a shift would be inappropriate. Contracting firms and contracting industries are not equivalent; there are many growing firms in contracting industries and vice versa. More important, for the most part, the largest U.S. industrials are so highly diversified that analysis on an industry level either becomes simplistic, if homogeneity is assumed, or impossibly complex, when the true level of diversity is represented.

Of the questions listed in table 2-1, those which seek to correlate contraction with increases or decreases in certain behaviors (increased requests for government assistance, for example) cannot be answered even on an industry level because the data have not heretofore been collected. Only a careful case by case analysis can generate such data in terms of current and past levels of activity. Even then, the problems of comparability remain acute because of the high degree of structural diversity that exists between firms of the same general type (single-product, related-product, or diversified) participating in the same industry or industries.

In Search of a Conceptual Framework

Why are the basic questions asked about the contraction process so varied? Why is the descriptive terminology so confusing and the level of specificity so disparate? This confusion arises because the questions are generated from fundamentally different concepts or models of firm behavior. Different assumptions lead to different hypotheses about what has gone awry and why. Decision criteria, the role of the corporate decision maker, the level of decision interdependence, and the extent of strategy flexibility can differ sharply with perspective. Assumptions of *steady-state growth* (that is, once strategy variables have been set the firm grows at a constant exponential rate with constant profit levels and retention ratios) characterize many conceptual frameworks and theoretical models that attempt to predict or explain corporate behavior. Some models assume decision rules that result in automatic decision criteria to single out the best course of action. Other models focus attention on the nature and characteristics of the decision-making agent or agents under conditions of uncertainty. Still other models view corporate strategy as the result of the rational response to broad historical patterns of change in the economy.

In the search for the most persuasive frame of reference for undertaking the interpretation of the corporate studies that follow in part II, the view of the corporate decision maker is of primary importance. The corporate studies, which detail cases of the contraction process, focus on executive decision makers and the corporate strategies they pursue in response to the environmental uncertainty created by contracting revenues. The following review of pertinent theories of firm behavior is intended to develop a frame of reference. The aim is not to appropriate specific assumptions, hypotheses, or models of variable interaction but rather to assess the usefulness of general conceptual schemes for systematically approaching the questions under consideration.

The Economic Theory of the Firm

Derived from the work of Alfred Marshall (1890) and subsequent marginalists, the neoclassical theory of the firm posits an a priori model from which firm behavior can be deduced. The firm is a purely theoretical construct embedded in an interactive system of *perfectly competitive markets* (atomistic competition, free entry and exit, homogeneous goods, perfect knowledge and information). Based on specified changes in market conditions, neoclassical theory can predict the direction of change in prices, inputs, or outputs for a large number of firms. But the theory provides no explanation of how or why firms grow or contract in size and the neoclassical model assumes steady-state growth. Neither are factors such as differential firm size, market concentration, or *uncertainty* (imperfect knowledge) taken into account. Firm behavior represents the application of a single decision criterion, profit maximization. No other decision rules are posited. Hence, the view of the decision maker and of the decision process is very limited. Neoclassical theory assumes that the profit maximization rule will *automatically* single out the best course of action for the firm as market conditions change.[5] Although neoclassical theory does not directly contribute to an understanding of corporate contraction issues, it does provide the starting point, or the assumptions that define the terms of debate, for consequent theoretical frameworks that consider decision criteria and firm behavior under conditions of imperfect competition and differential rates of growth.

Behavioral Revisions. During the last fifty years, various revisionist efforts have contributed to the development of descriptive models of firm behavior, which reflect market structure, human decision processes, and differential corporate strategies. The intent of the two major revisionist efforts, behavioral and managerial, has been to heighten the predictive power of the theory of the firm by introducing empirical content. Early revisionist efforts began in the 1930s in Great Britain and the United States. Dissatisfaction with the limitations of neoclassical theory led, on the one hand, to the development of macroeconomics as a separate field of study, and, on the other, to the development of new microtheories of the firm.[6] The new microtheories released assumptions of pure competition and homogeneous goods and led to models of firm behavior under conditions of monopolistic and oligopolistic competition. These theories changed the focus of analysis by raising the issue of interdependent decision criteria (between firms).[7]

The critical assumption of profit maximization also came under attack with the publication of *The Modern Corporation and Private Property* in 1932 written by Adolf Berle and Gardiner C. Means. Among other arguments, Berle and Means presented evidence of the degree of separation of ownership from management in the United States. They questioned whether the professional manager, whose self-interest logically diverged from that of the owner-entrepreneur, could be expected to behave as a *profit maximizer;* that is, to maximize owner welfare.[8] But because it was nearly twenty years before the Berle and Means study had a significant impact on the economic theory of the firm, the development of the behavioral school of revisionists is generally dated from 1939 and the publication by R.L. Hall and C.J. Hitch of a descriptive study of pricing behavior in British firms. Hall and Hitch found that managers actually based their prices on *full costs;* that is, average fixed costs plus average variable costs plus a margin for *normal* profits. They found that managers believed this method of pricing kept prices stable in the short term, changing only when costs for most firms in the industry moved in the same direction.[9] Although full-cost pricing can be consistent with profit maximization, it is a quite different process from the marginal analysis method of price determination posited by neoclassical theory. After Hall and Hitch, empirical studies which closely examined managerial behavior within the firm gained credibility.

Subsequent research found that profit maximization behavior, though plausible, required a rather special psychology on the part of corporate decision makers. Observation and analysis of the decision processes within corporate organizations indicated that professional managers were more concerned with sales growth and their own goals (stability, risk aversion, power, prestige, and the leisure-income tradeoff) than with profit maximization per se; that decision processes within the firm were plagued by information bias; that competition for organizational resources led to compromise decisions which could not easily be equated with profit maximization; and that exchange relationships between the firm and various claimant groups (employees, suppliers, creditors, regulators, and so on) entailed a level of interdependence that constrained managerial discretion and frequently led to deviation from maximization goals.[10]

Herbert A. Simon's early study of corporate decision making (1945) and later study of the human decision process (1955) pushed behavioral theory forward another step. Unlike the rational man posited by neoclassical theory, Simon's decision maker, as revealed in the choice processes exhibited by actual corporate executives, is not only constrained by environmental factors but also by his own *bounded rationality* (that is, the neurophysiological limits of cognition). Simon determined that organizational decision makers have multiple goals and that the decision process involves the resolution of conflicting goals among subunits on a continuing basis. He found that organizational decision makers must act under conditions of uncertainty and that the search for information and problem solution is a biased, myopic, and simplistic process. Simon discovered that corporate managers do not know whether they are in fact maximizing profits because they have neither perfect information not pure rationality. Consequently Simon argued that managerial behavior can more accurately be described as *satisficing* rather than optimizing in nature. In the real world, when profit levels are unsatisfactory in terms of manager, creditor, or investor expectations, search activity is undertaken as a corrective measure. Simon determined that corporate goals are not given but discovered through a continuous process of analysis and search.[11]

Additional consideration of the corporate decision-making process was undertaken by Richard M. Cyert and James G. March (1956, 1963) who emphasized the role of *groups* (those who have a stake in the firm's performance: managers, workers, creditors, investors, and customers) in the setting of corporate goals and strategy. From this perspective, the firm becomes a coalition of interest groups with often conflicting values and goals. Cyert and March found that organizational decision making is a continuous bargaining and learning process. Hence the firm, rather than having one overriding goal such as profit maximization, has a series of more or less independent goals: a production goal, a sales goal, a market share goal, a profit goal, an inventory goal. These goals exist in a state of actual or potential conflict. Building on Simon's work, Cyert and March argued that conflict resolution, uncertainty avoidance, problemistic search, and learning were the important elements of a general theory of firm behavior. They characterized the firm as an adaptive entity wherein decision rules are reinforced and used again if performance is satisfactory (uncertainty avoidance). Unsatisfactory performance (failure to satisfy coalition goals) activates search activity to develop more acceptable alternatives or more efficient means. Search continues until participants in the organizational coalition are satisfied or goals are readjusted.[12]

Behavioralists make the assumption that the basic organizational features of structure and function evolve from the characteristics of human problem-solving processes. As with other behavioral research, the intent has been to develop a theory of firm behavior with generality beyond the specific firms studied. As a theoretical framework, the behavioral model developed by Simon, Cyert, and March has proven more successful in explaining behavior within firms than in predicting behavioral responses to common stimuli, such as increasing interest rates or declining markets. The merit of behavioral models has been their emphasis on bounded rationality and treatment of the firm as an adaptive entity in which decision processes change as personnel and the relative bargaining strengths of the groups in the organizational coalition change. For the purpose of predicting firm behavior under conditions of contracting revenues, the behavioral model is of limited value because steady-state growth is assumed. The conceptual framework developed by the behavioral revisionists, however, should prove useful in any interpretative scheme concerned with human decision processes. Because behavioral theories focus attention on the nature and characteristic of the decision-making agent or agents, they are relevant to any descriptive effort that seeks to characterize firm behavior in realistic terms.

Managerial Revisions. Revisionists in the managerial stream have built on the work of Berle and Means. They stress two factors in their analyses: the separation of management from ownership in the large joint-stock corporations; and that such corporations operate in increasingly concentrated or oligopolistic markets. Their models of firm behavior focus on top-echelon managers. They assume that since executive-level managers make the ultimate decisions in the firm, the study of such managers will provide a reliable guide to strategic action and firm behavior. They suggest that there is sufficient similarity between the motivations of executive-level professional managers in most firms to make managerial theories generally applicable. Major contributors include William J. Baumol, Oliver E. Williamson, and Robin Marris, in addition to those researchers who conducted the earlier empirical studies questioning the assumption of profit maximization.

In 1959 William J. Baumol presented empirical evidence that the typical firms operating in an oligopolistic market maximize gross revenues or sales rather than net revenues or profit. He argued that managerial utility functions are maximized subject to a minimum profit constraint. That is, *managerial rewards* (remuneration and prestige) are a function of *growth* (increasing sales revenue) as long as an established rate of return on investment is obtained. Baumol argued that managers can effectively resolve any conflict between growth and profit objectives by establishing and maintaining a minimum profit level.[13]

Baumol later refined his theory of managerial behavior by hypothesizing that managment groups, rather than simply maximizing current sales levels, maximize the growth rate of sales. Profit remains an instrumental variable or a means whereby management works toward its overriding goal of long-term growth. The retained earnings share of profits provide the capital needed to finance expansion. Therefore, an automatic limit exists as to how far profits can be encroached upon in order to enhance current sales. Baumol argued that profit levels must remain high enough not only to mollify shareholders but also to finance the investment required for long-term sales growth.[14]

Subsequent theorists have argued that managerial motivation is related to a composite managerial utility function. Oliver E. Williamson's (1964) managerial-discretion model of firm behavior suggests that firms that enjoy

an overall high level of demand in an environment of weak competition utilize *managerial slack* (the difference between actual profits and reported
profits) to support discretionary managerial behavior. Williamson argued
that discretionary spending for corporate investment and managerial
emoluments (perqs) is deducted from actual profits in the utility-
maximizing firm. Williamson posited that managerial slack is constrained
by the lowest level of profits consistent with retention of effective control
over the firm, including dividends to shareholders and necessary funds for
investment (*security constraint*). Hence, throughout the business cycle the
utility-maximizing firm is characterized by small variations in profits. When
profitability lags, Williamson's model predicts a reduction in managerial
slack and thus in discretionary behavior on the part of professional managers.[15]

Simultaneously, Robin Marris (1963, 1964) developed a dynamic-
growth theory wherein he determined the managerial utility function to be
composed of two elements: the growth rate or size of the firm, and the
valuation ratio, or the relationship between the market value of the firm
and the book value of net assets. Marris postulated that the valuation ratio
acted as a security constraint on growth. He argued that managers find satisfaction in being associated with a large firm that has stock market approval,
that is, when stock is valued at a high enough level to keep shareholders
satisfied and discourage takeover bids. According to Marris, professional
managers subject corporate strategy decisions to utility functions of their
own. Individually they value salary, power, and status, and as a group they
value aggregate profits, aggregate capital, share of the market, and public
image—all of which correlate more closely with size than with profit
level. The restraining force on size or growth, according to Marris, is the
felt need for security from takeover, shareholder dissatisfaction, or close
scrutiny by either creditors or the general public. Importantly, Marris also
postulated that growth demand, and hence growth in the size of the firm,
is a function of the firm's rate of diversification. He asserted that fast-
growing firms must continually acquire and launch new products as most
products follow a characteristic product life cycle where profitability and
price elasticity vary over time. At very high rates of diversification, the valuation ratio checks the rate of growth before either management or financial
resources become overextended and threaten the security or tenure of top-
echelon managers.[16]

Efforts to refine and empirically validate Williamson's static managerial model of firm behavior and Marris' dynamic growth model are currently underway. Given considerable managerial discretion and the indeter-
minancy and uncertainty of environmental conditions, validation may
prove difficult. According to Marris, specific criteria for determining pricing policies, diversification strategies, and growth rates must be developed

if the managerial models are to become more than merely descriptive. Nevertheless, criteria specification for Marris' model will be particularly difficult as the individual units under study interact in a dynamic self-organizing system in which stimulus and response are interdependent.[17]

Neither managerial model is determinate enough to be used as the sole means of analysis in a study of firm behavior under conditions of economic decline. However, the proposition than under conditions of oligopolistic competition, corporate managers enjoy considerable discretion in strategy and policy choices is useful. Observable variation in the behavior of individual firms is such that it is quite impossible to support a case that only particular narrowly defined strategies will result in specific outcomes. Williamson's notion that a decrease in managerial slack is related to a decrease in managerial discretion leads to the proposition that corporate contraction will considerably reduce managerial discretion. Marris' proposition that for professional managers there is a tradeoff between their own security and growth of the firm suggests that contraction episodes may prove difficult for top-echelon managers who cannot afford further diversification and cannot otherwise raise rates of return or profitability. It should be noted, however, that neither Williamson nor Marris actually direct the reader's attention toward the expected behavioral ramifications of reduced managerial slack or constrained growth.

Stages of Corporate Development

A major criticism leveled against behavioral and managerial revisionists is that their theories tend to ignore the real diversity of the corporate population. During the last twenty years, a group of theories has developed that argue changes in corporate size, structure, and managerial strategy are mediated by changes in the firm's external environment. Alfred D. Chandler's *Strategy and Structure* (1962) essentially set the parameters for the literature dealing with stages of corporate growth. Chandler outlined in four phases the general historical pattern of corporate administrative accommodation to changing environmental conditions in the United States between 1850 and 1950. Demographic changes in population, personal income, and evolving technology provided the opportunity for the firm's rapid expansion and for the more profitable deployment of existing resources. These changing environmental conditions acted to reshape the firm's internal characteristics and its role as a major economic institution. Before 1850, most economic decisions were made by entrepreneurs working alone or with one or two partners. Merchants operated much as they had in the Western world for the previous 500 years. Manufacturing, mining, and agriculture were carried out almost entirely by small, single-unit enterprises operated by their owners. These owner-entrepreneurs had little control over their supplies, markets, or prices. The neoclassical theory of the firm was relevant to this kind of production.[18]

According to Chandler, a new and different type of decision-making unit appeared after 1850. It was the large, multiunit enterprise operated by professional managers rather than owners. It was first seen in the major railroad and telegraph enterprises. By the 1880s, these businesses had built permanent work forces of tens of thousands of workers administered by hundreds of salaried managers. Similar large enterprises subsequently began to appear in industries and trades where the use of new technologies permitted high-volume production and where developing transportation and communication systems encouraged high-volume distribution. The centralized coordination, evaluation, and planning for the activities of a large number of subunits, which frequently carried out several different functions of production, distribution and transportation within a single enterprise, could not be run efficiently without a formal internal organization. The new enterprises required the creation of internal operating, financial, and cost data. The operational requirements of the multiunit enterprises required the services of a large number of technically trained managers who eventually replaced the original entrepreneurs as a new class of economic decision makers. Relations between the multiunit firm and the external environment also changed. With *vertical integration* (the move into new functions), transactions previously carried on between firms in the market place came to be carried out within the firm. Prices came to be based more on cost estimates than on the forces of supply and demand. The concentrated economic power of the new multiunit enterprises encouraged the growth of countervailing institutions in the form of labor unions and governmental regulatory commissions.[19]

Chandler's historical study of four large American firms (DuPont, General Motors, Standard Oil of New Jersey, Sears Roebuck), augmented by broader industry analyses, led him to propose that the role of professional management in the growth and development of the firm has been to plan and direct the use of resources to meet fluctuations and developments in the firm's external environment. His model of the firm is based on the two critical areas in which management exercises choice: strategy and structure. Chandler defines the basic determination of long-term goals and objectives of a firm and the appraising, planning, and coordinating actions undertaken by managers to affect growth plans as *strategy*. Decisions are *strategic* if they are concerned with the long-term health of the enterprise and *tactical* if they deal with the day-to-day activities necessary for efficient and smooth operations. He defines *structure* as the organization devised to administer these corporate activities and resources. Structure includes the lines of authority and communication between the different administrative offices and officers as well as the information and data that flow through these lines. Chandler argues that different organizational structures result from different types of growth; that is, organizational structure flows from administrative growth strategies. Chandler determined that successful growth strategies entailed a new or at least a refashioned organizational structure. He concluded that growth without structural adjustment led only to economic inefficiency.[20]

The four phases in the development of the large American industrial enterprise that Chandler discerned include: the initial expansion and accumulation of resources, the rationalization of the use of resources, the expansion into new markets and lines to help assure the continuing full use of resources, and the development of a new structure to make possible continuing effective mobilization of resources to meet changing short-term market demands and long-term market trends. Although each firm studied had a unique history, nearly all followed this general pattern. Chandler found that the strategy of vertical integration managed through a centralized structure tended to be succeeded by a strategy of diversification managed by a decentralized structure. His work suggests that a developmental model of the large, U.S. industrial firm would not be small-medium-large but rather small-integrated-diversified.[21]

Chandler's work inspired efforts to elaborate the role of strategy and structure in the behavior of the multidivisional diversified firm. Norman A. Berg (1965, 1969) distinguished between multidivisional firms in which upper-echelon managers are directly involved in decision making and planning for the divisions (*diversified major*) and those firms in which they plan growth strategies and manage divisions only in the financial sense of allocating resources, very much like a holding company (*conglomerate*).[22]

Williamson incorporated this distinction into his theory of managerial discretion (1970, 1971). He argued that excessive discretionary behavior occurs in diversified majors as the various operating units act to maintain their respective interests (status quo) by taking on advocacy postures that can result in inefficiencies. Williamson asserted that growth is more efficient for the multidivisional firm when strategic planning and resource allocation is carried out by independent, corporate-headquartered managers within a conglomerate structure. The conglomerate structure acts as a conventional *capital-market restraint* on the excessive discretionary behavior that characterizes the divisional competition for corporate resources. According to Williamson, the operation of a large firm under the conglomerate structure favors goal-pursuit and least-cost behavior (as opposed to excessive discretionary behavior). Williamson (1975) extended his views to a microeconomic analysis of the interaction of structure, managerial discretion, and transactions costs—both market and informational. He was interested in the efficiency tradeoffs related to a firm's growth preference for the development of organizational *hierarchies* (internal vertical integration) versus the utilization of *markets* (contractual relations between firms).[23]

In 1973, Bruce R. Scott presented a three-stage theory of corporate development based on Chandler's earlier work. According to Scott, entrepreneurial (stage I) and functionally-specialized (stage II) firms act as a single unit with one set of distribution channels in a single industrial or service market. Stage III firms have multiple product lines and hence multiple channels of distribution. Divisional units in stage III firms relate directly to their own markets and the various units have considerable independence from one another. Scott's model proposes that as firms grow they tend to pass through these three stages of development. The transition from stage I to stage II results from increased volume which eventually leads to increased levels of specialization. The stage II firm is characterized as vertically integrated with centralized management organized along functional lines. The essential difference between stage II and stage III firms is not a function of volume and specialization but one of divisional autonomy.[24]

Researchers associated with the Industrial Development and Public Policy Program at the Harvard Business School (including Scott) determined that most large American industrial firms were in stage III during the late 1960s. But, in an analysis of the *Fortune* "500" industrial firms, it became clear that those firms differed considerably in type and degree of diversification. Leonard Wrigley (1970), one of Scott's students, devised a classification scheme that allowed him to categorize his *Fortune* "500" sample population according to levels of diversification. He found that over 90 percent of the *Fortune* "500" major industrials were diversified to some extent, while over 80 percent maintained multidivisional structures.[25]

Another of Scott's students, Richard P. Rumelt (1974), analyzed a 40 percent sample of the *Fortune* "500" population in terms of changes in strategy and structure over time. As suggested by Wrigley's data, Rumelt found that the major U.S. industrials moved from dominant business toward increasing levels of diversification during the 1949–1969 period. When he sorted his sample according to growth strategy, he found that diversified firms performed better than dominant-product businesses in terms of sales, earnings, and earnings per share. As for structure, Rumelt determined that the product-divisional firms performed better on all of the conventional financial measures than did function-divisional firms.[26]

Subsequently Scott reported that four parallel research studies found that the largest 100 firms in the United Kingdom, France, Germany, and Italy were also moving toward diversification during the 1950–1970 period. These studies, based on the concepts and definitions developed by Wrigley and Rumelt, also indicated a decline in the population of firms in the dominant-product category. In Europe, the trend toward the diversified, multidivisional organization appeared to have progressed farthest in the United

Kingdom and the least in Italy, but in all countries the broad trends were similar. Scott concluded that diversification has become the most common growth strategy in Europe and the United States. The major forces inducing this transition appear to be similar in all five countries studied and relate to the need for managers to sustain growth despite declining competitiveness in basic industries. Scott concludes that the national interest would be better served if government regulators were to encourage dominant-product firms to merge with other firms in order to acquire new production. He believes public policies should encourage firms capable of generating high earnings.[27]

Dennis C. Mueller's (1972, 1977) life-cycle theory of firm growth is closely related to the Harvard diversification studies. Mueller hypothesized that young firms (new firms or firms that have recently experienced a technological or commercial breakthrough) go through a takeoff period of accelerated growth associated with good profitability. For these firms, the interests of managers and stockholders converge in maximum feasible growth. Later, as product-market cycles stabilize or wind down, a given firm may experience a mature phase for a very long if not indefinite period of time. As growth rates stabilize or decline during the mature phase, conflict may develop between stockholder and manager interests. Because stockholders tend to prefer dividends over retention of profits for internal investment when high rates of return cannot be guaranteed by management, mergers become the obvious way for managers to retain control and avoid the slowdown in growth that product maturity brings. Mueller's theory predicts that the mature firm will look to merger as a growth strategy when profitability declines or threatens to decline subject to the constraint of stock market valuation (price levels must be maintained to placate stockholders and avoid takeover bids).[28] It will be interesting to see if product-market diversification increases in response to contracting revenues in those firms examined in part II.

Whatever the merits of these particular classification systems, the stage-of-growth theories promote a greater awareness of the interaction between the stage of corporate development and the formulation of corporate strategy. They indicate that information about the firm's historical growth pattern is important to any analysis of firm behavior. The development concepts discussed above can enhance the analysis of firm behavior in either the behavioral or managerial modes. Chandler's work suggests that economic efficiency is lost when structural adjustment does not accompany growth. Hence, we can expect those firms that successfully adapt to contraction to have changed their organizational structure to fit their new contraction-related strategies. Williamson's work suggests that top-echelon managers experiencing a contraction episode may act to reduce inefficiencies by moving toward a conglomerate structure (essentially, to centralize financial

decision making at the corporate headquarters level) where resource allocation decisions can be depoliticized as a means of curbing excessive discretionary behavior within the firm. The Scott Wrigley, Rumelt, and Mueller
literature suggests that viability for a contracting firm may well be related to
management's ability to develop a strategy that will diversify the firm's
assets into growth businesses. Their work further suggests that stockholder-
manager interests will diverge with economic decline, and that strategy will
be constrained by stock market valuation.

The Process of Rationalization

Perhaps the most useful way to look at the firm, particularly during a
period when institutional relationships are under stress and subject to
change, is to conceptualize corporate decision makers as engaged in efforts
to rationalize the firm's environment. As previously discussed, Max Weber
was first to identify the rationalization process and its administrative corollary, bureacratization, as the primary industrial dynamic of capitalism.
Weber maintained an ambivalent posture toward the consequences of
rationalization. He believed that bureaucratic administration was the most
efficient form of organization, but predicted the inherent logic of the
rationalistic mode would ultimately constitute a grave threat to individual
freedom.[29]

The *process of rationalization* as the primary industrial dynamic of
advanced capitalism, can be defined as the pragmatic manipulation of
means to achieve a hierarchy of ends. That hierarchy includes goals such as
firm survival, stable growth, and job security for the group of managers
currently in power. In lieu of perfect control, the means employed would
include activities undertaken by corporate decision makers to maintain or
enhance environmental predictability, investment security, and price stability. There is no presupposition, however, that decision makers know automatically, as with the maximization assumption, which ends to pursue and
which means to employ. There is only the more general but more inclusive
presupposition that corporate decision makers will use whatever means
available to shape and manage the firm's external environment. They do so
to reduce environmental uncertainty, buffer the firm's internal decision
processes, and protect the firm's markets from disruptive external forces,
whether economic or political in nature.

To envision the firm and its professional managers as passive price
takers in an economy that is governed by the sovereign consumer or the
sovereign state is to ignore the American industrialization experience. Historically, both entrepreneurs and salaried managers have intervened in the

political realm in order to gain increased control over market conditions. By adopting strategies and structures that insulate the firm from competitive market pressures, the major U.S. industrial corporations have been able to forge and maintain oligopolistic markets, check the overproduction generated from excess capacity, and obtain considerable predictability in pricing. Through the development of systematic controls, long-range market planning systems, and the development of forecasting techniques, modern industrial managers have also succeeded in adapting the firm's internal decision-making processes to the rationalization mode.

The American Industrialization Experience: External Rationalization. The American industrialization experience, characterized by the rise of big business and regulatory government is a tribute to Weber's vision. The transformation of the economic system from one resembling the neoclassical model (*entrepreneurial capitalism*) to one of managerial capitalism illustrates the profound impact of the rationalization process on modes of organization and production. The term *managerial capitalism* is used to describe the mixed economies of North America and western Europe where production is concentrated in the hands of large joint-stock corporations operated by professional managers who are responsible for the current flows of goods and services as well as the allocation of resources for future production and distribution. Alfred D. Chandler's (1977) work on the managerial revolution describes the general pattern by which the visible hand of management replaced the invisible hand of market forces in the U.S. economy. According to Chandler, the modern business enterprise appeared when managerial hierarchies were able to monitor and coordinate the activities of a number of business units more efficiently than did market mechanisms. It continued to grow so that these hierarchies, increasingly staffed by professional managers, might remain fully employed. It emerged and spread, however, only in those industries and sectors where technology and markets permitted administrative coordination to be more profitable than market coordination. Because these areas were at the center of the American economy and because professional managers replaced families, financiers, or their representatives as decision makers, entrepreneurial capitalism evolved into managerial capitalism. Industrial concentration and oligopoly appeared as a consequence of the profitability afforded by rational administrative coordination.[30]

Chandler's historical studies indicate that in making administrative decisions, career managers preferred policies that favored the stability and growth of their enterprises to those that maximized current profits. For salaried managers, the continuing existence of their enterprises was essential to their lifetime careers. Their primary goal was to assure a continual flow of material to their facilities so as to insure full capacity utilization. Growth normally resulted from two quite different strategies of expansion. One was defensive and stemmed from a desire for security. Its purpose was to prevent sources of supply or outlets for goods and services from being cut off and to limit the entry of new competitors (horizontal and vertical integration). The other strategy was positive. Its aim was to add new units and permit, by means of administrative coordination, a more intensive use of existing facilities and personnel. Such expansion, in turn, led to the addition of still more workers and equipment. In this way the desire of the managers to keep the organization fully employed became a continuing force for its further growth.[31]

The rationalization process has received considerable attention from business historians. From colonial times, business interests have played a privileged role in the public policymaking process. Business leaders have tended to regard politics as an important part of their larger position in society. In consequence, utility has remained the dominant measure of corporate legitimacy.[32] The key economic role fulfilled by the corporate enterprise (capital accumulation and economic growth) continues to provide the rationale for special claims to consideration from elected officials and their appointed representatives who administer the federal regulatory agencies. From the turn of the century, dominant industrial interests (primarily in oil, steel, finance, and transportation) gradually began to understand that only the national government could stabilize economic and trade conditions to the extent required to support their increasing capability to plan over the long term and efficiently manage their extensive resources. The previously unorganized small-business interests responded to the monopoly market conditions and private planning systems established by dominant industrial interests with demands that government also act to protect their interests vis-á-vis the powerful oligopolists. In the rhetoric of the time, government was asked to step in and regulate in order to preserve the free market. These demands resulted in the passage of the first major pieces of regulatory legislation aimed at curtailing the economic power of big business: the Interstate Commerce Act (1887), the Sherman Antitrust Act (1890), the Federal Reserve Act (1914), the Clayton Act (1914), and the creation of the Federal Trade Commission (1914).

In an effort to further rationalize industrial conditions (organize markets, establish limits to competition, stabilize financial activities), at least one segment of the business community supported each major mandate for increased federal regulation of business activity in the marketplace. Long-range strategic planning, a prerequisite of long-term growth with profitability, became a viable possibility for the large business enterprise only with a stable economy—one free from erratic fluctuation. Although specific conditions varied from industry to industry, internal problems that could have been solved only by political means were the common denominator in those industries whose leaders advocated greater federal regulation. Leaders of the regulated industry were frequently in a position to direct the regulatory efforts toward ends they deemed acceptable or desirable. In fact, the nearly universal belief among political leaders in the basic justice being accorded to business leaders as owners (or representatives of owners) of private property, along with the felt legitimacy of business claims to special consideration, acted to limit the reach of the reform impulse embodied in the Progressive Era and the New Deal legislation.[33]

After World War II, the fear of postwar recession and mass unemployment produced broad support among the populace (including for the first time small business interests) for the national stabilization policies that sought to maintain full employment and aggregate demand. With fiscal and monetary policies and an ever-increasing body of regulatory law, the federal government became the coordinator of aggregate demand and the allocator of resources whenever the managers of the private sector failed to achieve desired employment and demand levels. By the 1950s, managerial capitalism, the embodiment of the rationalization process, was well entrenched in the U.S. economy. The process of administrative consolidation was apparent in every sector. Large industrial operations for the most part were predictable, secure, and stable under the systematic control of professional managers. The government set goals, influenced the pace of growth, and regulated procedures throughout the economy.[34]

However, as inflation significantly began to undercut real economic growth and exacerbate underlying structural problems in the economy during the late 1960s, cracks appeared in this highly rationalized interdependent order. If past historical patterns can predict anything about the future, the pressure of slow growth should lead business leaders, particularly those from firms or industries that have experienced contracting revenues, to become involved in political efforts to restabilize the conditions of competition. We should expect such business leaders to step up efforts to rationalize their firms' external environment with requests for further government intervention in the form of tariffs, quotas, wage and price controls, tax relief, or special assistance programs, depending on specific circumstances. Short of inside knowledge of a specific firm's public relations and government lobbying strategy, the outside observer can best interpret the external rationalization process through a study of the firm's exchange relationships with its shareholders, employees, suppliers, creditors, competitors, consumers, regulators, and elected officials. An analysis of top management's efforts to balance the often divergent interests and competing claims of stakeholders should provide useful insights to an analysis of the strategic response to contracting revenue. (*Stakeholders* are those who have some type of legal relationship with the firm who merely because they are a part of the same polity cannot help being affected by the actions of the firm[35]).

Organizational Theory: Internal Rationalization. Whether by organizational or political means, the rationalization process is subject to the constraints of human decision processes and the firm's internal decision-making system or structure. Organizational theorists who have studied the decision-making process maintain that organizational decisions are goal oriented and adaptive. But because of the approximating and fragmented character of human decision processes, only a few elements of the system are adaptive at any one time; the remainder are inflexible in the short run. Organizations have a limited capacity to gather and process information and to predict consequences of alternative courses of action. This limited adaptive capacity is a function of the gap between the capacity of the human mind for formulating and solving complex problems and the great complexity of the problems that individuals and organizations face in the real world. As Simon (1958, 1978) has indicated, organizational decision processes are characterized by uncertainty and the neurophysiological limits of rationality. Simon asserts that the number of considerations that are potentially relevant to the effectiveness of a decision is so large that only a few of the more salient of these lie within the circle of awareness at any given time, that the membership of this subset changes continually as new situations arise, and the learning in the form of reaction to perceived consequences is the dominant way in which rationality is exhibited.[36]

James D. Thompson (1967) has proposed a model of organizational administration that is primarily concerned with the interface between organizational structure, policy formulation, and decision processes. He describes the norms of rationality that exists within the firm that must manage a high level of interdependence with the external environment. Thompson has argued that instrumental action is rooted on the one hand in desired outcomes and on the other hand in beliefs about cause-effect relationships. *Technical rationality* is related to a firm's production technology and is determined by managers' ability to develop means-ends utility hierarchies that rank various production methods. Desired outcomes are linked to appropriate production processes by constructing cause-effect relationships. The extent to which a firm selects production activities that efficiently lead to desired outcomes is a measure of its technical rationality.[37]

According to Thompson, *organizational rationality* involves efficiency in acquiring the inputs necessary for production and dispensing with the outputs of the production process. Organizational rationality integrates input, throughput, and output activities, facilitating construction of systemwide means-ends utility functions. To maintain technical and organizational rationality, administrative *norms of rationality* direct managers to try to protect or buffer the technical core of the firm from environmental contingencies; control or manage disruptive environmental fluctuations; and reduce the firm's dependence on exchange relationships with suppliers, customers, competitors, and regulators. That is, to attain any significant measure of self-control, the firm must manage its dependency. Under norms of rationality, managers seek to minimize the power of those involved in the firm's exchange relationships by seeking greater power relative to those on whom they are dependent. Subject to the nature of the interdependence, managers resort to contracting with, coopting, or coalescing with those on whom they are dependent. Thompson argues that the more managers are constrained by one of their exchange relationships, the more power they will seek over remaining relationships. When they are unable to achieve such power, managers will seek to enlarge the domain of the firm into areas in which they can maintain control.[38]

In a recent article concerned with organizational governance as a consequence of organizational structure, William G. Scott, Terence R. Mitchell, and Newman S. Peery (1981) have refined and expanded the concepts of rationality developed by Thompson. They maintain that three distinct forms of rationality have emerged in modern organizations. *Technical rationality* becomes synonymous with efficiency, the minimization of means to accomplish ends. Technical rationality pervades all organizational decision-making tasks and dominates all other forms of rationality in terms of its impact on organizational structure during the early growth phase of structurally simple organizations. *Organizational rationality* concerns the means for achieving and maintaining a cooperative system. The existence of a cooperative system is critical to the health of the organization and crucial to the satisfaction that members derive from participating in the organization. As the organization becomes more complex and differentiated in response to technical demands, problems of integration take precedence over and may conflict with the imperatives of technical rationality. Organizational rationality dominates in organizations of moderate maturity which are structurally complex. *Political rationality* as defined by Scott, Mitchell, and Peery is concerned with regime maintenance, or with organizational structures that are intended to achieve consensual support for the management of the organization. Political rationality can be construed as maximizing political support for the normative order. To gain such support, management must persuade individuals and subunits within the organization to accept its goals and the distribution of status, privilege, and scarce resources. These authors argue that political rationality can come to dominate other forms of rationality in fully mature, structurally complex organizations because as the imperative for systems integration increases, it carries with it the propensity for more intense political behavior.[39]

William G. Scott (1976) had argued earlier that the three forms of internal organizational rationality should be sufficient to cope with the management of decline, assuming changing values and sensitivities among the managerial elite. He is concerned, however, that given the very high level of organizational interdependence in our technical, urbanized economic sys-

Table 2-2

The Conceptual Framework: Definitions, Propositions, and Issues

---

Definitions

1. The firm is a purposive organization that seeks to adapt to environmental change and avoid environmental uncertainty (Simon, Cyert, March).

2. Optimal firm behavior cannot ever really be defined in a situation-specific setting. Managers necessarily make *satisfying* decisions in a world characterized by uncertainty, imperfect knowledge, and bounded rationality (Simon).

3. Firm behavior is conjointly determined by the individual firm's historical pattern of development, external or market circumstances (including exchange relationships with constituent groups), organizational structure and strategic decision-making processes, and the self-interests of management, or, in Williamson's phrase, the extent of *internal discretionary behavior.*

4. Organizational members maintain a set of expectations about what the organization will and will not do, in Thompson's phrase a *domain consensus.* This concept enables us to deal with organizational goals and mangerial strategies without imputing to the organization the human quality of motivation, or assuming a group mind.

Propositions

1. To the extent possible given rationality and security constraints, managers will seek to maximize the growth rate of sales and the level of firm diversification as means of ensuring security and enhancing their power to manage the firm's dependencies on exchange relationships. Managers will seek to avoid sales revenue contraction and return the firm to a growth trajectory (Marris, Williamson, B. Scott, Mueller).

2. Managers will attempt to avoid uncertainty by rationalizing the firm's dependencies on exchange relationships that represent external constraints or contingencies for the firm (Thompson). Hence, managers will rationally respond to the uncertainties created by changing environmental conditions by devising strategies designed to insulate the firm from competitive market pressures; that is, to organize markets and influence public policymakers (Williamson, Chandler).

3. Managers will attempt to counteract external uncertainty by increasing the firm's internal level of technical rationality. Hence, during the contraction process efficiency imperatives will effectively reduce the internal levels of discretionary behavior and organizational slack experienced under growth conditions (W. Scott, Williamson, Cyert).

4. It will be assumed that the underlying causes of the contraction process are variable and interactive. The corporate studies that follow will focus on the managerial response to the contraction process itself rather than initiating factors.

Table 2-2 continued

5. It will be assumed that the level of management skill and acuity is equivalent among major U.S. industrial firms. That is, creditors, the stock market, takeover threats, and the greater willingness of directors to intervene and dismiss top management act as a check against irresponsible management.

6. It will be assumed that self-disclosure in the form of public statements, reports to shareholders and government agencies, as well as press and trade journal accounts present management views, intents, and purposes in an accurate rather than deceptive manner.

Issues

1. To what extent do major U.S. corporations experience prolonged periods of sales revenue contraction?

2. What are the patterns of internal resource allocation during the contraction process?

3. What strategic responses result from the contraction process:
   divestiture?
   merger?
   acquisition or further diversification?
   penetration of new markets (foreign, domestic)?
   participation in cartels or other price fixing arrangement?
   requests for government subsidies, loans, or additional regulation?
   requests for deregulation?

4. What are the internal governance consequences of the contraction process:
   reorganization, new top management team?
   restructuring to increase degree of centralization (impulse to tighten controls and executive level decision circle)?
   restructuring to increase degree of decentralization (impulse to delegate authority to discourage exits, enhance organizational adaptiveness, or *political rationality*)?

5. How does the contraction process affect the demand for government intervention into the marketplace? Does management attempt to externalize costs associated with the contraction process?

6. How does management handle its dependency on exchange relationships during the contraction process?

tem, the real threat to the integrity of organizations and the stability of existing managerial regimes is from intersystem crises external to the firm. Scott
argues that technical rationality will come to dominate other forms in a contracting environment as managers respond to the increasing need for efficiency with every resource in the technological repertory, solving problems
with engineering, economic, organizational, and eventually behavioral technology. He fears that increasing centralization and administrative control
will result at every level in society. In other words, given the imperatives of
modern technology, economic decline will lead to ever-increasing levels of
totalitarian control. Participants will be forced to remain in organizations,
regardless of satisfaction level, as mobility opportunities contract.[40]

At a public administration symposium concerning organizational
decline and cutback management held in 1978, Charles H. Levine made the
point that managers must decide whether to adopt a strategy of resistance or
adaptation. The best choice, of course, is situation specific and dependent
on the degree to which managers can expect to be able to control the environmental fluctuations that contribute to the decline situation. Levine notes
that the second horn of the decline dilemma involves the selection of who
will be let go and/or which programs or subunits will be curtailed or terminated. The process of choosing among these alternatives introduces an
equity-efficiency tradeoff. Equity cuts distribute the pain across the organization with an equal probability of hurting all units and employees irrespective of impact on the long-term capacity of the organization. Efficiency cuts
affect only those people and units in the organization whose termination
would minimize the long-term losses to the organization as a whole, irrespective of their distribution. Making cuts on the basis of equity is easier for
managers because it is socially acceptable, easier to justify, and involves few
decision-making costs. Equity decision making avoids costs from sorting,
selecting, and negotiating cuts. In contrast, efficiency cuts involve costly
triage analysis because the distribution of pain and inconvenience requires
that the value of people and subunits to the organization be weighed in
terms of their expected future contributions. One would expect to find efficiency cuts in the private sector, but it will be interesting to see if indications
of equity cutbacks (political rationality) also occur in corporations experiencing contracting revenues.[41]

Richard M. Cyert contributed to the same symposium and, though his
topic was the management of universities of constant or decreasing size, his
discussion of organizational slack is relevant here. He argued that it is best
to begin the cutback process before *organizational slack* (the difference
between total resources and total necessary payments to coalition members)
is completely dissipated, as it is always possible to use some of the slack to
ease the transition of the organization to new paths or as side payments to
gain the cooperation of subunits. According to Cyert, when the organiza-

tion fails to achieve some well-defined goal such as specified rate of output, the organization will then be motivated to search for explanations. Only when organizational members are convinced that a real problem exists, that the structure of the environment has somehow changed, will they prepare the organization to engage in serious search. Cyert believes that where solutions are hard to find—and they are more difficult to find the greater the contraction—the danger is that aspirations for the organization and individuals within the organization will be reduced. Cyert maintains that the major problem of managing a contracting organization is to break the circle of declining expectations and performance, which tend to disintegrate the organization very quickly. Those individuals who do not lower their aspirations are easily lured to other organizations that are in an expansionary phase and can offer opportunities for advancement. If organizational slack is completely dissipated, managerial performance cannot be differentially rewarded.[42]

There are many other aspects of organizational theory that are potentially relevant to the study of contracting firms. The conflict literature, the organizational-change literature, and the strategic-choice literature are examples. This material is concerned with internal organizational processes that require direct observation and measurement and, therefore, access to the internal workings of the firm. Consequently, consideration of these theories is beyond the scope of the corporate studies presented in part II that are developed entirely from public source data.[43]

Definitions, Propositions, Issues

A systematic approach to the analysis of the corporate response to sales-revenue contraction can be outlined in terms of certain key assumptions, propositions, and issues. Interpretation of the corporate studies that follow in part II is guided by the conceptual framework set forth in table 2-2, with particular emphasis on efforts to rationalize the firm's environment. However, the definitions, propositions, and issues presented in table 2-2 are drawn from the previous review of economic, historical, and organizational theories of firm behavior.

Notes

1. Fritz Machlup, "Theories of the Firm: Marginalist, Behavioral, Managerial," *American Economic Review (AER)* (March 1967):31.

2. Kenneth E. Boulding, "The Management of Decline," *Change* (June 1975):8.

3. See Richard M. Cyert, "The Management of Universities of Constant or Decreasing Size," *Public Administration Review (PAR)* (July/August 1978):344–349; Charles H. Levine, "Organizational Decline and Cutback Management," *PAR* (July/August 1978):316–325; William G. Scott, "The Management of Decline," *Conference Board Record* (June 1976): 56–59. Note that the danger of reification arises whenever language is used such as "the firm's response to declining revenues." The intent here is to employ terms of purpose and motivation usually reserved for human actors in descriptions of firm behavior for analytic and expository convenience. Action on the part of the firm in terms of decision making and problem solving is conceptualized as the aggregate result of interactive social processes taking place within the firm among its members. No anthropomorphic entity over and above the individual members of the firm is envisioned.

4. Jeffrey D. Ford, "Occurrence of Structural Hysteresis in Declining Organizations," *Academy of Management Review (AMR)* (October 1980): 589; Kathryn R. Harrigan, *Strategies for Declining Businesses* (Lexington, Mass.: Lexington Books, D.C. Heath and Company, 1980). In addition to the work of Cyert, Levine, and Scott cited above and discussed later in this chapter see David A. Whetten, "Organizational Decline: A Neglected Topic in Organizational Science," *AMR* (October 1980):577–588. For suggestive examples of the corporate failure/turnaround literature, see John Argenti, *Corporate Collapse* (New York: John Wiley, 1976); Joseph Eisenberg, ed., *Turnaround Management* (New York: McGraw-Hill, 1972); Charles W. Hofer, "Turnaround Strategies," *Journal of Business Strategy (JBS)* (Summer 1980):19–31.

5. See Alfred Marshall, *Principles of Economics* (London: Macmillan and Co., 1920); Richard M. Cyert and Charles L. Hedrick, "Theory of the Firm: Past, Present, and Future; An Interpretation," *Journal of Economic Literature (JEL)* (June 1972):398; Machlup, "Theories of the Firm," pp. 9, 31.

6. See J.M. Keynes, *The General Theory of Employment, Interest and Money* (New York: Harcourt Brace, 1936).

7. See E.H. Chamberlin, *Theory of Monopolistic Competition* (Cambridge, Mass.: Harvard University Press, 1946); Joan Robinson, *The Economics of Imperfect Competition (London: Macmillan and Co., 1948).*

8. A.A. Berle and G.C. Means, *The Modern Corporation and Private Property* (New York: Harcourt Brace, 1932).

9. R.L. Hall and C.J. Hitch, "Price Theory and Business Behavior," *Oxford Studies in the Price Mechanism,* ed. T. Wilson (London: Oxford University Press, 1939), pp. 107–138.

10. For discussions of the goals of corporate managers, see Chester I. Barnard, *Functions of the Executive* (Cambridge, Mass.: Harvard University Press, 1938); Tibor Scitovsky, "A Note on Profit Maximization and its Implications," *American Economic Association: Revised Economic Studies* (Winter 1943):57–60; R.A. Gordon, "Short-Period Price Determination in Theory and Practice," *AER* (June 1948):265–288; A.G. Papandreou, "Some Basic Problems in the Theory of the Firm," *A Survey of Contemporary Economics,* ed. B.F. Haley, vol. 2 (Philadelphia: Blakiston, 1952), pp. 183–219; R. Joseph Monsen and Anthony Downs, "A Theory of Large Managerial Firms," *Journal of Political Economy (JPE)* (June 1965):221–236. For discussions of resolution of conflicting goals among organizational subunits, see M. Reder, "A Reconsideration of the Marginal Productivity Theory," *JPE* (October 1947):450–458; Kenneth E. Boulding, *A Reconstruction of Economics* (New York: John Wiley and Sons, 1950); Richard M. Cyert and James G. March, *A Behavioral Theory of the Firm* (Englewood Cliffs, N.J.: Prentice-Hall, 1963). See works by Gordon, Papandreou, Monsen and Downs for discussions of constraints on managerial discretion.

11. Herbert A. Simon, *Administrative Behavior* (New York: Macmillan Co., 1945); idem, "A Behavioral Model of Rational Choice," *Quarterly Journal of Economics (QJE)* (February 1955):99–118.

12. Richard M. Cyert and James G. March, "Organizational Factors in the Theory of Oligopoly," *QJE* (February 1956):44–46; idem, *A Behavioral Theory of the Firm.*

13. William J. Baumol, *Business, Behavior, Value and Growth* (New York: Harcourt, Brace, 1959).

14. William J. Baumol, "On the Theory of the Expansion of the Firm," *AER* (December 1962):1078–1087.

15. Oliver E. Williamson, *The Economics of Discretionary Behavior* (Englewood Cliffs, N.J.: Prentice-Hall, 1964).

16. Robin L. Marris, "A Model of the 'Managerial' Enterprise," *QJE* (May 1963):185–209; idem, *The Economic Theory of 'Managerial' Capitalism* (New York: Macmillan Co., 1964). For antecedent growth models of the firm, see Baumol, *Business Behavior;* idem, "Theory of Expansion," pp. 1078–1087; Jack Downie, *The Competitive Process* (London: G. Duckworth, 1958); Edith T. Penrose, *The Theory of the Growth of the Firm* (Oxford: Blackwell, 1959).

17. For examples of refinement and validation, see Robin Marris, "An Introduction to Theories of Corporation Growth," pp. 1–36; idem, "The Modern Corporation and Economic Theory," pp. 270–317; John Lintner, "Optimum or Maximum Corporate Growth under Uncertainty," pp. 172–241; Robert M. Solow, "Some Implications of Alternative Criteria for the Firm," pp. 318–342 in *The Corporate Economy* ed. Robin Marris

and Adrian Wood (Cambridge, Mass.: Harvard University Press, 1971). The stock market as a dependent variable is a common feature of this class of models.

18. Alfred D. Chandler, Jr., *Strategy and Structure* (Cambridge, Mass.: MIT Press, 1962).

19. Alfred D. Chandler, Jr., "Decision Making and Modern Institutional Change," *Journal of Economic History (JEH)* (March 1973):1–15. For a more detailed accounting see Alfred D. Chandler, Jr., "The Beginnings of 'Big Business' in American Industry," *Business History Review* (Harvard) (Spring, 1959):1–31; idem, *Strategy and Structure,* pp. 19–51.

20. Chandler, *Strategy and Structure,* pp. 383–384, 7–17.

21. Ibid., pp. 385–386.

22. Norman A. Berg, "Strategic Planning in Conglomerate Companies, *Harvard Business Review (HBR)* (May/June 1965):79–92; idem, "What's Different About Conglomerate Management," *HBR* (November/December 1969):112–120.

23. Oliver E. Williamson, *Corporate Control and Business Behavior* (Englewood Cliffs, N.J.: Prentice-Hall, 1970); idem, "Managerial Discretion, Organization Form, and the Multi-division Hypothesis," *Corporate Economy,* pp. 341–386; idem, *Markets and Hierarchies* (New York: Free Press, 1975). For a more detailed discussion of Williamson's work, see Robin Marris and Dennis C. Mueller, "The Corporation, Competition, and the Invisible Hand," *JEL* (March 1980):32–62.

24. Bruce R. Scott, "The Industrial State: Old Myths and New Realities," *HBR* (March/April 1973):133–148.

25. Ibid., p. 138. See Leonard Wrigley, "Divisional Autonomy and Diversification," D.B.A. thesis, Harvard Business School, 1970.

26. Richard P. Rumelt, *Strategy, Structure, and Economic Performance* (Boston: Division of Research, Graduate School of Business Administration, Harvard University, 1974). Rumelt's diversification categories, a refinement of Wrigley's earlier work, are discussed in chapter 3.

27. B. Scott, "Industrial Strategy," p. 141. Scott does not consider the problems of political power and economic control associated with the large, diversified firm. For additional detail, see Richard E. Caves, "Industrial Organization, Corporate Strategy and Structure," *JEL* (March 1980):70–77.

28. Dennis C. Mueller, "A Life Cycle Theory of the Firm," *Journal of Industrial Economics* (July 1972):199–291; idem, "The Effects of Conglomerate Mergers: A Survey of the Empirical Evidence," *Journal of Banking Finance* (December 1977):315–347; Marris and Mueller, "Corporation, Competition," pp. 44–45.

29. Max Weber, *The Protestant Ethic and the Spirit of Capitalism,* trans. Talcott Parsons, (New York: Charles Scribner's Sons, 1958).

30. Alfred D. Chandler, Jr., *The Visible Hand* (Cambridge, Mass.: Harvard University Press, 1977), pp. 11, 489.

31. Ibid., pp. 10, 486.

32. James W. Hurst, *The Legitimacy of the Business Corporation* (Charlottesville: The University Press of Virginia, 1970).

33. For historical treatments of the complexities of the various corporate reform movements, and, at minimum, the tacit approval of federal regulation by business interests, see Richard Hofstadter, *The Age of Reform* (New York: Random House, 1955); Robert H. Wiebe, *Businessmen and Reform* (Cambridge, Mass.: Harvard University Press, 1962); Gabriel Kolko, *The Triumph of Conservatism* (London: Collier-Macmillan, 1963); Robert H. Wiebe, *The Search for Order* (New York: Hill and Wang, 1967); James Weinstein, *The Corporate Ideal in the Liberal State* (Boston: Beacon Press, 1968); Louis Galambos, *The Public Image of Big Business in America* (Baltimore: Johns Hopkins University Press, 1975); Thomas C. Cochran, *200 Years of American Business* (New York: Basic Books, 1977); Chandler, *Visible Hand.* For analyses of more current arrangements, see George J. Stigler, "The Theory of Economic Regulation," *Bell Journal of Economics and Management Science* (Spring 1971):3–21; James Q. Wilson, "The Politics of Regulation," *Social Responsibility and the Business Predicament,* ed. James W. McKie (Washington, D.C.: The Brookings Institute, 1974); James Q. Wilson, ed., *The Politics of Regulation* (New York: Basic Books, 1980).

34. Chandler, *Visible Hand,* p. 497.

35. Arthur Selwyn Miller, *The Modern State* (Westport, Conn.: Greenwood Press, 1976), p. 25.

36. James G. March and Herbert A. Simon, *Organizations* (New York: John Wiley and Sons, 1958), p. 169; Herbert A. Simon, "Rationality as Process and as Product of Thought," *AER* (May 1978):8.

37. James D. Thompson, *Organizations in Action* (New York: McGraw-Hill, 1967), pp. 32–38.

38. Ibid.

39. William G. Scott, Terence R. Mitchell, and Newman S. Peery, "Organizational Governance," *Handbook of Organizational Design,* ed. Paul C. Nystrom and William H. Starbuck, vol. 2 (New York: Oxford University Press, 1981), pp. 135–151. The purpose of governance according to the authors is to establish *consensus* (the integration of interests) among organizational participants about the normative structure of the organization. Organizational participants must accept the rules, regulations, and behavioral expectations of an organization if it is to survive. The ways in which management allocates resources, defines the nature of equity, and determines the means for controlling arbitrariness in the administration of justice are tangible evidence of governance policies regulating the consensus issue.

40. William G. Scott, "The Management of Decline," *Conference Board Record* (June 1976):56–59. Also, see Albert O. Hirschman, *Exit, Voice, and Loyalty: Responses to Decline in Firms, Organizations, and*

States (Cambridge, Mass.: Harvard University Press, 1970).

41. Charles H. Levine, "Organizational Decline and Cutback Management," *PAR* (July/August 1978):316–325.

42. Richard M. Cyert, "The Management of Universities of Constant or Decreasing Size," *PAR* (July/August 1978):344–349.

43. For relevant material from the organizational process-strategic choice literature, see Lee E. Preston and James E. Post, *Private Management and Public Policy* (Englewood Cliffs, N.J.: Prentice-Hall, 1975); James E. Post, *Corporate Behavior and Social Change* (Reston, Va.: Reston Publishing Co., 1978); Raymond E. Miles, Charles C. Snow, Alan D. Meyer, and Henry J. Coleman, Jr., "Organizational Strategy, Structure, and Process," *AMR* (July 1978):546–562; Dan E. Schendel and Charles W. Hofer, *Strategic Management* (Boston: Little, Brown and Co., 1979); Richard E. Caves, "Industrial Organization, Corporate Strategy and Structure," *JEL* (March 1980):64–92; William D. Guth, "Corporate Growth Strategies," *JBS* (Fall 1980):56–62.

Part II
Corporate Response
Patterns

After an examination of the incidence of prolonged sales-revenue contraction among U.S. corporations in chapter 3, three studies of the corporate contraction process are presented in chapters 4 through 6. The conceptual framework developed in chapter 2 provides the means for a comparative analysis. The corporate studies represent distinct categories of corporate strategy and structure for a crucial period of time, chosen to illustrate patterns of response to declining rates of growth. Given the basic strategic and structural differences of the firms considered in the studies, the narrow range of variation in their patterns of response was an unexpected finding.

3

Sales-Revenue Contraction among Major U.S. Corporations

To what extent is the corporate population affected by prolonged periods of contraction? A preliminary study of sales-revenue contraction patterns among major U.S. corporations was undertaken in an effort to provide an answer to this question. The American corporate population is vast and diverse. In any study of the corporate population, it is important to distinguish between the few very large firms and the many small businesses and manufacturing firms. The 500 largest industrial firms are often regarded as representative of industry as a whole because of their exaggerated impact on the economy. During the period considered in the preliminary study, 1967 through 1977, the 500 largest industrials accounted for approximately 65 percent of the sales and 75 percent of the employees of all U.S. industrial corporations. In turn, industrial sector sales (including manufacturing, mining, and construction firms) represented approximately one-third of total national income.[1]

Defining the Parameters

The firms selected for inclusion in the preliminary study included 600 of the largest U.S. firms: the 500 largest industrials, the fifty largest retailing firms, and the fifty largest transportation firms, ranked according to sales revenues for 1967 by the editors of *Fortune*. (See appendix A for a complete listing.) To qualify for the *Fortune* listing a firm must be based in the United States, provide public reports of its financial status, derive at least 50 percent of its revenues from manufacturing and mining (industrial listing), or retailing, or transportation operations. The 1967–1977 time frame was selected in 1978 as the most recent period reflecting high inflation rates and generally declining measures of industrial vigor.

Industry coding and financial data were obtained for each of the 600 firms from the Compustat Industrial File computer-readable tapes. Compustat is the registered trademark of Investors Management Science, Inc. (IMS), a Denver-based subsidiary of Standard and Poors Corporation, which compiles financial data for 2,700 American corporations. Compustat data is primarily obtained from corporate financial reports filed by publicly owned corporations with the Securities and Exchange Commission. Corporate annual reports, Standard and Poors' publications, and inside corporate contacts supplement the quarterly updated data. Sales data represent gross sales and other operating revenues. Royalty income is included when considered operating revenue (as for most oil firms, extractive industries, and publishing firms). For cigar, cigarette, oil, rubber, and liquor producers, excise taxes collected by the firm for the federal government are deducted. Sales data for consolidated subsidiaries are included. IMS maintains a policy of not restating annual data.[2]

Membership in the original 1967 *Fortune* population changed over time as the result of bankruptcy, merger, and acquisition activity. IMS maintains financial data only on active firms and only under the current corporate name. Consequently, historical data for firms that either filed for bankruptcy or merged with other companies between 1967 and 1977 were expunged from its data files. Research indicated that 392 of the 600 firms remained active; forty-one firms remained active under a changed name; 125 firms merged with or were acquired by other firms.[3] Deleted from the original population were fourteen firms that filed for bankruptcy; eleven firms that came under foreign ownership; six firms (or the 125 total merger/ acquisitions) that merged with or were acquired by firms not included on the Compustat tapes; fifteen firms still doing business but not included on the Compustat data tapes; and two firms that no longer issued public financial statements. In the case of merger or acquisition, the new firm or the acquiring firm was added to the final research population. Hence, six nonindustrials made their way into the research population. For example, in 1969 Transcontinental Bus System (original population) was merged into the nonindustrial Holiday Inns of America, Inc. which was included in the research population. Also, each partner to a merger included in the original *Fortune* list was counted as a merger/acquisition. For example, in 1968 Canada Dry, Hunt Foods, and McCalls (each in the original population) merged to form Norton Simon, Inc., the only firm represented in the research population. The total number of firms in the research population was reduced considerably by such merger activity and by the acquisitive behavior of such firms as ITT which absorbed Rayonier and Continental Baking in 1968 and Grinnell in 1969 (all four on the original list). See table 3-1 for a summary of original population activity during the 1967–1977 period.

Treatment

The total number of firms in the final research population for which financial data were retrieved was 475. Included were 403 industrials, six nonin-

Table 3-1

Corporate Activity (Original Population):1967-1977

	Industrial Firms	Retailing and Transportation Firms	Percentage of Total (600 Firms)
1967 *Fortune* firms that remained active under same name:	332	60	65.3
1967 *Fortune* firms that remained active with name change:	36	5	6.8
1967 *Fortune* firms that merged with or were acquired by Compustat listed firms:	98	21	19.8
1967 *Fortune* firms that merged with or were acquired by firms not listed by Compustat:	5	1	1.0
1967 *Fortune* firms that filed for bankruptcy:	4	10	2.3
1967 *Fortune* firms that came under foreign ownership:	11	0	1.8
1967 *Fortune* firms still doing business but not listed by Compustat:	12	3	2.5
1967 *Fortune* firms that no longer issue public financial statements:	2	0	.3
Totals:	500	100	100.0

dustrials, thirty-seven retailing firms, and twenty-nine transportation firms. (See appendix B for a complete listing.) In order to identify those firms that had experienced contraction due to declining revenues during the 1967-1977 period, current dollar sales data were retrieved from the Compustat files and then restated in constant dollar terms employing the implicit price deflators for gross national product (GNP) compiled by the U.S. Department of Commerce, Bureau of Economic Analysis. Since we measure growth in real terms, it seemed appropriate to do likewise when attempting a measure of decline. The GNP price deflators were chosen over specific industry wholesale price index (WPI) measures after a review of the literature concerning the structural deficiencies of the WPI. The GNP deflators were also preferred because the majority of the firms under consideration were diversified and active in a variety of industries.[4]

The GNP deflators cover all prices in the economy including exports. They reflect changes in the composition of national output as well as pure price movements. They constitute a conservative measure of inflation when compared to the widely cited consumer price index (CPI). The CPI has been

used by publicly held corporations to compute constant-dollar depreciation
and profit data since 1980 when the Financial Accounting Standards Board
mandated the inclusion of such data in annual reports. There is, however,
considerable evidence that the CPI tends to overstate inflation. Consequently, there is resistance to its continued use.[5]

The 475 firms in the research population were categorized into forty-
two industry groupings. Compustat industry codes conform to the Bureau
of the Budget's Standard Industry Classification (SIC) codes. See table 3-2
for a breakdown of the final population by industry.

Trends

In real terms, 56 percent or 266 of the 475 firms in the research population
experienced two or more consecutive years of contracting sales revenue during the 1967-1977 period. This finding alone is surprising because we are
accustomed to thinking of the major industrial, retailing, and transportation firms as continually growing and expanding regardless of any aggregate
measures that may signal economic decline. Traditional financial accounting methods have tended to camouflage the stagnation of U.S. industry for
managers, shareholders, and analysts alike. Of course, two consecutive
years of negative growth in sales revenue cannot be equated with stagnation
or decline. More often than not, a two-year contraction episode merely
reflects strategic divestiture or a firm's struggle to cope with inflation. But
a single factor, even the impact of inflation which presumably would affect
all firms in the same industry in a similar manner, cannot explain the variation found in contraction patterns of firms operating in the same industries.

Of those industries in which more than one firm was represented in the
research population, only three, including metal mining (code 10), house-
hold furniture (code 25), and publishing (code 27) were characterized by
contraction of all firms. The timing and duration of contraction episodes
varied in all forty-two industrial categories. There were no instances where
every firm in a particular industry experienced simultaneous contraction
and recovery episodes. There were also frequent examples of growth firms
in generally contracting industries and vice versa. Even in the troubled steel
industry (code 33), eight of the twenty-nine firms in the research population
avoided sales contraction altogether during the eleven-year period under
study. The other twenty-one firms experienced contraction episodes ranging
from severe (contraction each year from the 1967 sales revenue level) to
moderate, with the bulk of the firms indicating contracting reveneus for five
or six consecutive years.

Table 3-3 gives details of the duration of contraction episodes for each
industry represented in the 475-firm population. Table 3-4 summarizes the
same data in tabular form.

Table 3–2
Industrial Codes and Descriptors

Industry Code	Industry Descriptor	Number of Firms in Research Population
10	Metal mining	4
12	Coal mining	2
13	Crude petroleum and natural gas	4
14	Nonmetallic minerals	1
16	Construction	2
20	Food, beverages, and kindred products	50
21	Cigarettes	2
22	Textile mill products	11
23	Apparel and other finished products	7
24	Lumber and wood products	5
25	Household furniture	2
26	Paper and allied products	16
27	Publishing and printing	9
28	Chemicals, drugs and allied products	47
29	Petroleum refining, paving, and roofing materials	28
30	Rubber and miscellaneous plastics	7
31	Footwear (except rubber)	4
32	Glass, cement, abrasives, asbestos	14
33	Blast furnaces and steel smelting, refining, rolling and drawing of nonferrous metals	29
34	Fabricated metal products	9
35	Industrial machinery and equipment (including electronic computing equipment	39
36	Electrical machinery, household appliances, and electronic components	31
37	Motor vehicles, parts and accessories, aircraft, boat, railroad, guided missile/space vehicles, parts, auxillary equipment and repair	41
38	Industrial measurement, medical and photographic equipment, supplies and instruments	8
39	Toys and sporting goods	2
40	Railroad lines	11
42	Trucking	4
44	Water transportation	2
45	Air transportation	12
48	Telephone communication, radio and television broadcasters	3
49	Natural gas transmission	3
50	Wholesale metals, minerals, scrap and waste materials	2
51	Wholesale drugs, groceries, and nondurable goods	3
52	Retail lumber and building materials	1
53	Retail department stores	16
54	Retail grocery stores	17
59	Retail stores (other)	3
61	Licensed small loan lenders	3
70	Hotel-motels	1
72	Linen supply services	1
73	Equipment rental and leasing	1
99	Conglomerates	16
42	Totals	475

Table 3–3
Patterns of Contracting Sales Revenue (Research Population):1967–1977

Industry Code:	10	12	13	14	16	20	21	22	23	24	25	26	27	28	29	30	31	32	33	34	35
Total in Population: 475	4	2	4	1	2	50	2	11	7	5	2	16	9	47	28	7	4	14	29	9	39
Total Experiencing Contraction:266	4	0	2	1	1	25	1	9	5	3	2	6	9	17	9	4	2	3	21	6	25
Patterns																					
10 cons. yrs. (5)						1													2		1
9 cons. yrs. (19)								1					1			1			1		1
6 + 3 yrs.[a] (1)																			1		
5 + 4yrs. (1)				1																	
8 cons. yrs. (14)						1		1	1	1			2	2							2
5 + 3 yrs. (5)						1								1							1
4 + 4 yrs. (1)																					1
7 cons. yrs. (12)						1		1						1							
5 + 2 yrs. (7)						1			1			1	1								2
4 + 3 yrs. (10)	1																1		3	1	1
6 cons. yrs. (8)	1						1						1	1							
4 + 2 yrs. (25)						4		2	1			1			1	1			1		2
3 + 3 yrs. (18)	1											1		1	1	1			7		1
5 cons. yrs. (9)									1				1	2							1
3 + 2 yrs. (26)			1			3		3	1	1	2		1	1	1	1		1	4	2	
4 cons. yrs. (23)												2	2	3	5			1	1	1	2
3 cons. yrs. (47)			1			5				1		1		5	1			1		1	5
2 cons. yrs. (35)					1	8											1		1	1	5

Industry Code:	36	37	38	39	40	42	44	45	48	49	50	51	52	53	54	59	61	70	72	73	99
Total in Population: 475	31	41	8	2	11	4	2	12	3	3	2	3	1	16	17	3	3	1	1	1	16
Total Experiencing Contraction: 266	23	36	2	1	4	1	1	4	1	0	1	0	0	12	8	1	2	0	1	1	11
Patterns																					
10 cons. yrs.	1																				
9 cons. yrs.		8												1	1						3
6 + 3 yrs.[a]		1							1					1							
5 + 4 yrs.																					
8 cons. yrs.	2																				
5 + 3 yrs.											1			1	1						1
4 + 4 yrs.						1															
7 cons. yrs.		4													2						2
5 + 2 yrs.	1			1				1													
4 + 3 yrs.		2						1													
6 cons. yrs.		1												1							
4 + 2 yrs.	6	2												1						1	2
3 + 3 yrs.	2	1			1																
5 cons. yrs.	2							1											1		
3 + 2 yrs.		7			1		1	1													
4 cons. yrs.	2	7	1											2	1	1					1
3 cons. yrs.	4	2			1										2		1				1
2 cons. yrs.	3	1	1		1									5	1		1				1

[a]6 + 3 yrs. = six consecutive years plus three more consecutive years.

Table 3–4
Summary of Contraction Patterns (Research Population):1967–1977

Patterns of Consecutive Years of Contracting Sales	Number of Firms Involved	Percentage of Total Research Population (475 Firms)	Cumulative Percentage of Total Research Population (475 Firms)
10 consecutive years	5	1.1	1.1
9 consecutive years	19	4.0	
6 + 3 cons. yrs.[a]	1	.2	
5 +4 cons. yrs.	1	.2	
	21		
		4.4	5.5
8 consecutive years	14	3.0	
5 + 3 cons. yrs.	5	1.1	
4 + 4 cons. yrs.	1	.2	
	20		
		4.2	9.7
7 consecutive years	12	2.5	
5 + 2 cons. yrs.	7	1.5	
4 + 3 cons. yrs.	10	2.1	
	29		
		6.1	15.8
6 consecutive years	8	1.7	
4 + 2 cons. yrs.	25	5.3	
3 + 3 cons. yrs.	18	3.8	
	51		
		10.7	26.5
5 consecutive years	9	1.9	
3 + 3 cons. yrs.	26	5.5	
	35		
		7.4	33.9
4 consecutive years	23	4.8	38.7
3 consecutive years	47	9.9	48.6
2 consecutive years	35	7.4	56.0
Totals	266 firms	56.0	

[a]6 + 3 cons. yrs. = six consecutive years plus three more consecutive years.

Short periods of contraction were frequent among this group of corporate giants. More significantly, longer periods of contraction characterized a substantial number of firms. If during the eleven-year period, a firm experienced six years (more than half of the study period) in which real revenues fell below the 1967 level, it is reasonable to assume that the firm was having some trouble maintaining growth, whether the actual level of contraction was large or small. This was true for 26.5 percent of the 475 firms included in the research population. When those six years were consecutive, the case is stronger. Fifty-nine firms, or 12.4 percent of the population, experienced six or more consecutive years of declining revenue. In addition, some of the 125 firms that dropped from the original population (600 firms) because of merger or acquisition activity may well have undertaken such strategies in response to declining sales growth on the part of one or both parties. It is not surprising to find a considerable number of firms in industries hard hit by foreign competition or excess capacity during the last decade suffering from contraction, for example, the textile (code 22), paper (code 26), chemical (code 28), footwear (code 31), steel (code 33), consumer electronics (code 36), and automotive (code 37) industries. The data also indicate a significant number of contracting firms in industries which experienced declining rates of investment in plant and equipment during the same period; for example, the food processing (code 20), textile (code 22), apparel (code 23), chemical (code 28), tire and rubber (code 30), steel (code 33), automotive and aerospace (code 37), and retail food (code 54) industries.[6]

The data in table 3-3 indicate that conglomerate firms have not been immune to sales-contraction episodes. Eleven of the sixteen conglomerates in the study experienced contracting revenues for three or more consecutive years (including the very acquisitive Gulf Western and ITT). Conglomerates with well-publicized financial problems such as Avco, Kaiser Industries, LTV, Signal Companies, Teledyne, and Textron experienced contracting revenues for seven or more consecutive years during the eleven-year period under study, largely the result of divestiture after periods of heavy acquisition.[7]

Selecting Corporations for Study

Another way to look at the data is in terms of those firms that had a lower level of sales activity in 1977 than ten years earlier at the beginning of the study. This was true for 10.1 percent, or forty-eight of the 475 firms in the research population. These firms may have expanded revenues from one year to the next, but real revenues declined absolutely during the period. These firms remained financially viable even though they may have contracted each year during the study. Changing environmental conditions resulting in contracting revenues may or may not lead to financial insolvency. Bankruptcy is associated with many factors and is not necessarily related to changes in revenue levels. These forty-eight firms, representing cases of absolute contraction, were selected for further study in the belief that corporate response patterns would be more readily apparent in the more extreme instances. See table 3-5 for a listing of the forty-eight research population firms that experienced absolute contraction.

In order to reduce to a manageable number the firms to be considered in a more detailed analysis of corporate response patterns, firms other than

Table 3-5
Firms Experiencing Absolute Contraction (Research Population):1967-1977

Industry Code	Firm	1967 Sales (Constant $, million)	1977 Sales (Constant $, million)	Percentage Decline 1967–1977
20	Am. Bakeries	376.740	338.760	10.1
	Rath Packing	299.038	258.418	13.6
	Ward Foods	349.532	244.687	30.0
22	Burlington Industries	1726.905	1689.909	2.1
26	Fibreboard	175.525	161.307	8.8
27	Cadence Industries	73.652	71.579	2.8
	Grolier	220.071	156.659	28.8
28	Olin	1140.344	1041.962	8.6
30	Am. Biltrite	179.701	136.087	24.3
31	Genesco	1103.645	718.077	34.9
33	General Cable	472.285	439.078	7.0
	Kaiser Steel	507.593	465.835	8.2
	Porter, H.K.	354.720	338.648	4.5
	Reading Industries	56.433	39.995	29.1
	Revere	426.221	422.873	.8
35	Addressograph-Multigraph	455.581	421.915	7.4
	Curtiss-Wright	219.818	219.292	.2
	Ex-Cell-O	332.954	316.046	5.1
	FMC	1661.605	1622.003	2.4
	Midland-Ross	423.437	333.457	21.3
	Stewart-Warner	217.540	206.828	4.9
	Warner and Swasey	185.776	185.121	.4
36	Ampex	295.368	200.865	32.0
	Bunker Ramo	292.372	241.446	17.4
	Zenith	827.522	683.270	17.4
37	Boeing	3744.250	2843.760	22.0
	GATX	455.075	412.890	9.3
	General Dynamics	2851.602	2052.918	28.0
	Grumman	1225.761	1098.709	10.4
	Lockheed	2955.581	2386.641	19.3
	Maremount	235.955	224.696	4.8
	McDonnell-Douglas	3712.731	2508.348	32.4
	Rohr	315.363	239.448	24.1
	Todd Shipyards	245.664	150.887	38.6
	United Aircraft	12.782	10.674	16.5
	White Motor	974.184	887.114	8.9
48	Cowles Comm.	185.016	9.751	94.7
53	Allied Stores	1372.394	1363.580	.6
	Arlen Realty	770.292(1971)	601.464	21.9
	Vornado	882.941	699.445	20.8
54	Allied Supermarkets	753.860	635.024	15.8
	First National Stores	810.068	702.402	13.3

Table 3–5 continued

Industry Code	Firm	1967 Sales (Constant $, million)	1977 Sales (Constant $, million)	Percentage Decline 1967–1977
	Food Fair	1736.016	1724.244	.7
	Great Atlantic and Pacific Tea	6908.119	5120.191	25.9
	National Tea	1451.784	591.285	59.3
72	Sears Industries	41.508	37.112	10.6
99	Avco	1261.706	1088.231	13.8
	Kaiser Industries	1006.238	758.792(1976)	24.6

basic industrials were deleted from the list of firms experiencing absolute contraction. Consequently, food products (code 20), publishing (code 27), broadcasting (code 48), retail department stores (code 53), retail grocery stores (code 54), and services (code 72) firms were deleted. In addition, the firms in industry code 37 including motor vehicles, parts and accessories; aircraft; boat; railroad; guided missile/space vehicles, parts, auxillary equipment, and repair firms were deleted because of the extraordinary impact of the Vietnam War winddown and the aerospace cutbacks that negatively affected this industry during the period under study. Kaiser industries was also deleted from the list because it operated primarily as a holding company. Contraction episodes for the remaining twenty-one firms were explored in more detail.

Annual Reports

U.S. securities laws require that publicly held firms produce annual documents that disclose operating statistics and information regarding securities issues. Annual reports to shareholders and the Securities and Exchange Commission, together with any stock prospectus issued by a corporation, provide a good deal of useful information about corporate goals and strategy. There are legal sanctions against deliberate distortion, and these reports are generally agreed to provide accurate documentation of corporate operations and activities. Readers of these reports should be aware, however, that the potential for biased statements also exists given the promotional nature of much of the narrative. Securities analysts are considered the main audience for these reports along with stockholders, employees, customers, and regulatory officials.

Annual reports for the remaining twenty-one firms of the research population were analyzed. The reports almost always included discussions of the growth problems confronting the firms, although such explanations are not mandated by law. In instances where dividends were cut back or eliminated because of sales revenue contraction, lengthy explanations and descriptions of turnaround plans were frequently the centerpiece of the reports.[8]

Diversification Categories

Information gleaned from the corporate annual reports indicated that diversification level made a significant difference in the response alternatives available to managers of contracting firms. That is, managers of firms that were diversified at a low or a moderate level could consider further diversification into new high-growth markets as an option if current debt levels were manageable. On the other hand, managers in highly diversified firms rarely suggested further diversification as an alternative. Retrenchment to basic industries was a dominant theme in the annual reports of the highly diversified firms such as Olin Corporation.

The foregoing analysis made it clear that the criteria for selecting representative firms for more detailed analyses should include diversification level. Diversification level was designated as an independent variable and the remaining firms were categorized according to their operational diversification level in 1967, the first year of the study. The traditional product-count measure of diversification (gauged by the number of industries in which a firm is active in addition to the distribution of the firm's annual sales among those industries) is based on the SIC system at the two-, three-, or four-digit level (increasing order of specificity). There are, however, several serious problems connected with any measure based on the SIC, which when applied uniformly tends to create anomalies in the definition of markets. SIC-based measures give no weight to what can be great differences between various firms' activity patterns in a given industry at any level of SIC specificity.[9]

In their recent studies of diversification in U.S. industry, Leonard Wrigley (1970) and Richard P. Rumelt (1974) developed a system of categorization based upon the concept of *diversification strategy,* defined as the firm's commitment to diversity per se, together with the strengths, skills, or purposes that span this diversity demonstrated by the way new activities are related to old activities.[10] The Wrigley-Rumelt diversification categories were utilized to group the twenty-one firms in the study that had experienced absolute contraction. The diversification categories may be described as follows:

Dominant-Product: Such firms may have diversified to a small degree but are still quite dependent upon and characterized by their major product-market activity.

Related-Product: Firms which have diversified by adding new activities that are tangibly related to the collective skills and strengths possessed originally by the firm.

Unrelated Product: Firms that have diversified (usually by acquisition) into areas that are not related to the original skills and strengths, other than financial, of the firm.[11]

The qualitative analysis of corporate activity as described in the 1967 annual reports resulted in the following categorization of the twenty-one firm population that experienced absolute contraction between 1967 and 1977:

Dominant-product
  Addressograph-Multigraph
  American Biltrite Rubber
  Reading Industries
  Zenith

Related-product diversification
  Ampex
  Burlington Industries
  Bunker Ramo
  Curtiss-Wright
  Ex-Cell-O
  Fibreboard
  General Cable
  Genesco
  Kaiser Steel
  Midland-Ross
  Porter, H.K.
  Revere Copper and Brass
  Stewart-Warner
  Warner and Swasey

Unrelated-product diversification
  Avco
  FMC
  Olin

One firm was chosen from each diversification category for more detailed study drawn from public source information. Zenith Corporation was selected as an example of a dominant-product firm and Avco Corporation was selected as an example of an unrelated-product firm. Both firms had experienced absolute contraction. In order to broaden the analysis, Boise Cascade Corporaton was selected as an example of a related-product firm that had recouped (or accomplished a turnaround) after a lengthy period of severe decline. Boise Cascade differs from Zenith and Avco in that after turnaround was accomplished, annual revenues eventually exceeded the 1967 level. Corporate studies describing patterns of response to declining rates of growth for Zenith, Boise Cascade, and Avco are found in chapters 4, 5, and 6, respectively.

The corporate studies are concerned with the process of adaptation and change over time. In contrast to deductive models of explanation, the pattern model of explanation employed is appropriate for gaining an understanding of changing or evolving relationships within open systems during the early stages of inquiry.[12] Explanation is generated from the data rather than from formal hypotheses. Meaning is a function of the relationship between variables, not of precise definition of variables or boundaries. The corporation, or the firm, is envisioned as a rational system of control and motivation within the conceptual framework developed in chapter 2. The corporate response to the stimulus of sales-revenue contraction is analyzed in terms of efforts by management to reduce environmental uncertainty or rationalize the firm's changing environment. Although a useful analytical distinction can be made between the firm's internal and external domains, it should be stressed that they are highly interdependent. Any change in one has ramifications for the other. Financial statistics included in the corporate studies are in current dollars unless otherwise stated.

Notes

1. Phillip I. Blumberg, *The Megacorporation in American Society* (Englewood Cliffs, N.J.: Prentice-Hall, 1975), pp. 21, 24.

2. Financial data for previous years is frequently *restated* (revised) from year to year in corporate annual reports.

3. Typically the name change involved an effort by the firm to get away from the one-industry connotations of the original name. Thus Pet Milk became just Pet, Automatic Sprinkler became ATO, United Shoe Machinery became USM, and Pittsburgh Plate Glass became PPG Industries.

4. For discussions of the structural deficiencies of wholesale price index measures, see U.S. Office of Management and Budget, Statistical Policy Division, "Price Statistics," *Statistical Reporter,* no. 77-6 (Washington, D.C.: Government Printing Office (GPO), 1977), pp. 201-202;

U.S. National Bureau of Economic Research, *Price Statistics Review Committee, The Price Statistics of the Federal Government,* general series, no. 73 (Washington, D.C.: GPO 1961).

5. For discussions of the consumer price index as an overstated measure of inflation see *Business Week (BW),* 14 October 1979, pp. 120–122; *BW,* 4 May 1981, pp. 84–86; William Nordhaus, *New York Times,* 12 July 1981, p. F-3. Compare the CPI with the GNP deflators used in the preliminary study of corporate contraction for the 1967–1977 period.

Implicit Price Deflators for Gross National Product, 1967–1977

1967	79.02	1973	105.80
1968	82.57	1974	116.02
1969	86.72	1975	127.18
1970	91.36	1976	133.88
1971	96.02	1977	141.32
1972	100.0		

Source: Council of Economic Advisers, *Economic Report of the President,* January 1978, no. B–3, p. 260.

Consumer Price Index, 1967–1977

1967	100.0	1973	133.1
1968	104.2	1974	147.7
1969	109.8	1975	161.2
1970	116.3	1976	170.5
1971	121.3	1977	181.5
1972	125.3		

Source: Council of Economic Advisers, *Economic Report of the President,* January 1981, no. B–50, p. 289.

6. See Peter O. Steiner, *Mergers: Motives, Effects, Policies* (Ann Arbor: University of Michigan Press, 1975); Stanley C. Vance, *Managers in the Conglomerate Era* (New York: John Wiley and Sons, 1971) for discussions of merger motives including *hyperdepressed* investment opportunities. Also see *BW,* 17 October 1977, p. 5 for an investment inventory of U.S.

industry between 1967 and 1977 (computations are based on comparable Compustat data).

7. The term *conglomerate* is used here to describe the firm that has accomplished broad spectrum diversification into products unrelated to the initial technology and market of the firm. The convention is to classify a firm as a conglomerate if it produces goods in five or six two-digit industries (SIC codes).

8. For recent discussions of annual report and use and validity see William C. Glueck and Robert Willis, "Documentary Sources and Strategic Management Research," *Academy of Management Review* (January 1979): 95–102; Edward H. Bowman, "Strategy, Annual Reports, and Alchemy," *California Management Review (CMA)* (Spring 1978):64–71. For discussions of annual report preparation from management's point of view, see Joseph Poindexter, "Circus Time at W.R. Grace," *Saturday Review* (1 April 1978):46–47; *BW,* 16 April 1979, pp. 114–118. For a general discussion of the relationship between business and various news media, see S. Prakash Sethi, "Business and the News Media," *CMR,* (Spring 1977):52–62.

9. For a discussion of diversification measures and data analysis problems, see Adrian Wood, "Diversification, Merger and Research Expenditures: A Review of Empirical Studies," *The Corporate Economy,* eds. Robin Marris and Adrian Wood (Cambridge, Mass.: Harvard University Press, 1971), pp. 428–453; Charles H. Berry, *Corporate Growth and Diversification* (Princeton, N.J.: Princeton University Press, 1975).

10. Richard P. Rumelt, *Strategy, Structure, and Economic Performance* (Boston: Division of Research, Graduate School of Business Administration, Harvard University, 1974), p. 11.

11. Ibid.

12. Abraham Kaplan, *The Conduct of Inquiry* (New York: Chandler Publishing Co., 1964), pp. 327–335.

4 The Dominant-Product Firm: Zenith Corporation

Management strategy and corporate operations of a dominant-product firm, the Zenith Corporation, are described here for the 1967–1980 period. On the basis of consolidated revenues, Zenith was ranked as the 134th largest U.S. industrial firm in 1967. As a measure of relative decline, Zenith had fallen in rank to the nation's 277th largest industrial by 1980 after a ten-year struggle with contracting sales revenues.[1]

Conservative Growth Strategies

Zenith was founded as a partnership under the name of the Chicago Radio Laboratory by R.H.G. Matthews and Karl Hassel in 1918. The partners first project was the construction of a long-wave radio receiver for the *Chicago Tribune*. The receiver was used to pick up news dispatches from the Versailles Peace Conference beamed from a long-wave station in France. By avoiding the congested trans-Atlantic cable, the *Tribune* was able to beat the competition by twelve to twenty-four hours on conference news stories.

In 1921, Eugene F. McDonald, a former lieutenant commander in the navy, joined the partnership as general manager. McDonald provided funds badly needed for expansion. In 1923, he incorporated Zenith Radio to serve as a sales agent for Chicago Radio Laboratory products. Zenith Radio soon absorbed the original partnership and built a reputation as a manufacturer of innovative, high-quality radio receivers.

The early depression years brought on Zenith's first experience with retrenchment. The firm reported losses from 1930 through 1933, but it survived the depression relatively unscathed mostly because of an extremely conservative financial strategy. Expansion during the 1920s had not involved long-term debt, and investment in inventories had been kept to a minimum. Furthermore, new low-priced table and portable radio receivers, the latter selling for as little as $19.95, were well-suited to the times. Aside from a loss in 1946, the firm experienced no other net deficits until the 1970s.

During the 1930s the notion of television began to generate excitement. Although Zenith carried out some research and even set up Chicago's first television station in 1939, the firm made no attempt to market a commercial television set. According to Zenith's 1938 annual report to shareholders, the firm refused "to be stampeded into the premature production of television receivers for sale to the public." Management's stand on the matter of television greatly increased the firm's good will with radio dealers, and the trade in general, as they began to realize the threat posed by television technology.

After World War II, Zenith expanded to meet the demand for consumer audio products: coils, loud speakers, record changers, and the like. Finally, in 1948, Zenith put its first television receivers on the market. To assure a picture tube source, Zenith acquired the Rauland Corporation in the same year. Continued expansion enabled the firm to profit from the initial surge of demand for monochrome television sets. Building on a reputation for high quality and a capable distribution network, Zenith gradually increased domestic monochrome television market share to 20 percent and became a leader in that segment of the consumer electronics industry. Later the firm held back again, and it was not until mid-1961 that it introduced a color television line, seven years after the first color sets became commercially available. By then Zenith had gained the reputation of never being first with new products.[2]

Between 1961 and 1965, two major expansions of color television manufacturing capacity took place. Annual capacity reached a rate of approximately 1.5 million monochrome tubes and 1 million color tubes. The firm also continued to produce a range of high-fidelity audio products. Zenith operated six manufacturing plants in the Chicago area in addition to its five wholly owned subsidiaries: Rauland Corporation, Wincharger Corporation, Central Electronics, Inc., Zenith Radio Distributing Corporation, and Zenith Radio Research Corporation. During 1962, Zenith launched a successful national advertising campaign that stressed the firm's quality control systems and unique hand-wired chassis. Hand-wired circuits, as opposed to the printed circuit boards used by competitors, were said to be more easily repaired at less cost to the consumer. Zenith's advertising motto, "the quality goes in before the name goes on," was credited with obtaining a large degree of consumer acceptance for Zenith products.

Joseph S. Wright, formerly with the Federal Trade Commission in Washington, D.C., became Zenith's third chief executive in 1964. He had joined the firm eleven years earlier as an assistant to Zenith's general counsel. Sam Kaplan served under Wright as president and chief financial officer. Leonard Truesdell was given responsibility for all Zenith marketing activity. These three men were Zenith's top decision makers until 1968 when Truesdell resigned amid conflict of interest charges. At a time when most other large American firms were enthusiastically pursuing diversification growth strategies, Zenith's management team was proudly insisting that its strength came from concentrating all efforts on the radio, stereo, and television businesses. Prior to 1967 the firm was clear of long-term debt and was reported to have more than $100 million in excess cash on hand.[3]

Before the Deluge: 1967–1969

Zenith's annual report for 1967 presented a rosy growth picture to shareholders. Production of monochrome and color television sets exceeded 1 million units and a newly completed manufacturing plant increased production capacity to 2 million color units per year. Approximately 78 percent of total sales revenue was generated by television-related products; another 20 percent from radio, phonograph, and hearing instrument products; and 2 percent from military and medical instrument products. Demand was strong for Zenith phonographs, stereos, and hearing aids, but radio sales were gradually declining. Rather than cut prices as other major U.S. competitors had done during the preceding year (primarily RCA with a 30 percent market share), Zenith broadened its color television line to include smaller, less expensive sets. During the year, Wright centralized Zenith's research and engineering facilities. Research continued on Zenith's Phonovision decoders and other equipment designed to bring subscription television into the home. Zenith representatives, including Wright, were highly visible in lobbying efforts to convince the Federal Communications Commission to authorize subscription television on a permanent basis.[4]

The rosy picture was interrupted when production at a Zenith manufacturing plant in Hong Kong (radio components) was interrupted by riots and labor strife. Chinese dissidents charged that American electronics firms were exploiting low-wage workers in order to produce electronic equipment cheaply for the Defense Department's "war of aggression in Vietnam." In addition, a partially owned Zenith assembly plant in Israel was shut down when workers were mobilized for the June Arab-Israeli war. Such incidents no doubt contributed to Zenith's admitted "innate cautiousness" when later it became necessary to establish major production facilities abroad.[5]

Another troubled note was sounded by investment analysts who reported that dealers, distributors, and manufacturers were stockpiling color television sets. When the anticipated sales boom did not materialize, the consumer electronics industry was forced to learn, once again, that the rate of sales volume increase rarely exceeds the annual GNP growth rate. The stockpiling episode indicated that the potential for productive overcapacity existed in the domestic consumer electronics industry in 1967, prior to the heavy onslaught of foreign imports during the 1970s. With only a 22 percent market share for color sets and declining sales of monochrome sets, radios, phonographs, and stereos, investment analysts labeled 1967 as a disappointing year for the firm.[6]

Sales revenue in 1968 increased 3.2 percent (constant dollars) over the

1967 level. Zenith was able to increase its color television market penetration to approximately 25 percent because of a "continuing emphasis on quality products, modern production techniques, tight inventory control, and a strong marketing organization." Investment analysts advised that Zenith stock had excellent growth potential. Structurally, Zenith merged its former subsidiaries Rauland Corporation and Zenith Sales Corporation and thereafter operated each unit as a corporate division. In conjunction with the earlier centralization of research and engineering, management began a program of tightening financial controls.[7]

During 1969, revenue from sales decreased 8.7 percent (constant dollars). But, since Zenith had no long-term debt, the impact of declining revenue on operations was initially less traumatic than for Boise Cascade or Avco (described later) where creditor interests immediately acted to constrain management flexibility in response to mounting debt. Chairman Wright commented in the 1969 annual report that "progress had been affected by the general slowdown in economic growth resulting from the government's anti-inflation measures." He also pointed to high labor and material costs, a two-month strike at one of Zenith's manufacturing plants, the federal 10 percent income tax surcharge, and the recently enacted Illinois state income tax as factors cutting into profits.

Subscription television was finally authorized by the Federal Communications Commission during 1969. Wright arranged to have Teco, Inc., a 1948 Zenith spin-off, begin production of the home decoders needed to unscramble subscription broadcast signals. And in another matter suggesting Zenith's eagerness to maintain orderly market conditions, the firm's antitrust suit against Hazeltine Research, Inc. was decided in favor of Zenith by the U.S. Supreme Court. The action, originally filed against Hazeltine in 1959, was similar to a previous suit won against RCA in 1948. Both damage actions claimed that Zenith had been prohibited from competing in certain markets due to the participation of competitors (RCA and Hazeltine) in foreign and/or domestic patent pools. Finally, Wright announced that Zenith would follow its major domestic competitor (RCA) and establish manufacturing operations overseas in low-wage countries in order to protect the firm's position in the domestic electronics market. Whereas in 1960, 94.4 percent of all consumer electronic products had been supplied by domestic manufacturers, by 1970 that figure had fallen to 68.4 percent. Zenith's long and arduous battle against Japanese imports was officially underway.[8]

Operating statistics documenting Zenith's contraction experience are shown in table 4–1. In constant dollars, Zenith's sales revenue contracted 22 percent between 1967 and 1978. Simultaneously, Zenith's stock prices plummeted from $72.13 to $7.89 per share.

Table 4-1
Zenith Corporation's Consolidated Operating Statistics, 1967-1978 in Constant Dollars

Year	Sales and Operating Revenues ($ million)	Percentage Change over Previous Year's Sales	Fortune "500" Ranking	Number of Employees	Common Stock Year-end Price-Close ($)	Earnings per Share ($)	Net Income ($ million)
1967	827.522	—	134	22,900	72.13	2.76	51.913
1968	854.311	3.2	141	23,900	67.34	3.03	57.303
1969	780.186	(8.7)a	166	22,500	38.05	2.40	45.688
1970	627.347	(19.6)	202	19,700	40.50	1.42	27.038
1971	638.470	1.8	203	18,200	43.95	2.05	32.609
1972	795.908	24.7	176	20,400	54.40	2.55	48.579
1973	951.988	19.6	164	27,500	24.76	2.74	54.140
1974	784.800	(17.6)	218	27,800	8.79	.60	9.826
1975	708.057	(9.8)	222	22,928	18.48	1.29	24.218
1976	730.638	3.2	231	23,365	20.69	1.53	28.831
1977	683.270	(6.5)	243	23,900	10.19	(.18)	(3.324)
1978	644.371	(5.7)	259	22,700	7.89	.82	15.348

Table 4-1 continued

Year	Long-term Debt ($ million)	Interest Expense ($ million)	Common Dividends ($ million)	Research and Development Expense ($ million)	Capital Expenditures ($ million)	Current Assets ($ million)
1967	n/p[b]	n/p	32.163	n/a[c]	22.792	275.578
1968	n/p	n/p	32.030	n/a	16.246	318.411
1969	n/p	n/p	30.650	n/a	24.855	305.685
1970	n/p	n/p	29.146	33.384	9.357	286.601
1971	8.091	.746	27.737	31.660	23.888	296.555
1972	6.635	1.340	26.653	23.100	14.591	353.608
1973	7.268	2.041	26.641	24.834	44.557	360.633
1974	8.468	9.622	22.520	25.435	35.292	343.245
1975	39.314	7.497	14.780	21.849	16.733	280.136
1976	37.347	4.724	14.060	22.871	22.407	266.170
1977	37.968	4.307	13.329	22.553	15.896	249.739
1978	32.875	4.340	12.361	19.472	11.243	318.232

Source: Compustat.

Note: GNP implicit price deflators were used to convert current dollars to constant 1972 dollars.

[a]Figures in parentheses are negative.

[b]n/p = data not made public by firm.

[c]n/a = consolidated data not available.

The Consumer Electronics Trade War: 1970-1978

During 1970, Zenith experienced a near 20 percent decline in sales revenue. In the words of Chairman Wright, "1970 was a disaster year for the industry." Wright attributed Zenith's depressed profits to the slowdown in U.S. economic growth, the dumping of imports, a trucking strike in the second quarter that closed down most Zenith manufacturing plants for six weeks, startup costs for two new chromocolor picture tube sizes, and unsatisfactory performance on several government and other special product contracts.[9]

In March 1970, Wright complained in a letter to Commerce Secretary Maurice Stans that Zenith would be forced to lay off 3,000 U.S. employees while simultaneously creating 4,000 new jobs in Taiwan with a new plant scheduled to start production in 1971. He blamed Japanese imports for the layoffs and for the need to turn to offshore sourcing in Taiwan and Mexico. Wright pleaded with Stans to have the Commerce Department look into Japanese dumping activity. He criticized the U.S. government for its lack of support "in the life and death struggle with the Japanese." Wright maintained that his was "not a protectionist view, but rather an insistence that the U.S. obtain fair and equitable trading terms with other nations." Wright's letter to Stans was made public in a speech delivered by the assistant commerce secretary for domestic and international business before the Electronics Industry Association.[10]

On 3 April 1970, Zenith petitioned the U.S. Treasury Department asking for the imposition of countervailing duties on Japanese television imports. The petition argued that the Japanese government assessed a commodity tax that equaled 15 to 20 percent of the value of all television sets produced for the home market. This tax was then refunded to firms that exported their sets. Zenith contended that under U.S. law, the remission of the commodity tax amounted to a "bounty or grant" to Japanese exporters who then, as a means of gaining entrance to foreign markets, passed on this savings to importers. Thus, Zenith argued, imported Japanese sets should be subjected to countervailing duties at a similar rate. Attached to the Zenith petition was a description of more than a dozen special programs through which the Japanese government encouraged exports and, in effect, lowered costs to exporting firms (subsidies for insurance, plant and equipment, overseas market development, entertainment of foreign buyers, and so forth).[11]

Wright made it very clear in his president's letter to stockholders in the 1970 annual report that the Taiwan and Mexican plants were a direct result of the U.S. government's failure to quickly respond to the Japanese import problem. Though Zenith's competitors had responded to the import threat by locating manufacturing plants abroad in cheaper labor markets, Zenith held out until 1970, hoping for government intervention on behalf of the entire industry. In June, Wright testified before Congress in oversight hearings on the Trade Act of 1969 regarding Zenith's projected decline in employment and its effect on the training and employment of minority groups. Approximately 38 percent of Zenith's projected layoffs would be racial minorities during a year when nonwhite unemployment reached 8.2 percent. Wright also testified regarding the effects of Japan's combined protectionism and dumping practices. He requested upward revision of tariffs and enforcement of the countervailing duty law. Wright succeeded in making the Japanese import problem highly visible during 1970—he became known as a spokesman and crusader for the domestic industry.[12]

Reorganization, Long-Range Planning, and the
Elimination of Basic Research

While 1970 was a disaster year for the consumer electronics industry, Zenith had some special problems of its own. Sam Kaplan, Zenith's president, died unexpectedly in April. Before the end of the month Wright had reorganized Zenith's top management in a self-described attempt "to broaden into new manufacturing and marketing areas." This action was interpreted in the business press as a response to outsiders who had been critical of Wright's failure to diversify Zenith beyond radio, stereo, and television. Wright's reorganization and his efforts to get Zenith ready for a more diversified future included a shift away from triumviral management (Wright, Kaplan, and Truesdell) toward a centralized, functional structure. Wright appointed four new executive vice-presidents (operations, marketing, product development, and corporate development) all of whom reported directly to Zenith's new president and Wright himself. According to Wright, the new executive vice-president for operations would be responsible for engineering, purchasing, and manufacturing, "centralizing for the first time everything necessary to get our product out on time." Only the Zenith hearing aid sales corporation remained outside of Wright's centralization effort.[13]

Wright's push for formal, long-range planning began with the hiring of James R. Collier as vice-president in charge of corporate development. Collier was directed "to plan for internal and external growth." Collier had previously been director of commercial development for the Raytheon Corporation when that firm launched its successful acquisition program during the 1960s. He defined his principal role at Zenith as "worrying about diversification in areas it is not in and establishing a planning system for the businesses it is in now." During 1970 Zenith acquired L. Berman & Company,

Inc., one of the largest manufacturers of television and stereo cabinets (a former supplier); and, a minority interest in Electronic Industrial Engineering, Inc., a producer of community antenna television equipment.[14]

Wright's reorganization was completed in May of 1971 when John J. Nevin, previously a corporate vice-president for marketing at Ford Motor Company, was appointed Zenith's new president. Nevin was then forty-four years old, held a Harvard M.B.A., and had seventeen years experience at Ford Motor Company as a financial analyst, controller, divisional product planning manager, and corporate vice-president. He shared Wright's indignation at the "government's dallying over protecting the American electronics and auto industries from foreign dumping." In a *New York Times* interview in July, Nevin described himself as a free trader in favor of fair price competition. He described the government as "diddling" around for the last three years over the dumping of Japanese radios and television sets at prices far below those charged in Japan. Nevin stated that dumping was "just as unfair to American business as monopoly practices are to the American consumer."[15]

For Zenith, 1971 was a year of redirection and reorganization. Sales revenues increased only 1.8 percent (constant dollars) over the previous year, but net income was increased $6.3 million by the initial payment in the Hazeltine settlement. The firm also took a $2.2 million extraordinary charge against income as the result of the termination or redirection of several production facilities. In order to reduce manufacturing costs, all U.S. color television picture tube production was centralized in one plant. Other production plants were closed. The manufacturing and marketing of medical electronic products was discontinued altogether. Despite Zenith's previous $20 million plus investment in subscription television hardware, management's renegotiation of the licensing agreement with Teco, Inc. left Teco solely responsible for financing future efforts to market the Phonovision subscription television system. Research activities at the Zenith Research Corporation and the Zenith Radio Research Corporation Ltd. were terminated. Those research and engineering programs that were continued involved applied technology related to what were considered to be high-growth potential markets.

Wright's response to threatened contraction was to reorganize, centralize decision making, cut manufacturing costs, and eliminate basic research. The deluge of lower-priced imports on the market prohibited any possibility of compensating with price increases. In the attempt to maintain its market share for color receivers, Zenith's primary market, Wright undertook an aggressive price-cutting strategy supported by heavy advertising expenditures. Heedless of Zenith's troubles, the Federal Trade Commission, acting on complaints from U.S. competitors, began a probe into the veracity of Zenith's advertising claims.[16]

The Swiss Watch Diversification Move

Concurrent with Wright's reorganization efforts, Zenith acquired a 93 percent interest in Movado-Zenith-Mondia Holding Company, a Swiss firm that owned several watch-making companies together forming Switzerland's fourth largest watch manufacturer. Part of Collier's diversification plan was to utilize Zenith's research capability in electronics in conjunction with the Movado-Mondia brand name and distribution system to market electronic wrist watches around the world. A second international move was made to enter the Mexican television receiver market, officially closed to imports, through a joint venture with Elementos Electronicos Mexiconos, S.A. (Elmex). Zenith licensed Elmex to produce its major television products in return for a substantial equity interest in the Mexican firm. As a result, at year-end 1971, Zenith had incurred $8.1 million (constant dollars) in long-term debt.[17]

Reprieve, Capacity Expansion, and Antitrust

On 4 March 1971, the U.S. Tariff Commission (later the International Trade Commission), a nonregulatory agency whose major function was to carry out investigations for the president and the Congress, found that the U.S. television industry was being injured by Japanese imports that were being sold at less than fair value. Both U.S. law and the General Agreement on Tariffs and Trade (GATT), signed in 1947 by the U.S. and Japan among others, prohibited dumping and provided for assessment of penalties when discovered. Following the Tariff Commission finding, the U.S. Treasury Department became responsible for assessing penalties. The Treasury Department required that importers of Japanese receivers post a bond to cover duties that might ultimately be assessed. At this point Zenith's management expected not only redress for past dumping, but also hoped that the Treasury Department would impose countervailing tariffs covering future imports. In fact, Treasury officials continued to deliberate but made no final determination for six years.

The following May, Chairman Wright testified in hearings before the Subcommittee on International Trade wherein the Congress was considering the changing world economy and its influence on the domestic economy and foreign policy. Wright testified that U.S. consumer electronics producers had been forced to buy components from Japan and move factories to Asia in order to meet Japanese import competition. He pointed out that the United States had lost the entire small radio market to the Japanese and he emphasized the dramatic 26 percent increase in U.S. market share gained by importers of consumer electronic products over the past decade. Relief arrived in August when President Nixon moved to slow the pressure of imports on the economy by initiating steps to revalue the dollar with respect to other currencies. He also imposed a temporary 10 percent surcharge on all imports. As a result, the dollar was devalued about 10 percent on the average, and more like 20 percent in comparison with the Japanese yen. These monetary changes so altered the economics of offshore production that Zenith began to reevaluate plans designed to relocate 75 percent of productive capacity outside the United States by 1975.[18]

The U.S. television industry had a record year in 1972 with total sales of color sets to dealers reaching 8.5 million units (including U.S. and import brands) compared to 7.1 million units sold in 1971—a 20 percent increase. Zenith's sales revenue increased 24.7 percent from the previous year. Zenith was able to capture 20.5 percent of the U.S. color receiver market, compared to arch rival RCA's 19.5 percent share. The significant upturn in sales resulted partly from generally improved economic conditions, partly from the surcharge on imports, and partly from the fact that Zenith cut prices, undertook the biggest advertising campaign in its history, and added low-priced portables to its line of high-priced consoles. The Japanese had spotted this gap in U.S. product lines during the late 1960s and had then successfully flooded the market with low-priced portables, often sold under private labels.[19]

The rapid improvement in Zenith's operating environment allowed Nevin to announce as early as February that the firm would no longer need to transfer production offshore. He felt "confident we can now make color sets in the U.S., market them here and show a profit." Zenith's 1972 acquisitions included: H.R. Basford Company, a wholesale distributor of Zenith products in the San Francisco area, as well as the Zenith-related assets of the distributors who had represented Zenith in the Sacramento and Newark markets. These acquisitions increased to four the number of markets in which wholly owned subsidiaries were distributing Zenith products. The remaining eighty markets in the United States were served by independently owned distributors. The announced purpose of these acquisitions was to strengthen Zenith's distribution system. Zenith also acquired Movado Watch Agency, the New York-based distributor for Movado time pieces in the United States. Again the stated purpose was to strengthen marketing efforts for watches and "to build a foundation for the U.S. introduction of the new Zenith watch line." Collier was sent to Switzerland to reorganize and streamline the administrative structure of the new subsidiary which was renamed Zenith Time S.A. He was charged with updating and restyling Zenith Time's entire product line. Zenith Time S.A. and the marketing of the new electronic watch became Zenith's first major attempt at product-market diversification under the new management regime. Riding high on the Swiss watch diversification strategy, management turned down the opportunity to acquire the American Broadcasting Company at a fraction of its real value.[20]

Sales revenue increased another 19.6 percent (constant dollars) during 1973, and Zenith appeared to be well on the road to recovery. With the second devaluation of the dollar early that year and the subsequent upward float of the Japanese yen, the American consumer electronics industry seemed to be regaining ground lost to imports. Japanese color television manufacturers saw their share of the U.S. market decline from 19 to 11 percent between 1970 and 1972, and then further to 10 percent during 1973. The economics of production changed so drastically that Sony Corporation, historically Japan's principal exporter of color television receivers, established production facilities in San Diego, California.[21]

In an effort to shake up conservative Zenith, Nevin mounted an aggressive spending campaign to capture the top spot in the U.S. color television market from RCA. He undertook a $47 million capital expansion program—the largest in Zenith's history. He also acquired a color television picture tube plant from Philco-Ford. Productive capacity reached 2.5 million color and 1 million monochrome receivers, output valued at approximately $1.3 billion. The installation of a totally automated, computer-controlled assembly line in Zenith's major Chicago plant helped to lower production costs. Zenith's successful cost reduction effort led observers to predict that the offshore assembly of U.S. consumer electronics production would soon end. During 1973, 90 percent of the components incorporated into Zenith color sets were assembled in the United States. Color sets provided 73 percent of Zenith's total sales revenue. Nevin succeeded in taking 24 percent of the U.S. color set market, exceeding RCA's 21 percent. The firm earned nearly 22 percent on its invested capital in 1973, one of the best showings of any firm in any industry.[22]

Simultaneously, devaluation of the dollar had a negative impact on Zenith's unprofitable Swiss watch subsidiary. Marketing Zenith brand watches in the United States was consequently delayed pending new pricing plans, the correction of supply problems, and continuing development of the electronic watch itself. During the year, with the help of C. Itoh & Co., one of Japan's largest trading companies, Zenith attempted to develop a plan for exporting Zenith color receivers to Japan. That plan was put on the shelf, however, once management fully understood the conversion rates (dollars to yen) required for the sale of foreign-made television receivers in Japan would double the cost of the product to the consumer. The firm received some bad press when the U.S. Consumer Products Commission issued a mandatory recall for three monochrome television models during 1972. Another 12,000 color sets were voluntarily recalled during 1973 because of the fire hazard presented by improperly located high voltage capacitors. Zenith acted after several reported fires and before any fire-caused injuries occurred.[23]

During 1974, a year of economic slowdown and inflation, Zenith experienced a sharp 17.6 percent decline in sales revenue (constant dollars). This was in stark contrast to the previous two-year period of sales growth and exuberant capacity expansion. Zenith was stuck with expensive unused capacity. Before year-end, Nevin closed the newly acquired Landsdale, Pennsylvania plant and laid off 600 employees. Three price increases during the year were insufficient to offset inflating material and labor costs. The extent of Zenith's earnings decline shook the investment community as the price range for Zenith shares declined from $24.76 per share at year-end 1973 to $8.79 at year-end 1974 (constant dollars).[24]

In his annual 10-K Report, filed with the Securities and Exchange Commission, Nevin complained that in recent years the consumer electronics products industry had been confronted by increases in the costs of labor and materials similar in magnitude to the increases experienced by other industries. But whereas the prices of home appliances had increased by about 15 percent between 1967 and 1974, prices of home furnishings by more than 30 percent, housing by more than 50 percent, and food by more than 60 percent, prices of television receivers had declined about 1 percent during the same period. He argued that the inability of many consumer electronics firms to recover higher costs through price increases contributed to the pressures that during late 1973 and 1974 led to Admiral's acquisition by Rockwell International Corporation, the purchase of Motorola's television activities (renamed Quasar) by the largest Japanese television manufacturer (Matsushita Electronic Industries Company, Ltd.), the acquisition of Magnavox by an affiliate of Europe's largest television manufacturer (N.V. Philips), and the purchase of Philco's television operations by GTE Sylvania. RCA had terminated the manufacturer and sale of radios, phonograph, and modular and console stereo units. General Electric had terminated its participation in the portable phonograph market in which it enjoyed a leadership position; and Teledyne, Inc. had ceased television manufacturing and marketing operations entirely.[25]

Earlier in the year, Wright and Nevin had publicly assailed Motorola's plans to sell its television line to Matsushita. In a seven-page letter to the Justice Department, Nevin called the proposal a "flagrant antitrust violation." He complained that Matsushita was the world's largest television manufacturer with total annual sales of $4 billion, $2 billion of which were generated from consumer electronic products. The proposed acquisition immediately would permit Matsushita to increase its share of the U.S. color television market from about 2 percent to about 9 percent and increase its share of the U.S. monochrome market from about 8 percent to about 14 percent. Nevin confirmed that Zenith had notified Motorola that it would be interested in acquiring certain assets of Motorola's consumer products division. Nevin complained in a *Wall Street Journal* interview that the proposed acquisition would permit Matsushita to more than quadruple its share of the U.S. market while maintaining its domestic position in Japan, where the Japanese government effectively refused entry to foreign-owned competitors. He also made it clear that Zenith had no intention of forfeiting any of its rights to seek relief from the anticompetitive aspects of the proposed sale through the Justice Department, the Congress, or if necessary, the courts. Zenith would fight the acquisition. Motorola rejected Zenith's bid for its properties and the acquisition by Matsushita went forward. In September 1974, Zenith sued Motorola and Matsushita charging violation of the antitrust laws and seeking $900 million in damages. In Washington, D.C., a representative of the Japanese Electronic Manufacturers characterized the suit as "harassment."[26]

In spite of Zenith's difficulties, management acquired one of its former distributors (Kansas City), a one-third interest in Televisores Venezolanos S.A. (Maracaibo, Venezuela), an assembler of Zenith products, and a Philco-Ford furniture plant (Watsontown, Pennsylvania), which produced television and stereo cabinets. In a *Forbes* interview, Wright explained Zenith's failure to diversify beyond consumer electronics in the positive terms of management commitment to one field. He admitted that the strategy exposed Zenith to market fluctuations to a greater extent than major competitors, but, he added, the strategy left Zenith's managers free to concentrate all of their efforts on one basic product. Nevin concluded, "No one here is desperately looking around for a market to be in when TV dies." Zenith Time, S.A. had another unprofitable year and Collier quietly left the firm.[27]

The New Chairman

Recession in conjunction with inflation decreased demand for consumer electronics products during 1975 and produced sizable losses for many of Zenith's domestic competitors. Zenith's sales revenue fell 9.8 percent (constant dollars) below the 1974 level as Nevin pursued the strategy of automating U.S. production facilities and fighting in the courts the incursion of low-priced Japanese sets. RCA returned to an offshore sourcing strategy. Nevin acted to reduce levels of support personnel in all areas of the firm. Production costs were reduced through design improvements, integration actions, and more efficient plant utilization. In pricing, the firm was able to recover virtually all its labor and materials price increases for the first time in three years. But even market share gains could not compensate for lower unit volume. Zenith was able to enter into a fifteen-year, $50 million loan agreement with the Prudential Insurance Company, which provided Zenith with needed long-term financing. Total domestic debt was reduced from $114 to $50 million.[28]

Both *Financial World* and *The Wall Street Journal* reviewed Zenith's operations and found Zenith shares to be sound with excellent growth potential once consumers responded to economic recovery. Neither analyst was concerned with the potential for overcapacity in the industry; both were convinced that replacement and second-set demand would pick up the slack.[29]

After twenty-four years with Zenith, Wright retired as chairman of the board and chief executive officer. He was replaced by Nevin. Wright was questioned about Zenith's long-term strategy before his departure. He admitted that Zenith had "overfacilitated and underdiversified" in recent years. He explained that Zenith's efforts to diversify with some of the by-products of research efforts had been very disappointing. Hence both research and diversification tended to be put aside while management concentrated on maintaining volume and building market share for its dominant product.[30]

At year-end 1976 after sales revenues had increased a mere 3.2 percent (constant dollars), Zenith's new chairman and president commented that the American electronics industry was facing a "threat of extinction every bit as real as that facing coyotes and bald eagles." Nevin was referring to the fact that imports of color sets had jumped from 19 percent of the domestic market in 1975 to 37 percent in 1976. He calculated that more than 60,000 U.S. jobs had been lost to color imports. That figure reached 100,000 when monochrome set production was included. Sanyo Electric Co. acquired Whirlpool Corporation's majority share in Warwick Electronics, Inc., the major supplier of receivers to Sears, Roebuck & Co., decreasing again the number of domestic suppliers.[31]

Early in 1976, after a delay of almost six years, the Treasury Department issued a "final negative determination" denying Zenith's 1970 petition for the imposition of countervailing duties against Japanese importers. Zenith appealed the Treasury finding to the U.S. Customs Court asking that Treasury be required to impose countervailing duties to offset benefits that accrued from commodity tax remissions. The case raised legal issues involving the authority of the secretary of the Treasury, the resolution of which would have substantial international economic consequences. The GATT treaty permits signatory nations to rebate *indirect* taxes (value added, commodity, excise, sales taxes) when a product is exported. *Direct* taxes (levied on wages, property values, or profits) may not be rebated. Treasury maintained that imposing countervailing duties to offset rebates of indirect taxes would violate GATT and act to disrupt world trade. Zenith asserted that U.S. law and Supreme Court interpretations of that law required rebated taxes to be countervailed. Zenith's lawyers further maintained that U.S. law superceded any GATT commitments.[32]

Import Quotas

In September 1976, eleven labor organizations and five corporations representing the domestic color television industry filed a petition with the International Trade Commission (ITC) urging that quotas be established to limit television imports. Initially, Zenith's management did not support the petition on the grounds that Zenith and most other domestic manufacturers could compete successfully in the U.S. market if "unfair methods of competition were identified and terminated." A second ITC investigation was actively opposed not only by Matsushita, Japan's major exporter, but also by the U.S. State, Treasury, and Justice Departments. Matsushita representatives argued that the Japanese firms could sell sets more cheaply because of labor-saving manufacturing techniques and innovative engineering design. They argued that the impact of Japanese imports on the American market had been exaggerated.[33]

Nevin personally responded in a *Wall Street Journal* interview and with a *Harvard Business Review* article in which he argued that there was no evidence that the Japanese manufacturers were any more efficient than American manufacturers. He noted that much of Japan's technology was developed in the United States, where Japanese firms had paid more than $200 million to domestic firms under licensing and technological assistance agreements. He argued that the exclusion of foreign competitors from domestic markets provided Japanese producers with profits substantial enough to permit them to sell their domestic products abroad at prices so low they displaced local competitors. He suggested that the same pattern applied in such industries as steel, motorcycles, CB radios, sewing machines, calculators, various passive electronic components, as well as television receivers and high-fidelity electronics. He noted that the Japanese Ministry of Finance forbade the importation of television receivers from Taiwan where labor costs were substantially lower than on the Japanese islands. Matsushita, Hitachi, Sanyo, Sharp, and other Japanese television manufacturers with plants in Taiwan exported their output. Nevin concluded that neither the Department of Treasury nor the Department of Justice was willing to actively enforce the Trade Act of 1974, wherein the Congress sought "to assure a swift and certain response to foreign import restrictions, export subsidies, and price discrimination (dumping)." He characterized Treasury and Justice officials as "free traders" who sought only "to accommodate diplomatic conveniences."[34]

By the end of the year, Zenith changed its position and publicly supported the petition for import quotas. Nevin stated that economic conditions in the U.S. television industry had become so critical that any further government delay in responding to the problem was intolerable. However, he maintained his former position that a permanent solution depended on government's discharge of its responsibility to eliminate unfair competition rather than in its authority to impose quotas on imports. It is interesting to note that RCA did not support the quota petition. RCA representatives stressed their firm belief in free trade, the need for self-reliance, and the determination to do a better job among domestic producers. Industry sources suggested that RCA's position derived from the fact that the firm received substantial earnings from its licensing agreement with Japanese companies. RCA denied that such agreements influenced its position.[35]

During 1976, securities analysts' reviews of Zenith's operations and their recommendations for purchase of Zenith shares became noticeably less enthusiastic. They continued, however, to recommend Zenith stock for purchase as a long-term investment. After a good deal of damaging press over a two-year period, the Federal Drug Administration determined that Zenith, among others, would not be ordered to recall color television sets that had been determined to leak minute amounts of radiation. At year-end, Nevin wrote stockholders that 1977 was likely to be the year in which the government would act to "relieve the domestic television industry and its employees of the burdens associated with dumping and other unfair acts that the television industry has borne so long." He promised that he would continue to make the facts of the situation highly visible to the ITC, the Congress, and the executive branch of the U.S. Government.[36]

With a 6.5 percent decline (constant dollars) in sales revenue, 1977 proved to be another difficult year for Zenith despite the 1 July 1977 Orderly Marketing Agreement under which the Japanese agreed voluntarily to reduce their exports to the United States. A quota of 560,000 completed units and 190,000 partially completed units was set for each year over a three-year period. The agreement proved to be ineffective in that imports from low-wage countries increased and took up the Japanese slack. In 1976, prior to the quota agreement, Japan supplied 90 percent of U.S. color television imports. By June 1978 the Japanese share had dropped to 57 percent, while imports from Taiwan, Korea, and Canada had more than doubled. In addition, Matsushita, Toshiba, Sharp, and Hitachi joined Sony in launching U.S. production facilities for their receivers. The Japanese factories were established as much in response to rising Japanese wages and the appreciating yen as to the Orderly Marketing Agreement. Zenith's competitors were also struggling to survive in the aggressively competitive domestic market. Rockwell International Corporation folded its Admiral subsidiary, acquired just three years earlier. General Electric was rumored to be looking for a buyer for its television business after a proposed joint venture with Hitachi was quashed by the Justice Department as anticompetitive.[37]

Layoffs

Nevin described 1977 operating results as "very disappointing." In an attempt to maintain color set market share, he had cut costs to distributors in January, again in February, and then three more times during the summer. Competitors began complaining that Zenith was setting off a price war. RCA, with a new lower-cost chassis and with most of its assembly operations in Mexico, had significantly lower manufacturing costs than Zenith. Zenith's U.S. assembly costs were higher even with its totally automated plant. Additionally, Zenith was forced to phase out its new "glass envelope" picture tube after less than a year of production because the tube design failed to provide the 8 to 10 percent cost reduction envisioned.

As a consequence, Zenith announced the reorganization of its engineering and research activities, which resulted in 600 more layoffs. Remaining research activities were incorporated into ongoing engineering projects and the vice-president for research was retired early. Nevin described the reorganization as a cost cutting move. He noted that, "We must get our costs in line because it is clear that we are not going to be able to depend on revenue improvements in this industry." The elimination of basic research was disturbing to many outside observers. Nevin maintained that the move would not affect Zenith's short-term future, but he conceded that it probably would eliminate the firm's chances to lead the industry in any new product development. He announced that Zenith planned to market Sony-made videotape cassette recorders (VCR) under the Zenith brand name.[38]

In September, Zenith succumbed to the realities of offshore production and announced the layoff of 5,000 additional workers (one-quarter of domestic workforce) and the transfer of a substantial part of its assembly operations to Mexico and Taiwan. Nevin commented: "We have no way of increasing revenues, so will have to cut costs." And, "It is clear that competitors have significant cost advantages from production activities in lower-labor cost areas of the world." In October, Zenith announced the sale of its Hearing Instruments Division (at book value) to Zenitron, Inc., a new company organized by former employees. In November, management was forced to cut the prices of Zenith's new Sony-made VCR by 20 percent in order to bring the selling price in line with RCA's version (manufactured by Matsushita).[39]

Countervailing Duties

In the countervailing duties case which Zenith had earlier appealed to the U.S. Customs Court, a three-judge panel of the court ruled unanimously in

Zenith's favor in April 1977. The Treasury Department appealed that decision to the Court of Customs and Patent Appeals which ruled against
Zenith by a margin of three to two. Zenith took the matter to the U.S.
Supreme Court, which agreed to review the case in February 1978. Zenith
argued throughout those hearings that the Japanese government's rebate-
to-exporters policy was in violation of Section 303 of the Trade Act of 1930
which prohibited all "bounties and grants." Zenith interpreted the
Japanese government rebates as a breach of that U.S. law. During a time of
growing apprehension over the drift toward national protectionism, the
Zenith case was closely followed throughout the industrial world as an important indicator of future U.S. policy. When the initial lower court verdict
was announced, a senior U.S. Treasury official felt it was necessary to
publicly indicate that a successful outcome of the case for Zenith would
leave the United States in violation of the terms of GATT. The official also
stated that the principles of trade involved in the Zenith case before the
Supreme Court could readily be applied to 70 percent of U.S. trade partners
who provided their domestic exporters with rebates in one form or
another.[40]

After the Customs Court decision, U.S. Steel Corporation petitioned
for a summary judgment that would apply the Zenith ruling immediately to
steel imports from western Europe—a move that drew a withering blast
from U.S. special trade representative Robert S. Strauss. Strauss predicted
that if the Zenith ruling were upheld by the Supreme Court it would be
necessary to completely rework U.S. trade law. The international reaction
came in a warning that the imposition of countervailing duties against
Japanese electronic products would not only go against international trade
law, but would no doubt prompt reprisals. It is not unreasonable to assume
that the Strauss-negotiated Japanese import quota plan was activated to a
considerable extent by Zenith's aggressive action in the federal courts during the immediately preceding years.[41]

Zenith's countervailing duties case was watched closely in the press during the first half of 1978. Bethlehem Steel joined U.S. Steel in support of
Zenith's bid for redress. The two largest domestic steel companies were
forced to compete with European imports that were exempt from the value
added taxes imposed on steel sold within the European countries. The two
U.S. steel companies wanted relief from the European practice of rebating
value added taxes on exports. On 22 June 1978 the Supreme Court was
unanimous in turning down Zenith's arguments that the U.S. should impose special penalty duties on television sets and other consumer electronics
imports from Japan that had been exempted from Japan's commodity tax.
The ruling was based on a strict interpretation of the 1897 Countervailing
Duty Statute. The Court supported Treasury's subsequent interpretations
of the statute as being "reasonable." Zenith's legal argument based upon
provisions of the Trade Act of 1930 was rejected. Prior to the final court
decision, the Carter administration let it be known that in the event Zenith's

arguments prevailed they were prepared to go to the Congress to seek legislation that would prohibit the Treasury Department from imposing any countervailing duties.[42]

Although Nevin promised Zenith shareholders "results" from his renewed offshore sourcing strategy, he received considerable criticism from the business press during 1978. He was criticized for having lost control of Zenith's aggressively competitive environment as a result of his steady political and legal war against Japanese imports. He was criticized for his overly ambitious production and marketing plants, for his strategy to make Zenith "the General Motors of the television business." He was criticized both for Zenith's failed new product strategies and for gutting the firm's research and development capability. It was argued that all Zenith had left was its brand image and topnotch distributor network.[43]

Other problems for Zenith during 1978 included a recall of 500,000 color sets in order to repair defective capacitors. Although the recall was ordered only for New York State by the New York State Agency of Consumer Frauds and Protection, Zenith voluntarily extended the recall nationwide. After a $7.5 million loss during 1977 (resulting in a $3.3 million consolidated loss for the firm), Nevin found a buyer for Zenith's Swiss watch operations. In August, Zenith, RCA, and Sony increased prices for color sets—the first sustainable price increase since 1974. Despite quota protection and good sales performance, profit margins remained slim for both Zenith and its major domestic competitor RCA. Zenith's sales revenues declined another 5.7 percent (constant dollars). But, the firm did increase color-set market share to 22.3 percent, while RCA was able to maintain only an 18.9 percent share.[44]

The good market share news for Zenith was clouded with the news that the Japanese quota system was working to keep down Japanese imports but not the even cheaper television imports from Taiwan, South Korea, Singapore, and Canada. Those Japanese firms that had significantly increased their U.S.-based production capability since the quotas were put in place joined the protest. U.S. trade negotiations reached quota agreements with the governments of Taiwan and South Korea during December 1978. However, many observers believed that extending quotas to Taiwan and South Korea would only stimulate other Asian nations to export. Again Nevin argued that there would not be any need for quotas or tariffs if the U.S. government would only enforce the dumping and unfair-practices laws already on the books.[45]

Concurrently, importers of Japanese receivers were battling with the U.S. Customs Service over the method used to calculate dumping penalties to be assessed against them for the period from April 1972 through April 1977. The $500 to $600 million assessment was going forward in spite of vigorous Japanese diplomatic protests. Political pressure exerted by the

Japanese lobbying groups resulted in the 31 March 1978 Treasury announcement that only $46 million in dumping penalties would be assessed for the time period from 1972 through June of 1973. Treasury's decision was made despite a strenuous written recommendation by the commissioner of customs that the Treasury proceed with the previously approved plan to assess television-dumping duties through April 1977. Nevin loudly objected and complained about the degree to which counsel for the importers and representatives of the Japanese government were able to influence Treasury and introduce procedural snarls which slowed the resolution process by seven years. Nevin noted that Treasury had not consulted with the Congress nor with representatives of domestic industry in reaching their decision. The ability of the Japanese lobby to influence U.S. policy is not surprising when one considers that a former CIA director, a former chairman of the International Trade Commission, a former assistant commerce secretary, as well as foreign policy advisers, trade negotiators, political advisers to former presidents, and several prominent Washington law firms were representing either the Japanese government or specific Japanese corporations during this period.[46]

Marketing the VCR

In another market share matter, it became clear during 1977 that the Sony-produced VCR marketed by Zenith, Sears, and Toshiba under their own brand names was losing market share to a new model developed by Matsushita and distributed in the U.S. by RCA, General Electric, Quasar, Sylvania, Magnavox, and JVC. Even though the Sony VCR had been on the market eighteen months earlier than the Matsushita model, the Matsushita model recorded for two hours longer and hence was more popular with consumers. Sony was forced to cut retail prices from the original $2,500 per unit to $1,100 in order to remain competitive. Zenith cut prices for its VCR units even lower to $995. But, even with those price cuts, the Matsushita model outsold the Sony model two to one. For the 1979 sales year, Sony and Zenith worked together to redesign their VCR model to record for a five-hour period. But, the fact that domestic manufacturers of all consumer electronics products gave up 50.6 percent of the U.S. market to imports, and that Japanese firms accounted for 33 percent of color television shipments in 1979, overshadowed recovery efforts. Drastic action was needed at Zenith and pressures on Nevin led to his resignation as chairman and chief executive during October. Exchairman Joseph Wright returned from retirement to try to put Zenith back together again. Revone W. Kluckman, a financial executive at Zenith for the previous thirteen years, took over from Wright the following November.[47]

Redirection: 1979–1980

Beginning in December 1979 with the acquisition of Heath Company, the nation's leading producer of do-it-yourself electronics kits, Wright and Kluckman mounted another turnaround effort. This debt-financed diversification move was geared to gaining entrance to the mass market for home computers which experts expected to grow at a 50 percent annual rate during the 1980s. Buying Heath rather than relying on internal research and development efforts to penetrate the home computer market was estimated to have saved the firm several million dollars and approximately two years time. At acquisition, only 25 percent of Heath's more than $80 million in annual sales was generated from computer products. But Heath already had two home computer units with word processing capabilities in production. Wright and Kluckman wanted to merge Heath's technology with Zenith's manufacturing and distribution strengths. They planned to price Zenith's home computers at the low end of the market, putting the firm directly in competition with Cromenco, Apple, North Star, and Tandy. Wright also announced plans to expand into European markets with Zenith's new home computers.[48]

Wright and Kluckman also undertook a strategy to buy videodisc technology from RCA and add videodisc players and large screen projection television to Zenith's product line. Their announced strategy was to spread Zenith investments broadly in order to gain flexibility. During 1980, the firm invested in several new television-related technologies with the potential to penetrate the "revived" home entertainment market: space phones, home security systems, home computers that hook into television receivers, projection television, and subscription television decoders (once again). Zenith's management was encouraged by estimates that the television industry would become a growth industry during the 1980s. Analysts predicted a transformation of the television industry based on the confluence of two major sociological and technological trends: advances in technology that would make it economically feasible to bring a vast array of entertainment and information processing services into the home, and rising gasoline prices that along with continuing inflation would force consumers to stay at home. The belief that the American consumer would soon begin to spend less money on cars and more money on home entertainment products directed Zenith's new recovery strategy.[49]

While outside observers continued to worry about Zenith's relatively small size in an industry of diversified giants, about the firm's inability to develop new technology through research and development, and about past failures to successfully diversify, Kluckman continued to try to redirect the firm on a very limited budget. He restructured the firm along product rather than functional lines, and then named three senior engineers as Zenith's top operating executives. Each was assigned a new-product development unit and a specialized marketing staff. Kluckman was clearly trying to exploit Zenith's production and distribution strengths by acquiring technology rather than by financing internal development. By gearing products to the mass market, where profits evolve from volume sales rather than technological leadership, he was also attempting to minimize Zenith's basic weakness.

Evaluating Zenith's Response Pattern

The Zenith story reveals a pattern of contracting revenues resulting from the interaction of many interdependent factors. The primary factors in Zenith's case, examined in detail later, are summarized here:

1. the slowdown of real growth in the domestic economy that adversely affected consumer demand for Zenith products particularly during the 1969–1971 and 1974–1975 recessionary periods;
2. increasing domestic labor and materials costs;
3. excess productive capacity in the domestic consumer electronics industry;
4. the increasing rate of foreign import penetration of the domestic market;
5. management's reluctance to move into offshore production in a timely manner and its heavy reliance on government officials and the courts to rationalize domestic marketing conditions;
6. the uncertainty surrounding U.S. trade policy, specifically the imposition of countervailing duties, dumping penalties, and quotas against importers of television receivers;
7. a belated and unsuccessful diversification strategy meant to provide both growth opportunities in international markets and to reduce the negative impact of cyclical downturns and declining growth potential in domestic markets;
8. various unproductive research and development projects (subscription television, glass tubes, electronic watch); and
9. the decreasing rate of successful innovation in the domestic consumer electronics industry coupled with Zenith's elimination of basic research expenditures.[50]

Internal Rationalization

Zenith's adaptive response to contracting sales revenue included several successive waves of reorganization, restructuring, and reformulation of basic strategy. The stated intent of the initial reorganization effort that began in 1970 was to make a sharp break with Zenith's conservative past by diversifying assets beyond radio and television into new manufacturing and marketing areas. Wright restructured the firm into four functional areas (operations, marketing, product development, corporate development) and initiated what became a continual effort to centralize and integrate Zenith's operations. In order to cut costs he instigated more stringent management control systems aimed at reducing overhead and inventory levels, and improving plant utilization and product design efforts. He also began to reduce basic research expenditures.

The new managerial talent brought into the firm with the initial reorganization effort led to Zenith's ill-fated diversification and capacity expansion strategies. Collier succeeded in divesting Zenith's marginal profit businesses such as government and special products contracting, medical electronics, and night vision instruments. However, his efforts to penetrate high-growth international markets with a new product (electronic watch) and to vertically integrate through acquisition (various distributorships and furniture-making plants) ultimately led to large losses and the need to finance debt during a period of tight money. Nevin's efforts to make Zenith the General Motors of the television industry, that is, to increase market share and reap the benefits of high volume sales, depended on an extensive capital expenditure program intended to reduce production and labor costs with the installation of computer-controlled automated technology in Zenith's main production facility. Nevin's strategy choice was certainly influenced by his underlying belief that government regulators would step in and favorably handle the import problem. In public statements, Nevin consistently referred to the government's "responsibility" to curtail dumping and rebate activities.

After the 1972-1973 respite from lagging U.S. sales caused by the temporary 10 percent surcharge on imports and the several currency devaluations, Zenith management was forced once again to reformulate strategy in response to contracting revenues. From 1974, Zenith management strategy focused increasingly on maintaining domestic market share for its television products. Revised cost-cutting programs resulted in plant closures and layoffs in the U.S. as production was realigned to offshore manufacturing plants in Mexico and Taiwan. When Zenith's new glass tube technology failed to reduce manufacturing costs, management suspended basic research altogether. Rather than continue the development of its own version of the videotape cassette recorder (VCR), Zenith contracted to distribute in the U.S. the VCR model developed and manufactured by Sony in Japan. This agreement left Zenith vulnerable when Sony's VCR lost the competitive edge to the superior model developed by Matsushita and distributed by RCA. In the struggle to retain market share, Nevin undertook a series of price reductions on color sets which in conjunction with the uneven results from the various cost-cutting programs resulted in a $3.3 million loss during 1977.

After Wright's return, he and Kluckman again restructured the firm, this time along product lines. They reorganized the resulting divisions in an effort to support Zenith's new growth and marketing strategies. As a relatively small consumer electronics firm with a very limited basic research and development capability, Zenith's new growth strategy is directed at volume sales priced to the low end of the market. Once again management is seeking diversification through acquisition with an eye on foreign markets. Rather than support in-house research, the new management team has adopted a policy of purchasing technology from rivals. They plan to exploit Zenith's manufacturing capability as well as its distribution and servicing network, considered to be one of the most efficient and reliable in the industry.

External Rationalization

The most salient characteristic of management's battle to exercise control over the firm's turbulent external environment was the failure to reach a compromise with government regulators that would protect Zenith from ruinous competition. In the matter of protection from imports, Zenith's interests were in direct conflict with the interests and policies of the U.S. Departments of Treasury, Justice, and State, as well as domestic producers with diversified interests and considerable foreign sales (RCA for example). Congressional and executive office lobbying efforts undertaken on behalf of Zenith's position failed to yield favorable results even with the support of Department of Commerce and Customs officials, industry associations, labor unions, and representatives of the politically powerful steel industry. Hence, Zenith's management sought redress through litigation—a course of action reflecting the failure of the traditional compromise process to preserve mutual interests. Zenith's pleas for protection clearly conflicted with free-trade policies as construed by most of the interested federal regulatory bodies and the executive branch of the government. This reflected the long-term strategic and economic objectives that have directed U.S. trade policy since 1945 and the postwar rebuilding effort. The judicial branch of government ultimately found against Zenith in a decision based on a strict interpretation of provisions of the long-standing Countervailing Duties Statute.[51]

Zenith's earlier successes in diminishing competitive threats through litigation (the RCA and Hazeltine cases in 1948 and 1969, respectively) was not repeated in the Japanese rebate issue. In fact, the Supreme Court decision included the statement that, ". . . it is not the task of the Judiciary to substitute its views as to fairness and economic effect for those of the Secretary [of the Treasury]." It should be noted, however, that, Zenith's antitrust suit seeking $1 billion in price-fixing damages from domestic importers of Japanese products remains unsettled. In that case, Zenith appears to have a stronger economic fairness argument given the intent of restriction of trade provisions in the antitrust laws.[52]

Failing renewed competitive vigor, Zenith's best hope for economic redress on the foreign competition issue will remain with the Judiciary. As long as U.S. trade policy favors free trade and open access to domestic markets, Zenith has little cause to expect protective regulatory action. As long as U.S. trade policy is biased in the direction of a gradual transition toward a world economy, one in which international specialization is encouraged, the consumer electronics import threat is unlikely to diminish—particularly as long as foreign competitors continue to concentrate on process innovation. The Zenith case suggests that the public policymaking process is being transformed by both the sheer number and the interdependence of the often conflicting interest groups affected by regulation of the U.S. corporation and the domestic marketplace. That transformation is manifest by the tendency of corporate and other interested parties to rely on litigation rather than compromise decision processes to settle disputes. In the Zenith case, the more parochial and traditional interests of Customs and Commerce officials were overridden by Executive, Treasury, State, and Justice Department representatives who reflected the free-trade, world market view—a view reinforced by the exigencies of increasing international economic interdependence. As it is improbable that the politically influential interest groups imbued with the free-trade view will cease to counteract protectionist pressures, it is unlikely that Zenith's managers and their protectionist allies will be able to rationalize domestic consumer electronics markets by restricting access.

During Zenith's contraction episode, management also moved to divest major foreign operations (Zenith Time S.A.) as part of their overall strategy to regain some measure of control over the firm's external environment. That action resulted in a sharp reduction of Zenith's international content as well as the firm's level of diversification. However, divestiture did succeed in ending mounting foreign losses for the firm and essentially eliminated the environmental uncertainties that characterize operations in foreign markets.

In terms of Zenith's exchange relationships with domestic competitors, the firm made no apparent attempts to stabilize domestic market conditions for consumer electronic products by way of price-fixing or market division arrangements with competitors. The domestic market for such products remained highly competitive during Zenith's most recent contraction episode. Exchange relationships with stockholders and consumers remained stable and seemed equally negligible in terms of impact on Zenith's overall contraction strategy. The consumer advocacy movement, however, did have some impact on the firm insofar as product recalls were undertaken during 1972, 1973, and 1978. Zenith's recall problems very likely enhanced the sense of loss of control in an increasingly uncertain external environment. Consumer pressure for safer products added weight to the already heavy burden of finding the road to profitability in a radically changed domestic marketplace.

As for the impact of the contraction episode on Zenith's work force, management was able to externalize to the public at large some of the costs surrounding the shift of Zenith's productive capacity from domestic to offshore facilities under provisions of the U.S. Trade Expansion Act of 1962 (liberalized in 1974). Under the act, the Trade Readjustment Assistance Program provides cash (up to 70 percent of a worker's annual salary for fifty-two weeks) plus retraining and relocation expenses for workers whose jobs are lost because of competition from imported goods. From its start in April 1975 through September 1981 the program paid out an estimated $2.7 billion to 1.2 million workers nationwide. In addition, Zenith sought special tax credits provided corporations under the Trade Act mandate.[53]

Ranked as the 277th largest U.S. industrial firm in 1980, Zenith's most recent contraction episode has nevertheless reduced the firm to marketing consumer goods developed by competitors and manufactured abroad. Although Zenith now shares the same cost advantages of offshore production enjoyed by both domestic and foreign competitors, questions remain as to whether the firm can survive in the long term without protected markets given its technological disadvantage and its past history of failed diversification. To the likely detriment of long-term strategy and planning efforts, management resources must necessarily continue to focus on the near term if turnaround is to lead to real recovery. Zenith's success at efforts to stabilize and diversify the firm with new strategies aimed at high volume sales in the new consumer electronics markets of the 1980s will interest all observers concerned with issues of industrial policy.

Notes

1. *Fortune,* 15 June 1968, p. 200; *Fortune,* 4 May 1981, p. 334.

2. Historical outline developed in the Harvard Business School Case no. 9-674-026 (rev. July 1978) entitled "Zenith Radio Corporation (AR)," copyrighted in 1973 by the President and Fellows of Harvard College and distributed by the Intercollegiate Case Clearing House; *Forbes,* 15 May 1975, p. 132.

3. *Business Week (BW)*, 16 May 1970, p. 62; *BW*, 23 February 1981, p. 102.

4. *Wall Street Transcript (WST)*, 5 August 1968, p. 14046; *Time*, 11 August 1967, p. 60; *Wall Street Journal (WSJ)*, 31 October 1967, p. 15; Zenith, *Annual Report: 1967*, pp. 26–27; U.S., Congress, House, *Subcommittee on Communication and Power*, 90th Cong., 2d sess., 20 Nov. 1969, H. Rept. 420, pp. 107–138.

5. *BW*, 27 May 1967, p. 34; *U.S. News and World Report*, 31 July 1967, p. 59.

6. *BW*, 16 September 1967, p. 154; *WST*, 5 August 1968, p. 14046.

7. *WST*, 5 August 1968, p. 14046; *WST*, 4 November 1968, p. 14847.

8. Zenith, *Annual Report: 1969*, pp. 3–4; *WSJ*, 3 November 1969, p. 12; *WSJ*, 3 January 1969, p. 7; *WSJ*, 5 February 1969, p. 21; *BW*, 24 May 1969, p. 39; *WSJ*, 29 October 1969, p. 19; Zenith, *Annual Report: 1969*, p. 3; *BW*, 30 June 1980, pp. 59–60.

9. President and Fellows of Harvard College, "Zenith Radio Corporation (C)," Case no. 9–674–095 (Rev. August 1977), distributed by Intercollegiate Case Clearing House, p. 3; Zenith, *Annual Report: 1970*, pp. 2–3.

10. *WSJ*, 10 March 1979, p. 40.

11. John J. Nevin, "Can U.S. Business Survive our Japanese Trade Policy?" *Harvard Business Review (HBR)*, (September/October 1978):169.

12. U.S. Congress, House, *Committee on the Proposed Trade Act of 1969*, 91st Cong., 1st sess., 8 June 1979, H. Rept. 14870, pp. 2945–2986; *WSJ*, 10 March 1970, p. 40; *Industry Week*, 6 April 1970, pp. 11–12.

13. *WSJ*, 24 April 1970, p. 24; *BW*, 16 May 1970, p. 62.

14. Zenith, *Annual Report: 1970*, pp. 2–3; *BW*, 16 May 1970, p. 63; *WSJ*, 17 June 1970, p. 2; *WSJ*, 22 December 1970, p. 2.

15. Seth King, *New York Times (NYT)*, 25 July 1971, p. F7.

16. Zenith, *Annual Report: 1971*, pp. 2–3; *WSJ*, 3 June 1971, p. 26; *WSJ*, 24 February 1972, p. 8; *WSJ*, 3 March 1972, p. 11; *Advertising Age*, 8 October 1971, p. 83.

17. Zenith, *Annual Report: 1971*, p. 2; *WSJ*, 6 April 1971, p. 25.

18. U.S., Congress, Senate, *Subcommittee on International Trade*, 91st Cong., 2d sess., 17 May 1971, pp. 84–119; *BW*, 30 June 1980, p. 60; *WSJ*, 19 May 1972, p. 2; "Zenith Radio Corporation (C)," p. 1.

19. Zenith, *Annual Report: 1972*, p. 4; *WSJ*, 8 February 1972, p. 17; *WSJ*, 24 February 1972, p. 8; *WJS*, 29 March 1972, p. 5; *WSJ*, 8 February 1972, p. 17.

20. *WSJ*, 8 February 1972, p. 17; *WSJ*, 24 April 1972, p. 11; *WSJ*, 19 July 1972, p. 6; *WSJ*, 13 July 1972, p. 8; *WSJ*, 4 May 1972, p. 25; Zenith, *Annual Report: 1972*, p. 27; Bob Tamarkin, *Forbes*, 31 March 1980, p. 33.

21. Richard M. Lilly, *WST*, 22 October 1973, p. 34745.

22. Zenith, *Annual Report: 1973*, p. 2; *WSJ*, 22 June 1973, p. 12; *WSJ*, 2 August 1973, p. 16; Lilly, *WST*, p. 34746; *BW*, 18 August 1973,

pp. 41–42; Zenith, *Annual Report: 1975,* p. 4; Lilly, *WST,* p. 34745; *Forbes,* 1 April 1974, p. 25.

23. Zenith, *Annual Report: 1973,* p. 3; Nevin, *HBR,* pp. 167–168; *WSJ,* 3 February 1972, p. 5; *WSJ,* 17 September 1973, p. 26.

24. *NYT,* 28 December 1974, p. 31; *Financial World (FW),* 8 May 1974, p. 15.

25. Zenith Radio Corporation, *10-K Report: 1974,* p. 4.

26. *WSJ,* 10 May 1974, p. 14; *WSJ,* 13 May 1974, p. 8; *WSJ,* 23 September 1974, p. 5.

27. *WSJ,* 7 January 1974, p. 23; *WSJ,* 17 January 1974, p. 6; *WSJ,* 14 November 1974, p. 38; *Forbes,* 1 April 1974, p. 25.

28. Zenith, *10-K Report: 1975,* pp. 8–9; idem, *Annual Report: 1975,* p. 2.

29. *FW,* 29 January 1975, p. 38; Charles J. Elia, *WSJ,* 24 July 1975, p. 35.

30. *Forbes,* 5 May 1975, pp. 131–132.

31. N.R. Kleinfield, *WSJ,* 16 December 1976, p. 1; Zenith, *Annual Report: 1976,* p. 1.

32. Nevin, *HBR,* pp. 169–170.

33. Zenith, *Annual Report: 1976,* p. 2.

34. Kleinfield, *WSJ,* p. 1; Nevin, *HBR,* pp. 165–168.

35. *NYT,* 12 January 1977, p. D7; Zenith, *Annual Report: 1976,* p. 2; Kleinfield, *WSJ,* p. 1.

36. *WST,* 1 March 1976, p. 43007; *WST,* 22 November 1976, p. 45421; *WSJ,* 2 October 1975, p. 6; *Plain Dealer,* 29 January 1976, p. 10B; Zenith, *Annual Report: 1976,* p. 2.

37. *WSJ,* 28 September 1977, p. 2; Zenith *10-K Report: 1977,* p. 7; *Nation's Business,* September 1979, p. 94; *BW,* 23 February 1981, pp. 89–91.

38. Zenith, *Annual Report: 1977,* p. 1; *BW,* 10 October 1977, p. 128; *NYT,* 12 September 1977, p. L51; Paul Ingrassia, *WSJ,* 25 October 1977, p. 1; *WSJ,* 13 September 1977, p. 20; *WSJ,* 19 September 1977, p. 7; *WSJ,* 2 February 1977, p. 14.

39. N.R. Kleinfield, *NYT,* 28 September 1977, p. D1; *WSJ,* 28 September 1977, p. 2; *WSJ,* 11 October 1977, p. 3; *WSJ,* 4 November 1977, p. 8.

40. *Financial Times (FT),* 27 July 1977, p. 30.

41. *Sales Marketing Management,* 11 July 1977, pp. 7–8.

42. David Bell, *FT,* 22 February 1978, p. 5; *WSJ,* 22 February 1978, p. 44; Jurek Martin, *FT,* 22 June 1978, p. 1; *WSJ,* 22 June 1978, p. 2.

43. Zenith, *Annual Report: 1977,* p. 3; Ingrassia, *WSJ,* p. 1.

44. *WSJ,* 14 August 1978, p. 5; *WSJ,* 14 September 1978, p. 4; *WSJ,* 28 February 1978, p. 10; Scott R. Schmedel, *WSJ,* 21 September 1978, p. 40; *WSJ,* 29 November 1978, p. 4.

45. Scott R. Schmedel, *WSJ,* 9 January 1979, p. 38.

46. Ibid.; Zenith, *Annual Report: 1978,* p. 1; Nevin, *HBR,* pp. 172–173; Clyde H. Farnsworth, *NYT,* 29 June 1980, p. F3.

47. Peter Nulty, *Fortune,* 16 July 1979, pp. 110–111; *BW,* 30 June 1980, p. 60.

48. Bob Tamarkin, *Forbes,* 31 March 1980, pp. 32–33.

49. *BW,* 23 February 1981, pp. 88–102.

50. See Raymond Vernon, *Storm Over the Multinationals* (Cambridge, Mass.: Harvard University Press, 1977), p. 24. Also note that Zenith's major competitor, RCA, has recently moved to decrease basic research expenditures for consumer electronics products. See Alice L. Priest, *BW,* 3 September 1979, p. 88.

51. Robert M. Kaus, "Getting Tough on Trade," *The Washington Monthly,* November 1978, pp. 22–27.

52. Zenith, *Annual Report: 1978,* p. 2. A number of Japanese television manufacturers, their U.S. subsidiaries, Motorola, Inc., Sanyo Manufacturing Corp., Sears Roebuck and Co., and Melco Sales, Inc., are defendents in that action.

53. Bernard Wysocki, Jr., *WSJ,* 5 April 1979, p. 1; *Mart Magazine,* 15 March 1978, p. 4; *BW,* 27 July 1981, pp. 24–26.

5

The Related-Product Firm: Boise Cascade Corporation

Management strategy and corporate operations of a related-product firm, the Boise Cascade Corporation, are described here for the 1967–1980 period. On the basis of consolidated revenues, Boise was ranked as the fifty-fifth largest U.S. industrial firm in 1969. As a measure of relative decline, Boise was positioned as the nation's 127th largest industrial firm in 1980 after a severe five-year contraction episode when management was forced to divest major assets for cash and 22,000 employees were dropped from Boise's payroll.[1]

The Three-Sawmill Lumber Company

When Robert V. Hansberger became president of the Boise Payette Lumber Company in 1956, the firm owned and operated three sawmills, six wholesale building materials plants, and seventy-eight retail outlets. At that time Boise could reasonably be characterized as a small lumber company with a troubled history. During its early years, the firm had been unable to penetrate the major U.S. lumber markets because of high freight and harvesting costs. Boise-owned timberlands were then distinguished by sparse growth, steep terrain, and poor location. The company recorded losses in eighteen of the thirty-two years from its incorporation in 1913 through 1944. Management had planned to liquidate during 1948, but market conditions changed as demand for timber species other than pine and Douglas fir developed. Moreover, logging technology had advanced to the point where previously inaccessible timber could be harvested economically. Rather than liquidate, a newly appointed management team set out to salvage Boise Payette. From 1948, management adopted a growth strategy increasingly dependent on harvesting timber from U.S. Forest Service timberlands. By the mid-1950s, however, management realized that if the firm was to remain competitive it would have to expand operations and take part in the growing industry trend toward greater by-product utilization.[2]

Surveys of Boise-controlled timberland revealed that the by-product (wood waste) generated would be insufficient to support a 400 ton per day pulp mill—the minimum size for an economically viable facility. When

Boise's president resigned in 1955 to accept a position with the Weyer-haeuser Company, the board began to search for a new president capable of instigating a growth and diversification program for the firm.

Hansberger, then thirty-six years old, was chosen and charged with expanding lumber operations to the point where the by-product generated would be sufficient to justify a paper mill. Hansberger's consequent and soon to be heralded diversification program began in April 1957 with the acquisition of Cascade Lumber Company. Cascade owned 192,000 acres of timberland and four sawmills. Through an exchange of common shares, Hansberger structured the corporate entity thereafter known as the Boise Cascade Corporation. During the next decade, Hansberger attempted to strengthen Boise through diversification as he led the firm along the merger and acquisition route. His first mergers were with other small lumber companies, which subsequently provided the borrowing base for a new pulp mill and entry into the paper business. Boise acquired the Columbia River Paper Company in 1962 (fine paper), Crown Zellerbach's St. Helens paper division in 1964 (kraft wrapping paper), and the Minnesota and Ontario Company in 1965 (newsprint and wood fibre insulation board). Thereafter, the strength of Boise's diversified paper holdings gave Hansberger considerable borrowing power. From paper he led the firm into packaging including plastic, metal, foil, and paper containers as he built up a system of wholesale and retail outlets for Boise's building materials and office supplies. As he acquired manufacturers of factory-built, on-site constructed, and mobile homes, the firm moved beyond the forest products industry.

By the mid-1960s, Hansberger's growth strategy included the construction of leisure-living communities, industrial parks, mobile-home parks, and condominiums. Boise was also involved in urban redevelopment projects in Harlem, Atlanta, and Los Angeles. Hansberger described his growth strategy as a reorientation, away from producing commodities and toward opportunities in the consumer market. He proclaimed that Boise would soon "cut its umbilical cord to trees."[3]

Hansberger's well-publicized success with Boise's growth and diversification program shaped his national reputation as an empire builder. Hansberger himself was occasionally referred to as something of a "renaissance man." He was involved in national affairs through President Johnson's urban housing committee and the Committee for Economic Development. As a Nixon appointee during the early 1970s, he was a member of two national environmental committees: the National Industrial Pollution Control Council and the Council on Environmental Quality, which he chaired. He was a member of the Business Council's executive committee, a trustee of the Aspen Institute of Humanistic Studies, and regional chairman of the Pacific Northwest Ballet Association. He served on several business school advisory boards. He was also a director of eight other private corporations. In September 1969, with the market price for Boise common stock at $70.00 per share, Hansberger's total personal holdings in Boise were reported to be approximately $20 million—considerably above par for chief executives of major U.S. firms.[4]

Hansberger definitely put his own stamp on Boise Cascade. As a Harvard M.B.A., he tended to recruit in his own image, primarily from the business schools at Harvard and Stanford. He eagerly sought out new management technologies, such as management information systems, computer simulation models, and decision scanning processes. Along with his top executives, he made annual three-day pilgrimages to Stanford where he submitted Boise's growth strategy and current operations to the scrutiny of academics and M.B.A. candidates. He also opened up operations to observation and critique by professors and students at the University of Washington.

In press releases and interviews Hansberger described his "free-form" management approach as the "Boise Cascade state of mind." He was confident that his managers would contribute more when treated as individuals within a corporate environment that was "relatively free of restrictions and policies or regulations." This philosophy resulted in a deemphasis on standard operating procedures and hierarchical channels of authority. Hansberger dropped formal organization charts, job descriptions, and set salary levels for managerial positions. He left it up to each of his managers to recognize when it was necessary to seek help. As he had adopted a product-division structure for Boise in 1959, each product group, and every division within the group, was operated autonomously with corporate headquarters staff available for consultation when necessary.[5]

Hansberger believed in promoting young and giving responsibility early. In 1968, the average age of his executives was thirty-nine years—more than one-fourth were under the age of thirty-five. Hansberger frequently referred to his cadre as his "young tigers." As "young tigers" his managers were expected to manage their autonomous divisional operations as profit centers with the goal of increasing profit levels by 20 percent compounded annually. Prior to 1970, Boise's eager acquisition policy meant that most managers were able to meet or exceed this criterion in most years. Hansberger's internal resource allocation process also pressed conformance to the 20 percent goal. Augmented by a central planning staff, Boise's five-man management council (Hansberger and executive vice-presidents Stephen Moser, William Agee, Gordon Randall, and John Fery) controlled investment decisions. Evaluation of the expected return on capital for the various profit centers was compared with the anticipated return for new projects waiting in the wings for capital. Hansberger's growth strategy demanded that operating units be phased out to make way for more profitable investments whenever they failed to obtain the 20 percent profit criterion.

Because performance-advancement criteria for individual managers were explicitly tied to attainment of the annual goal, commitment to growth was guaranteed. After ten years at the helm, Hansberger seemed to have succeeded in transforming Boise Cascade into an ideal of enlightened management policy.[6]

The Tigers Surge: 1967–1969

For Boise, the late 1960s were years of flamboyant growth and diversification via acquisition. Sales revenue in constant dollars more than doubled as the number of employees increased from 27,000 to 51,000. The previous major growth periods for the firm marked entry into the paper business in 1959 and into the shelter field in 1964. The next major growth phase began with the acquisition of U.S. Land, Inc., of Indianapolis and the Lake Arrowhead Development Company. Both firms were involved in resort development activities. By year-end 1969, Hansberger had also acquired R.C. Can Company, a manufacturer of plastic containers and fiber-foil cans; Divco-Wayne Corporation, a manufacturer of school buses, hearses, ambulances, and mobile homes; Theo. H. Davies, a Hawaiian-based insurance and travel agency (partial ownership); Union Lumber Company; West Tacoma Newsprint Company; United Lumber Company; Western Lumber Company; Sullivan Hardwood Company; Sikeston Ceramics; Aristocratic Travel Products, a manufacturer of mobile homes and travel trailers; American Buildings, Inc., Case Brothers, a construction firm; Crystal Bay Development, land development firm; Princess Cruises; and Ebasco Industries, Inc. Rather than borrowing money or handing over cash, Hansberger was able to negotiate the acquisition of thirty-three firms during his first twelve years with Boise primarily through the issuance of Boise's common and preferred stock. He characterized this growth-through-acquisition strategy as "a sophisticated way of selling stock."[7]

Concurrently internal growth was accomplished with large capital expenditures programs funded through retained earnings, long-term debt, and cash obtained from the new acquisitions. In addition to a new $12-million office building in Boise, Idaho, these programs resulted in the construction or expansion of several paper mills and shelter manufacturing plants. Hansburger also undertook several new joint ventures. One of these was with the Southern Natural Gas Company to explore for oil and gas to supply the newly constructed pulp and paper mill in Birmingham, Alabama; one was with the Burnett-Boise Corporation to participate in the urban redevelopment effort in New York City; one was with the R.A. Watt Company of Los Angeles; and another was with Perma-Built Enterprises of San Francisco. The Watt and Perma-Built ventures were home-building operations that eventually came under full ownership. By 1967 Boise owned large tracts of development land in Virginia, Nevada, California, Ohio, Illinois, Indiana, Maryland, Connecticut, New Hampshire, New York, Pennsylvania, Hawaii, and Costa Rica. Hansberger opened a new subsidiary, the Pacific Cascade Land Company, intended to help consumers finance recreational home purchases. All of this acquisition helped Boise to gain the reputation as the nation's "most thoroughly integrated company in the housing field."[8]

Entry into the international sphere (other than Canadian timberlands) resulted from experience gained through a management services contract with the Chase Manhattan Bank. Boise was asked to help straighten out a failing Guatemalan paper mill in which Chase had an equity interest. Hansberger was reported to be "quite enthusiastic about Latin American possibilities" after the Guatemalan experience and he bought into the paper mill. Subsequent press reports indicated that Hansberger was planning to take Boise into Costa Rica to develop industrial sites and produce low-cost, prefabricated housing from locally available timber as soon as he could raise the capital.[9]

To Hansberger's delight, the August 1969 merger with Ebasco Industries, Inc., plunged Boise directly into international operations. Ebasco, formerly Electric Bond and Share Company, had incorporated in 1905 as a subsidiary of General Electric. Subsequently the firm became one of the world's largest utility holding companies. At the time of merger, Ebasco was primarily an investment and management company that offered worldwide engineering, construction, and consulting services. It also operated several small manufacturing plants in Latin America as well as utilities in Ecuador, Chile, Guatemala, and Panama. Its liquid assets consisted of a marketable securities portfolio containing $66 million in blue chip stocks, $300 million in Latin American government bonds (payable in U.S. dollars), and $100 million in cash and short-term notes. Ebasco offered immediately liquidity to Boise during a time of tight money in the U.S. Ebasco had cash; Boise had prospects of putting the cash profitably to work. But Hansberger did have to assume the risk of collecting on Ebasco's foreign bonds and recouping its $97 million investment in Chile where political conditions could easily mean a loss. Hansberger thought that the $52 million in reserves on the Ebasco books would cover any future losses and therefore decided that the merger was a "pretty safe gamble" for Boise. In a *Fortune* interview, he discussed the "growth opportunities" provided by Ebasco's cash. He explained that while Boise had a large inventory of high-return projects waiting for financing, he would have to use some of the cash to pay off high-interest debt on previously committed land development projects. He noted that Ebasco offered Boise expertise in construction management and consulting services, which could be utilized in his planned building activities in Latin and Central America and eventually in Indonesia. He emphasized that he intended Boise's international growth to mirror patterns of domestic growth.[10]

A second noteworthy acquisition in 1979 concerned the West Tacoma Newsprint Company. West Tacoma was created in 1946 when eleven West Coast newspaper publishers bought an idle paper mill. West Tacoma's shareholders received $43.5 million in Boise common shares in return for the mill and timberlands in western Washington state. But 8 percent of West Tacoma's shareholders fought the acquisition, maintaining that the mill and timberlands were worth twice the Boise shares. The dissenting group did not want the "funny money" stock of a conglomerate like Boise Cascade in return for their earlier investment. The dissenters were overruled. Subsequently, Boise redesignated the timberlands along the Puget Sound as development land, which left the original owners feeling even more dissatisfied.[11]

Boise was lauded in the business press as one of the nation's best-managed and fastest-growing firms. Hansberger had gained a national reputation as the managerial whiz who had successfully diversified Boise from a small regional lumber company into a strong conglomerate. The firm was portrayed in *Time* magazine as having spread successfully into the "backward and fragmented housing industry" after other industrial giants (including Alcoa, Avco, Union Carbide, Humble Oil, Reynolds Metals, General Electric, National Gypsum, Certainteed, and Sunset International Petroleum) had failed with "formidable problems and elusive profits."[12] Industry analysts predicted that Hansberger's diversification and expansion strategy would enable Boise to escape its origins in the lumber industry and its historical dependence on construction for prosperity. Investment analysts recommended Boise common shares for long-term capital appreciation and stated that according to all indicators the rapid growth rate would continue or even accelerate in the near future. There were reports that a few members of the financial community felt that Boise was "too thinly capitalized and expanding too rapidly." Near consensus remained, however, that Boise's "young management and vast property holdings offer the best insurance for the long-term outlook.[13]

In his major public relations interviews during 1969, Hansberger argued that Boise was not diversified to the point of conglomeration, even after Ebasco. He explained that Boise had diversified in order to protect itself from the boom and bust cycles in raw materials. He characterized Boise as a company in an equilibrium position between the contracyclical movements of housing and paper. On the one hand, he explained, Boise had moved into packaging, newsprint, paper, and office supplies; and, on the other hand, it had advanced into on-site built, factory-built, and mobile homes, which led naturally into resort land development and leisure activities like cruises and recreational vehicles. Hansberger maintained that Boise's diversification was different from conglomeration in three important ways. First, he made acquisitions in accordance with a clearly defined plan, whereas most conglomerates were uninhibited about acquiring a variety of unrelated businesses. Second, he was an operating as well as a financially oriented executive; that is, he did not acquire companies merely for the purpose of managing their assets from a largely financial point of view. And third, he never made tender offers, only cooperative bargains. Hansberger revealed that Boise's assets were substantially understated, like most other timberland-owning companies, and that Boise's lenders had allowed the company to maintain a fairly high debt-to-equity ratio.[14]

By conventional standards, however, Boise was a conglomerate. Hansberger's defensiveness can be explained by the fact that by 1969 conglomerates were no longer the darlings of Wall Street as many were plagued with plummeting stock values largely caused by overextension and management failure. Clearly, Hansberger sought to develop an image for Boise distinct from that of other highly acquisitive, diversified corporations. Whether because of, or in spite of, Hansberger's and hence Boise's image, investment analysts continued to refer to the company's "highly regarded top management team" and to the "paradox" of Boise's great strength in the then depressed building industry. They continued to advise purchase of Boise shares. The market price for common shares climbed to over $80.00 per share at year-end 1969.[15]

The Tigers Falter: 1970–1973

Beginning in 1970 Boise experienced massive operating losses as management fought to survive contracting revenues and mounting debt. Real growth resumed in 1976 after a total realignment of Boise's resources and corporate strategy. Table 5–1 lists Boise's major operating statistics in constant dollars for the 1967–1978 period.

The Billion Dollar Debt

Hansberger continued to acquire new business throughout 1970: Communications Research Machines, Inc. (CRM), a publisher of *Psychology Today* magazine, college texts, and other educational materials; Manilla Mills, Inc.; Orange Coast Lumber Company; a plywood plant previously owned by St. Regis; a furniture manufacturing unit of Dolly Madison; Edinger Investment Company; and Hawaii Audio-Visual Center, Inc. Boise joined with Interlake Steel in a joint venture to construct 138 condominium units

Table 5-1
Boise Cascade Corporation's Consolidated Operating Statistics, 1967–1978 in Constant Dollars

Year	Sales and Operating Revenues ($ million)	Percentage Change over Previous Year's Sales	Fortune "500" Ranking	Number of Employees	Common Stock Year-End Price-Close ($)	Earnings per Share ($)	Net Income ($ million)
1967	973.424	—	117	27,300	52.14	2.53	67.923
1968	1,243.188	27.7	100	29,900	78.36	2.88	71.137
1969	1,990.083	60.1	55	51,900	81.87	3.29	94.149
1970	1,879.225	(5.6)[a]	61	47,889	50.60	1.31	37.161
1971	1,859.894	(1.0)	61	51,000	19.37	(2.85)	(97.066)
1972	1,150.900	(38.1)	74	29,000	11.10	(5.48)	(170.610)
1973	1,251.815	8.8	128	28,000	12.85	4.30	134.074
1974	1,252.844	.1	137	27,711	8.96	3.06	90.476
1975	1,146.446	(8.5)	143	28,977	18.48	1.70	50.236
1976	1,442.732	25.8	116	35,228	25.02	2.56	75.314
1977	1,638.677	13.6	107	37,314	17.90	2.83	81.807
1978	1,691.834	3.2	111	35,704	17.42	3.23	87.317

Year	Long-Term Corporate Debt Excluding Realty Debt ($ million)	Interest Expense Excluding Realty Debt ($ million)	Common Dividends ($ million)	Research and Development Expense ($ million)	Capital Expenditures ($ million)	Current Assets ($ million)
1967	396.348	21.425	3.075	6.581	106.935	258.162
1968	306.097	28.352	4.336	8.235	76.178	264.503
1969	457.555	46.494	17.032	n/a[b]	113.985	553.899
1970	534.216	60.424	8.134	4.926	144.842	530.899
1971	527.844	66.884	7.897	5.207	126.927	508.964
1972	523.183	36.244	3.892	2.099	58.510	505.302
1973	339.847	21.674	3.580	2.129	64.530	495.163
1974	275.474	18.322	11.130	2.258	140.543	405.989
1975	252.095	17.495	14.190	1.796	140.439	342.821
1976	328.261	23.865	16.769	2.462	196.722	465.556
1977	305.797	26.981	22.640	2.808	116.245	437.918
1978	271.276	24.873	22.371	n/a	159.961	445.274

Source: Compustat.

Note: GNP implicit price deflators were used to convert current dollars to constant 1972 dollars.

[a]Figures in parentheses are negative.

[b]n/a = consolidated data not available.

near Lake Tahoe in Nevada and Lake Arrowhead in California. Hansberger also formed another new subsidiary, Boise Cascade Credit Corporation and issued the firm's first public offering of a debt security ($75 million of 10 percent, five-year debentures—Moody's rating: Bbb). Boise Credit was intended to buy customers' notes and contract receivables from the recreational communities group and the recreational vehicles division. Hansberger continued to integrate forward to reach the ultimate consumer.[16]

During February 1970, Hansberger, Fery, and Agee presented projections of Boise's growth prospects to the Investment Analysts Society of Chicago. Their optimistic projections were based on what they described as the pent-up demand for housing needed by the postwar baby boom. Hansberger argued that sales and profits would continue to grow in spite of declining economic conditions because of his exceptional management team, because he was willing to invest heavily inside the firm, and because Boise had become oriented to the consumer market. Agee explained that Boise planned a major thrust into international markets during the coming year as a means of enhancing internal growth.[17]

In May, Boise disposed of its Chilean utility interests for $81.2 million ($3 million in cash with the remainder in notes) because of "unstable government conditions in that country." As Boise's chief financial officer, Agee revealed the sale at the annual shareholders' meeting. He stated that the company's financial position was better than at any time in its history. He said that Boise would be able to meet its near-term expansion needs without additional debt or equity commitment and without liquidation of the Mexican portion of the foreign bonds obtained in the Ebasco acquisition. At the meeting, shareholders criticized Boise's Incline Village development, north of Lake Tahoe, claiming that it substantially added to the area's serious pollution problems. Management easily defeated the shareholder's resolution aimed at stopping further development; and Hansberger tried to appease the dissident shareholders by expressing his sympathy for their view. He argued that Boise was one of the more environmentally aware corporations in the U.S., he cited his own environmental credentials, and indicated that he was really on the same side as the dissidents.[18]

The economic slowdown, coupled with high inflation and interest rates, promised sluggish results from Boise's traditional product lines during the year. As early as February management had predicted that improvements in the factory-built housing, paper, and recreational communities group would offset the downturn in building materials. Boise (among others) had been criticized in the business press for utilizing unsound accounting methods in its recreational communities operations. Consequently, Agee announced an increase from 5.5 to 8 percent of related revenues set aside to cover possible losses of receivables. Even as securities analysts waxed enthusiastic over Boise's future growth potential, the recreational communities group showed an operational loss in excess of $11 million for 1970. The loss was attributed by management to general economic conditions (high interest rates and softening of demand), to delayed construction activities, and to overall higher development costs (the result of increased environmental safeguards mandated by local governmental units at the California and Nevada sites). At that time, Boise had acquired thirty development projects in tracts of between 700 and 31,000 acres for a total of 129,000 acres. Eighteen of the thirty projects were located in California, a total of 72,000 acres. Consolidated sales revenues for the year decreased 5.6 percent (in constant dollars) from the 1969 level, but profits decreased a whopping 55 percent. In addition, management had totaled up $488 million in corporate debt, $596 million in realty debt, and $251 million in current liabilities for a $1.3 billion debt burden. Agee, Boise's thirty-two-year-old executive vice-president for finance, commented, "We still think it is a manageable kind of debt."[19]

Polluter of the Year

Hansberger continued to acquire firms through the early months of 1971. He picked up four more in exchange for 119,070 common shares: J.E. Elrod Lumber Company, Vaughn Lumber Company, Inc., Raygold Corporation, Rochester Envelope Company, Inc., and its subsidiary Detroit Tuller Envelope Company. In January 1971, management announced that it had completed a study of accounting practices among land development companies and was assured that its accounting methods were both "conservative and realistic." The study was completed with the aid of Arthur Andersen and Company.[20]

Then, in May, Hansberger publicly announced that Boise would be disengaging from the recreational development field by selling off all but about a half-dozen of the twenty-nine projects underway and the six projects acquired but not yet started. In June, he announced another $44 million extraordinary charge against income because of substantial losses on construction underway in the Burnett-Boise joint venture and write-downs in Boise's home-building and recreational land operations. He blamed environmentalist interference and the changed economic conditions in California and Washington states (both suffering from aerospace cutbacks) for the home-building and land development losses. He explained that Boise would increase production of factory-manufactured housing in other parts of the country in an effort to pick up some of the slack.[21]

By midyear Hansberger was forced to call off talks with Norton Simon regarding the acquisition of McCall Publishing, a Norton Simon subsidiary and publisher of the *Saturday Review*. During August, Boise was forced to rescind price increases on mobile home units which had been put into effect immediately prior to President Nixon's price freeze program. Then the Chilean government defaulted on its payment schedule for the Ebasco utility (semiannual payments of $1.566 million plus 6 percent interest). In response to all this, Hansberger was forced to divest the remaining Ebasco portfolio (approximately $50.5 million) and the firm's Lake Arrowhead holdings. Power Line Erectors and its subsidiary Tyee Construction (obtained in the Ebasco merger) were discontinued because of losses. Although sales revenues had decreased by only 1 percent (in constant dollars), Boise's corporate debt-to-equity ratio had increased from 56 percent in 1970 to 64 percent at year-end 1971. Long-term debt still exceeded $1 billion, half of it related to land development projects. The firm had taken a total of $48 million in extraordinary charges against income and had suffered a consolidated net deficit of $85 million. In addition to the urban and recreational development losses, Boise's engineering, construction, paper, packaging, and publishing units performed poorly. It became clear that the firm was being held together by the operational results of the timber, building materials, and manufactured housing units.[22]

Despite these problems, as late as October, investment analysts continued to evaluate Boise's stock as "neutral over the near-term and neutral-to-positive over the twelve to eighteen month period." Throughout, Agee made public statements to the effect that with tighter financial controls, tougher cost-cutting programs, and the proceeds from a few strategic liquidations, Boise would be able to meet all of its funding requirements with internal cash flow.[23]

As the major portion of Boise's $85 million loss resulted from land development activities, Hansberger was forced to dispose quickly of recreational land projects where the effects of environmental and consumer backlash had become even more threatening to the firm than the lost profit potential. Local land-use planning groups, environmentalists, and disgruntled consumers had effectively stopped development at the Washington, California, Nevada, Hawaiian, Connecticut, New Hampshire, and Maryland sites. A conservation-minded group of students at the University of California at Berkeley attracted considerable attention when it derisively gave Boise Cascade the "Polluter of the Year" award for the contamination of Lake Tahoe with silt. Viewing the situation in retrospect, Boise spokesmen attributed their problems to a "sudden, unforseen upsurge in ecological concern that literally changed the business overnight." Hansberger further explained: "Rather than risk more calumny, we'll never go to a spot of natural beauty again. The situation is just too emotional."[24]

The public outcry surrounding Boise's various developments, and recreational community development in general, revolved around the alleged lack of adherence to ecological constraints. Although claiming to have an ecological conscience, Boise was not viewed by outsiders as preserving the natural environment in "conventional ways." Questions concerning ecological damage and pollution arose on almost all projects, but protest was most apparent at the Lake Tahoe, Puget Sound shorefront (Washington), and Hawaiian beach sites. These sites became high-cost projects as the company was forced to respond to local demands for open spaces, underground utilities, and full sewage treatment facilities.[25]

The repeated charges of fraud and misrepresentation against Boise coupled with the nationwide oversupply of recreational lots resulted in the collapse of demand for Boise's product. The firm was investigated and indicted in several states. Convictions, injunctions, or consent agreements were obtained in nearly all cases. At first, management made protestations against what they considered to be "continuing harassment." Later, Fery admitted that Boise had "picked up some indifferent managers" along with the land companies it had acquired. "We had people running our operations who didn't give a damn about Boise Cascade's public image." Fery explained that high-pressure salesmen had indeed encouraged customers to buy lots for speculation purposes, and that Boise's management had originally envisioned recreational community sites as a speculative investment for the consumer. The land companies that Hansberger acquired were oriented to the "investment-sell" market. It was only after ecologists mobilized public opinion against Boise communities in 1971, and "after a lot of careful analysis of the land business," that Hansberger decided Boise would no longer develop land for speculation but rather would sell it as "a product for use."[26]

The most devastating consumer suit was filed by the California attorney general's office against four of Boise's recreational community projects. The suit alleged fraudulent promotional misrepresentation in the sale of approximately $46 million of lots between 1967 and 1969. The attorney general sought the return of all funds to customers and punitive damages. In response to the charges, a superior court judge ordered Boise to place all past and future profits from the sale of the land into a trust and prohibited any further foreclosures on the land in question. In April 1972, an injunction was issued restraining Boise from using misrepresentation in the sale of lots at any of its land development projects in the state of California. In February 1973, after several years of negative publicity, Boise consented to a $58 million out-of-court settlement that consolidated all the California misrepresentation claims as well as related suits charging conflict of interest and attempted bribery of certain public officials.[27]

A major corporate restructuring was disclosed during a midyear 1971 interview with Hansberger, Fery, and Agee who characterized the change as a "shift toward tighter control." The trio conceded that expansion had come too fast for Boise in the recreational land development field and that the resulting geographical dispersion had strained Boise's management team, which had also been too "timid about reaching in and seizing control" from the principals of acquired firms. According to Hansberger, the corporate restructuring process had begun in 1969 with a general tightening of managerial controls (about the same time that four prominent Wall Street figures, including Eugene R. Black, former World Bank president, had joined Boise's board). At Fery's suggestion, three committees had been set up under Boise's five-man management council: finance, strategy, and human relations. Hansberger explained that these committees were not meant to be operating committees, but rather were meant to handle policy formulation for the firm. He remarked that the committees "spread the decision process" resulting in better decisions and fewer mistakes. Hansberger had been forced to scrap his celebrated free-form management approach where "equals functioned almost interchangeably" for a more conventional decision-making mode. He acknowledged that a new computerized system of budgeting and a renewed long-range planning effort were being developed for Boise by an outside group of management systems consultants.[28]

Published case studies meant to describe Boise's strategic planning process during 1970 and 1971 indicate that executives throughout the corporation were having difficulty institutionalizing the generation of the incremental planning and budgeting documents required for the new system and its five-year planning cycle. The case studies also provide evidence that the Strategy Committee working with the Long-Range Planning Department, the group charged with drafting a diversification-strategy proposal to be submitted to Boise's five-man council, only half-heartedly believed that their recommendations would influence future acquisition plans. Clearly, it took a while for the organizational environment to adjust to more traditional decision-making and planning modes after the free-form experience.[29]

Divestiture

On 2 March 1972, Hansberger announced "substantial progress" in his plan to divest Boise of businesses which did not have adequate earnings potential. He blamed "a substantial portion" of the 1971 loss on the "direct or indirect" impact of the pending civil suits in California. On 6 March the Maryland Land Board imposed a ninety-day sales suspension on Boise because of licensing improprieties. Boise officials pleaded "administrative oversight," but the incident meant more bad press for the firm. Then at midmonth came the announcement that Hansberger had abolished his five-man management council along with the strategy committees. He commented, "When the corporate ship gets into trouble, the time for democracy has to be suspended." Outsiders speculated that Eugene R. Black was taking an active role in the restructuring and pruning efforts going on at Boise's headquarters.[30]

At the annual stockholders' meeting in April, Hansberger described plans to sell off another $100 million of Boise's assets in order to reduce the debt load. Boise executives were grilled by shareholders for 1971 financial losses and the loss of public credibility caused by projections of high profits while the firm was really racking up an $85 million loss. Hansberger tried to placate the shareholders with instances of unanticipated events. He finished by asking them to note carefully that, "We haven't made any glowing projections for 1972."[31]

In June a company spokesman announced an "expansion in executive leadership" at Boise. Stephen Moser, who had come to Boise with the original Cascade Lumber merger, was promoted to vice-chairman of the board and John Fery was made president. Fery assumed "certain administrative duties" in order to leave Hansberger free to "redirect the company and get it back on the track." Hansberger retained his chairman and chief executive titles. As the firm attempted to regain a public image of control and recovery, it was hit again with bad press. Charges were filed against Boise on behalf of the former shareholders of West Tacoma Newsprint for allegedly misrepresenting its debt position during merger talks in 1969. The plaintiffs sought $35.9 million in damages. Simultaneously, Deltec International filed suit against Boise charging that Boise's management had intentionally acted to cut its equity position in their joint venture, an Argentinian cattle ranch. Deltec claimed its investment had been watered down to nothing when Boise increased the number of marketable shares by tenfold.[32]

During July management announced a $200 million extraordinary charge against income to cover realty and Latin American losses. Hansberger attributed the largest portion of the charge to his decision to accelerate withdrawal from the recreational land development business, including the immediate discontinuance of retail land sales in California. A second and smaller portion of the charge involved adding to Boise's reserve for Latin American investments. The Chilean government had defaulted on a revised payment schedule, and Boise's Panamanian utility had been nationalized. The $200 million pretax writeoff was one of the largest single writeoffs in U.S. industry and, at the time, was compared to RCA's $490 million loss when it exited the computer business and Ford's $50 million Edsel writeoff. William Agee, Boise's chief financial officer, left Boise for the Bendix Corporation.[33]

Boise picked up even more bad press in July when the *New York Times* published a lengthy article about the Burnett-Boise Corporation, a joint venture construction firm that Hansberger had set up to undertake urban renewal and development projects in New York City in the wake of the 1968–1969 Watts, Detroit, and Newark riots. Winston A. Burnett, a 51 percent owner of Burnett-Boise shares, charged Boise's top management with racism, paternalism, and incompetence. Burnett claimed that the construction firm, which had been involved in thirty-seven renewal projects, involving contracts in excess of $500 million, had actually been controlled from Idaho. According to Burnett, Boise's management had maintained complete control of the purse strings and had given him very little discretionary decision-making power. He claimed that though Burnett-Boise had suffered losses because of late completion dates, Boise's managers were "looking for a scapegoat in which to dump other losses" and that they were taking Burnett-Boise down with them. Burnett further charged that the whole Burnett-Boise experience had been "a sad testament to the arrogance of white America" and that Boise executives had continually referred to his workers as the "failure-prone personality" of the urban slums. Asked to respond, Hansberger quipped: "Anything we might say would exacerbate the situation." There may have been some exaggeration in Burnett's charges, but the question of how Boise managed to turn a $600,000 investment into a $37 million extraordinary charge against income is a valid one.[34]

In October, Hansberger was replaced by Fery as chief executive. Moser was appointed chairman. Fery continued the planned sale of assets in order to raise the cash needed to meet the firm's heavy debt burden. All total, Boise ended up divesting assets which sold for $370 million between February 1972 and February 1973. See table 5-2 for details of the divestiture program. The company reported a 38 percent drop in sales revenue (constant dollars) and a $170.6 million net deficit for 1972. Employment levels fell from 51,000 to 29,000. And the market for Boise stock descended from the year-end high of $81.87 in 1969 to $19.37 in 1971, to a dismal $11.10 per share at year-end 1972 (constant dollars). Investment analysts were then describing Boise stock as "a long term speculative turnaround rather than an investment.[35]

Financial Restructuring

After three years of large writeoffs, two years of large losses, and a major divestiture program, Boise's reorganized management team dug in and fought to keep Boise solvent. They benefited greatly from record high prices in lumber and plywood and the improved profitability of Boise's pulp and paper operations. Early in 1973, Fery outlined the five basic problems confronting the firm:

Table 5–2
Boise's Divestiture Program

Sold	Buyer	Amount Realized (cash transactions, $ million)
Ebasco Services, Inc. and Vernon Graphics, Inc.	Halliburton	65.0
Chemical Construction Corp.	Aerojet-General	17.5
Mobile homes and recreational vehicles division	Bendix	61.3
Empresa Electrica de Guatemala	Guatemala	18.0
Panama Power and Light	Panama	18.5
Argentinian petrochemical plant	South American Consolidated Enterprises	9.0
Fort Bragg lumber operations (formerly Union Lumber)	Georgia-Pacific and Louisiana-Pacific	123.5
Guatemalan, Brazilian, and Columbian bonds	Various buyers	47.0
Subtotal		359.8
Detroit Automotive	Aspro, Inc.	
Detroit envelope plant	Seaman Patrick Paper	
Kansas City container plant	Hoerner-Waldorf	
Metal buildings division	American Buildings	
Subtotal		10.2[a]
Total		370.0
Liquidated		
Walter Kidde Constructors		
Power Line Erectors		
Tyee Construction		

[a]Derived from subtraction; individual prices undisclosed.

1. the extraordinary charges necessitated modifying the firm's many loan agreements;
2. debt had to be reduced quickly;
3. settlement of litigation involving the firm's discontinued recreational land developments had to be completed rapidly;
4. the firm had to operate its continuing businesses profitably; and
5. top management had to restore the firm's lost credibility with the investment community.[36]

By May, Fery was able to announce formal approval by Boise's creditors of a four-year financial restructuring plan that preserved the old interest rates but gave insurance companies and bank creditors an unusual 50 percent mortgage on Boise's remaining assets. Severe restrictions on the prerogatives of management were obtained by creditors including requirements that $100 million in working capital be maintained at all times and that 1973 dividends not exceed $2.5 million. In better days, the company had paid out as much as $17 million in dividends in one year. The firm negotiated the $58 million land litigation settlement in California. As for investment community credibility, Fery made several public statements to the effect that Boise had again become and would now remain a basic wood products and paper producer: "Boise isn't interested in investing in new businesses."[37]

In October, Fery announced that Boise would repurchase 1.5 million of the 31.5 million shares of outstanding common stock in order to bolster declining stock values which were negatively influencing the cost of capital for the firm. At year-end, Boise had repurchased 1.6 million shares. In response, investment analysts began to recommend buying Boise shares "on any significant market decline" although some persisted in describing Boise as a "zero growth" company, one that had managed "to just about break even over the past eight years."[38]

In the annual report for 1973, Fery explained that the company was now "rid" of all nonprofitable and nonstrategic operations. Boise's litigation problems, however, were not over. Along with twenty other major plywood producers, Boise was charged by the Federal Trade Commission with anticompetitive pricing and shipping tactics. Specifically, the charges concerned the maintenance of a system of delivered prices based on rail rates from the Pacific Northwest even though the plywood may have been shipped from a mill near the buyer. Boise was also named as a defendant in nine civil antitrust actions brought on behalf of various classes of consumers of lumber and plywood. Another misrepresentation at time of acquisition suit was filed against Boise on behalf of the former shareholders of the United Lumber Company, a firm acquired in 1969. In addition, Boise's Ocean Pines recreation community in Maryland was required to suspend sales by the Department of Housing and Urban Development on the grounds of withholding information from prospective buyers. According to the federal agency, Boise had failed to specify that buyers were to pay for improvements and that some lots were subject to flooding in heavy rain.[39]

Back to Basics: 1974–1980

Although real sales growth remained flat for the next several years, Boise's management held on and by 1976 returned the firm to a conservative growth position. The market for Boise shares strengthened as management effectively reformulated basic strategy.

Conservative Growth

John Fery, who had become Boise's chief spokesman in negotiations with lenders during the dark days of 1972, continued to act as Boise's major spokesman and chief financial officer, although he was not made chairman until May of 1978 when Moser retired. Fery made it clear, soon after he assumed control from Hansberger, that Boise's growth and diversification strategy would change dramatically, reflecting growth in the forest products industry where growth rates historically have reflected gross national product rates of change. He explained that Boise might do "modest acquiring for cash," but only of well-managed operations that would fit neatly into Boise's wood and paper operations. He added that Boise had no further plans for growth in international markets: "Our emphasis for future growth will remain domestic." He announced that Boise would be embarking on a five-year, $1.1 billion capital expenditure program that would be funded largely from cash and future cash flow from operations rather than from debt financing. Boise's managers were instructed to begin work on five- and ten-year strategies for controlled growth in terms of internal expansion in Boise's two basic product lines. Fery enumerated Boise's new corporate goals as follows:

1. becoming the most efficient operator in each of its two businesses;
2. maintaining a flexible financial structure with planned growth;
3. rewarding top management for results (return on assets employed); and
4. increasing productivity by upgrading skills.[40]

Rising construction costs and various start-up problems resulted in delayed profitability from Boise's new capacity. Despite record sales revenues and the firm's massive capital expenditure program, return on equity remained below the industry average. Given the depressed conditions in the construction industry, Boise's new strategy shifted resources toward the more profitable paper businesses to the extent that 60 percent of operating income was generated by the paper group in 1980. In the belief that the decline in the construction of new housing would continue through the 1980s, Fery acquired from Lone Star Industries fourteen wholesale and 112 retail building materials units located in twelve states for $50 million. He planned to utilize the units to tap into the burgeoning renovation and home repair market. Once again, Boise's growth strategy was formulated in terms of integrating forward to the ultimate customer.[41]

Under Fery's leadership, Boise undertook an informational advertising campaign designed to present Boise's new image to the public. Full-page informational ads were published in national newspapers and magazines describing Boise's new growth strategy in detail. According to the ads, Boise would be able to cushion the cyclical downturns in building materials with paper products, the demand for which increased with growth of the general economy. Slower growth in paper products, in turn, would be cushioned by further investment in paper packaging facilities, an area of production that was relatively less susceptible to market fluctuations. Fery was interested in creating an image of measured growth, stability, and security without diversification outside the forest products industry.[42]

Fery expanded efforts to protect Boise's access to public forest lands, the firm's major source of raw material. He vocally supported the continuation of the multiple-use approach to timber resource management by the U.S. Forest Service. In 1970, Boise derived 35 percent of needed raw material from owned forest lands. Five years later, after Hansberger's diversification program, that figure had dropped to a mere 23 percent. Remaining need had to be purchased from public forest lands where prices were escalating at a faster clip than inflation. By 1980, Boise owned 3.1 million acres of timberland throughout North America and controlled an additional 4.3 million acres through long-term leases, contracts, or licenses. On a sustained-yield basis, these timberlands are capable of providing for 54 percent of Boise's solid wood requirements and 43 percent of total fiber needs. In contrast, Boise's major competitors own a higher percentage of raw material need: Weyerhaeuser owns 100 percent of need outright; Crown Zellerbach, 65 percent; and Georgia Pacific, 55 percent.[43]

As conservationists across the country became involved in attempts to slow the cutting on public forest lands with the curtailment of clear cutting practices and the designation of large tracts of forest land as wilderness area, Boise officials responded as vocal advocates of the status quo. Constraints on the supply of harvestable timberland meant not only higher costs to Boise, but also signaled a significant loss of control over the firm's external environment, one that could negatively affect long-term viability. Consequently, Boise executives were involved in frequent testimony before congressional committees, federal agencies, and local land-use hearings whenever forest land management was at issue. Boise increased lobbying activities in 1974 and established a governmental affairs office in Washington, D.C. The new office was headed by a former congressional aide who had also served as an executive assistant to the secretary of the interior and a vice-president for governmental affairs of the American Paper Institute. Shareholders were informed that increased lobbying activities on behalf of Boise's interests had become mandatory in order to counteract the persuasive and effective lobbying efforts of environmental protection interests groups at all levels of government. In fact, the local threat to supply created by environmentalists in northern California had been one of the major reasons for choosing to sell Boise's prime Fort Bragg redwood holdings back in 1973 during the forced divestiture program. Much of the redwood timberland in California had already been put under some type of wilderness or park classification, and Boise executives did not relish the possibility of another long court battle with environmentalists in that state.[44]

Boise's growth-related position on public-forest-lands management was summarized by Fery in a quarterly report editorial: "Those who talk at wilderness hearings of preserving our natural heritage for future generations could well direct their energies to insisting on public policies which could expand the potential of our forest resources." Boise maintained a mutually supportive relationship with the U.S. Forest Service. Boise executives were always on hand to testify for higher appropriations for the agency. According to Fery, the agency was in need of an expanded budget if it was to efficiently plan for and manage U.S. timberland resources.[45]

Meticulous Planning

The organizational response to Boise's restabilization problems was fundamentally conservative. Fery adopted a back-to-basics approach and put aside most of Hansberger's theories about diversification and free-form management. Fery had specialized in finance at Stanford. As he put his mark on Boise, financial controls became preeminent and meticulous planning became the norm. Fery produced Boise's first organizational chart for shareholders in 1975. He swept aside one entire level of management and most standing committees. He designed a management control system that focused on accountability and rewarded on the basis of return on equity. He saw to it that his corporate staff received sophisticated training in long-range planning techniques, and then he geared up Boise's long-range planning systems to produce annual five- and ten-year blueprints. Elaborate income and expense projections, comprehensive quarterly reviews of business conditions, and strict budgets at all corporate levels became the starting point for the blueprints and the basis of the managerial control system.[46]

Fery reorganized again in 1978 with the announced purpose of giving the chief executive more time to cope with increased environmental complexity, "to recognize and reconcile all of the differing expectations of an increasingly complex society." According to Fery, this increased complexity was the result of the greater degree of government involvement with business, which required more discussion and more testimony on more regulations before Congress and federal agencies; the expanded level of communication with business expected by the many special interest segments of the public as well as the general public; the need of the chief executive to represent the firm's interests with industry associations; and the management time required to cope with corporate litigation. Fery appointed

Jon Miller to be president and chief operating officer as he happily announced that he had succeeded in moving the firm "closer to a traditional management alignment." Fery also directed the repurchase of approximately three million additional shares of outstanding common stock.[47]

Loose Ends

In December 1976, a Federal Trade Commission administrative judge ruled that Boise Cascade, Georgia Pacific, Weyerhaeuser, Champion International, and Willamette Industries (five of the twenty originally charged) were guilty of price-fixing activities. The judge ruled that their "phantom rates" were ". . . simply a convenient private arrangement for maintaining southern plywood prices at a satisfactory level . . . while facilitating the traditional oligopolistic objective of containing price cutting and limiting price uncertainty." The companies appealed the decision, but the Federal Trade Commission affirmed the earlier ruling in February of 1978. The case is now under appeal in the federal courts. In a related case, a Dallas jury indicted two Boise employees for destroying documents sought by private parties who had consolidated in a class action suit claiming to be injured by the price-fixing activities of the above firms. The local plant manager and controller were charged with removing and destroying subpoenaed documents.[48]

Of the private antitrust suits that were filed against Boise during the 1974–1978 period (charging the firm had conspired with others to fix prices, split up markets, allocate customers, rig governmental contract bids, and make reprisals against nonconforming wholesalers for plywood, paper, and cardboard boxes), the bulk were negotiated to settlement by mid-1979. These settlements cost Boise $25.9 million. Boise's management also agreed to settle the West Tacoma Newsprint and the United Lumber suits for misrepresentation of liabilities at the time of acquisition for $6.6 million. Additionally, Boise voluntarily admitted to the Securities and Exchange Commission "questionable foreign payments" amounting to $376,000 between 1971 and 1976 when the firm was involved in international operations. No litigation was instigated in that matter.[49]

Evaluating Boise's Response Pattern

A review of Boise's activities indicates the extent to which a basically healthy firm in a growth industry can be negatively influenced by a slow-growth economy. Management's acquisition strategy and the consequent emphasis on short-term profitability contributed significantly to Boise's immediate and long-term problems. The primary interdependent factors that shaped Boise's most recent contraction episode include:

1. the slowdown in real growth of the domestic economy that led to Hansberger's drive to diversify assets beyond the forest products industry where historically growth rates have reflected the general economy (real GNP increased at an annual rate of 3 percent during the 1967–1980 period);[50]
2. the slowdown in real growth of the domestic economy in conjunction with rising interest rates and a tight money market, which led to depressed revenues and increased operational costs (including interest on debt) in Boise's recreational development and consumer finance operations;
3. the mid–1960s shift of major producers in the forest products industry away from the utilization of the more costly Northwestern timberlands toward the less costly Southern timberlands in conjunction with the escalating price of timber cut from federally owned forests;
4. a slow rate of growth in productivity in the domestic paper products industry in conjunction with chronic conditions of excess capacity (interspersed with brief periods of shortage);
5. the softening of demand for Boise's building materials and paper products during the 1969–1970 and 1974–1975 recessionary periods;
6. Management's overly ambitious diversification program, which led not only to some dubious acquisitions (foreign and domestic) and negative press (related to land developments and stock mergers) but also overextended Boise's management resources;
7. management's emphasis on short-term financially oriented measures of performance and its initial nonresponsiveness to consumer, shareholder, and environmentalist claims; and
8. the various illegal activities on the part of managers and employees (related to land development sales, price fixing, and market allocation practices), which negatively influenced the firm's public image, and ultimately, the market for Boise common shares.

Internal Rationalization

After twelve years of rapid expansion through acquisition, Hansberger's diversification program left the firm seriously overextended in terms of managerial and financial resources. His original strategy of vertical integration into related-product markets with significant growth potential had been accomplished. But the rapidity with which he acquired firms and the rather haphazard way in which he also picked up firms in unrelated-product markets (everything from South American utilities to recreational vehicles and financial services) led to his demise at Boise Cascade. Hansberger's decision to integrate forward to the ultimate consumer (paper, packaging, wholesale and retail building supply outlets, construction, recreational community development, publishing) was a rational one. Yet, his failure to integrate backward (purchase timberlands) left Boise overly sensitive to escalating raw materials costs once the firm was forced to divest the majority of its new holdings. Diversification into international markets was too superficial to be of much aid when domestic markets faltered and the money troubles began.

On the whole, the internal managerial response to contracting revenues at Boise was straightforward and predictable. The first indication of a structural change came as early as 1969 after the election of new board members and the early reports that Boise was financially overextended in the land development field. Hansberger restructured the office of the president and delegated specific policymaking responsibilities to his newly formed finance, strategy, and human relations committees. From that point until Fery had completed his own restructuring program in 1973-1974, Boise managers were involved in a continual effort to broaden the top management team within an increasingly traditional structural framework. Various financial control systems of increasing stringency were instigated. Long-range planning and budgeting mechanisms overtook the computer-enhanced yet free-form decision style of earlier times. Either as a result of these financially oriented control systems or because of the ascendency of executives with training and experience in finance, a marked increase in the dominance of financial imperatives can be observed in Boise's postcontraction operations. Under Fery, managerial performance criteria and budget were explicitly linked and "controlled growth" came to be equated with five- and ten-year planning budgets.

In the face of a billion-dollar debt burden, Hansberger, Fery, and Agee significantly reduced Boise's international content and overall diversification level. In order to remain solvent, they were forced to divest the bulk of Boise's growth-producing assets. Pressure from Boise's creditors led not only to the departure of Hansberger and Agee but to the unusual 50 percent mortgage on Boise's remaining assets, controls on dividend payouts and cash flow, and to the early negotiated settlement of the California land litigation. Management control was essentially salvaged by the profitable operation of Boise's paper products divisions and the record high prices obtained for timber and plywood during 1971-1972. It was not until 1973 that Boise was officially charged with participating in price-fixing and market-allocation schemes. After the frantic period of asset contraction, the reckless impulse to grow initiated by Hansberger was replaced by a restrained growth strategy that focused on internal expansion and consolidation. Fery's success was in stabilizing a firm of reduced size and scope. Boise was again essentially a commodities firm that could be expected to produce annual earnings in the 4 to 6 percent of sales range. Boise's manager of corporate communications, Robert B. Hayes, commented that Boise's top executives no longer expected to be able to attract the young management talent that had flocked to Boise during times of exciting growth. An outside observer, Professor Charles E. Summer, commenting on Boise's new organizational climate indicated that the firm's contraction experience presented the central and critical question of whether an informal, group dynamics approach to management can only be sustained by affluent companies in affluent times.[51]

Fery's reformulated strategy for growth retains Hansberger's notion of forward integration to the ultimate consumer. Growth goals are conservative and officially framed in terms of the domestic market and cash acquisition. Boise has recently, however, taken on $287 million in long-term debt in order to help finance capital expansion. Boise's research and development expenditures (both in absolute terms and as a percentage of total revenue), however, have remained below average for the forest products industry and below par for Boise's major competitors. Boise expended $5 million for research and development during 1980 compared to International Paper's $37 million, Weyerhaeuser's $52.2 million, and Crown Zellerbach's $12.6 million.[52]

Boise's relative lack of owned timberlands has led Fery to focus consolidating operations, fine tuning output, and emphasizing distribution. Fortunately, Boise's northwestern owned timberlands are well positioned for exploitation of the expanding Japanese export market, which it is estimated will grow at twice the rate of domestic markets during the 1980s. The firm exported approximately 10 percent of its total plywood production during 1980. But again, Boise's relative lack of owned timberlands may prohibit increased export activity. Boise must purchase more than half of its current raw material supply from federal timberlands where prices have been escalating rapidly; federal timber prices are estimated to have increased 74 percent between 1978 and 1980. Despite Fery's stock repurchase program and Boise's considerable public information efforts, the market now values Boise common shares at approximately one-third of their 1967 value (constant dollars).[53]

External Rationalization

Under Fery, management fought hard to regain a modicum of control over what had become an increasingly hostile external environment for the firm.

Divestiture reduced the firm's diversification level and consequently the level of environmental uncertainty. Boise's withdrawal from foreign operations (except owned Canadian timberlands) and from the community development field improved the firm's relationships with disgruntled creditors and stockholders. Initial efforts to revamp the board, replace Hansberger, restructure the firm, and renegotiate loan and credit arrangements were meant to appease those constituencies. Fery's stock repurchase program and the informational advertising campaign which stressed Boise's more conservative financial structure and growth plans were supportive efforts aimed at improving stock market expectations. Desirous of avoiding any further negative publicity for the firm, Fery pushed for negotiated settlements in the various fraud and antitrust suits facing Boise.

Likewise, Boise's relationships with consumer and environmentalist groups were stabilized. The degree to which those groups could further impinge on Boise's activities was diminished by the firm's withdrawal from the community development business and the $58.3 million settlement in the state of California land litigation (including $24 million in refunds to dissatisfied land purchasers, $13 million for completion of improvements, and $21.5 million for operation and maintenance). Hansberger and Fery later acknowledged that by becoming the largest land company in California, if not the nation, Boise was too visible in an industry that became the focal point for the environmental and consumer movements in the early 1970s. According to Hansberger, "As the largest company, we became the target of everybody: the consumer movement, environmentalists, politicians, and newspapers." Fery acted to reduce the potential impact of environmentalists on the firm when he chose to divest Boise's valuable Fort Bragg, California redwood holdings (225,000 acres) in 1973. The extent to which consumer, environmental, and dissident stockholder groups were successful in influencing Boise's policies as well as the firm's activities in the marketplace is noteworthy.[54]

As Boise retreated from diversification, the firm became increasingly sensitive to the uncertainties surrounding its major source of supply for raw materials. At one point during the period under study, Boise was obtaining as much as 70 percent of its timber from public lands regulated by the Bureau of Land Management and the U.S. Forest Service. Boise's considerable dependence on federal decisions affecting the amount of cutting allowed on public lands led to an activist lobbying role for the firm. In 1973, a Forest Service study recommended withdrawals of forest lands for preservation as wilderness areas. If adopted, that recommendation would have reduced the allowable cut by 300 million board feet per year, mostly in the western United States. The Sierra Club, an environmentalist group, actively lobbied for larger withdrawals. In an effort to secure and stabilize its major source of supply, Boise representatives urged increased cutting with consequent replanting programs and less extensive withdrawals for wilderness preservation. Boise's only other alternatives were to reduce output or purchase the more costly cutting rights to privately held timberlands.

According to Frank Keane, a vice-president for the Bank of America (Boise's largest creditor), because nearly 90 percent of Boise's lumber and plywood production occurred in the Pacific Northwest, the firm was forced to enter what had become a "bidding war for trees." Prices for both private and publicly owned timberlands escalated after 1973 as withdrawals for wilderness preserves increased. From that time forward, Boise has been heavily involved in a federal lobbying effort to influence Forest Service policy. Boise representatives have argued that withdrawals of forest lands from the nation's commercial timber base should not be continued until a national land-use policy has been formulated. Boise spokesmen also argued for a revision of the 1897 federal statute that governs timber harvesting in the national forests. In 1977, lobbyists for the firm undertook an extensive effort to discredit the Carter administration's recommendation to expand the nation's Wilderness System from 14.5 million acres to the more than 300 million acres.[55]

From 1974 to 1977, management used Boise's quarterly journal and a nationwide advertising campaign to advocate the firm's viewpoint in the dispute over the withdrawal of public forest lands for preservation. Journal editorials urged stockholders and employees to write their congressional representatives on Boise's behalf and become politically involved in the issue at every governmental level. Boise employees were urged to run for local public office and use any suitable public forum to present Boise's case. The firm's most recent reorganization was undertaken with the expressed purpose of freeing up Fery to deal with Boise's increasingly complex and politicized external environment. In a milieu of competing interests, the firm's vulnerability to the regulation of raw material supply by the federal government has apparently become one of the primary concerns of Boise's chief executive.[56]

Notes

1. *Fortune,* 15 June 1968, p. 202; *Fortune,* 4 May 1981, p. 328.

2. For a detailed firm history through 1966, see Robert L. Katz, "Planning Corporate Strategy: Boise Cascade," *Cases and Concepts in Corporate Strategy* (Englewood Cliffs, N.J.: Prentice-Hall, 1970), pp. 345–499.

3. Ibid., p. 498.

4. Herman L. Boschken, *Corporate Power and the Mismarketing of Urban Development* (New York: Praeger Publishers, 1974), pp. 29, 327; *Business Week, (BW)* 24 February 1968, p. 152; John McDonald, "Boise

Cascade," *The Game of Business* (Garden City, N.Y.: Doubleday, Anchor Press, 1975), p. 144.

5. *BW,* 24 February 1968, pp. 148–150.

6. John McDonald, *Fortune,* October 1969, p. 135; *BW,* 1 June 1974, p. 72.

7. McDonald, *Fortune,* pp. 134–136.

8. *Time,* 21 July 1967, p. 70.

9. *Business International,* 14 April 1967, p. 117.

10. *Forbes,* 15 March 1969, pp. 41–42; *New York Times (NYT),* 24 July 1969, p. 48; McDonald, *Game,* p. 155; McDonald, *Fortune,* p. 202. The penultimate source contains a description of the Boise-Ebasco merger negotiations.

11. *BW,* 25 October 1969, p. 41.

12. *Time,* 21 July 1967, pp. 69–70.

13. Noel Hemming, *Wall Street Transcript (WST),* 16 December 1968, p. 15206; *WST,* 5 August 1968, p. 14032; *BW,* 24 February 1968, p. 150.

14. McDonald, *Fortune,* pp. 138, 198; *Forbes,* 15 March 1969, p. 41.

15. *WST,* 26 May 1969, p. 16731; *WST,* 29 December 1969, p. 19074.

16. Boise Cascade, *Annual Report: 1970,* p. 18.

17. *WST,* 18 May 1970, pp. 20581–20582.

18. *Wall Street Journal (WSJ),* 1 May 1970, p. 5.

19. *WSJ,* 20 February 1970, p. 14; *WST,* 19 October 1970, p. 22073; *BW,* 15 May 1971, p. 90; Boise Cascade, *Annual Report: 1970,* p. 3; Boise Cascade Credit Corporation, *Prospectus,* 15 May 1970, p. 11.

20. *WSJ,* 21 January 1971, p. 12.

21. *BW,* 15 May 1971, p. 90; *WSJ,* 21 June 1971, p. 10.

22. *WSJ,* 9 July 1971, p. 3; *WSJ,* 20 August 1971, p. 4; Boise Cascade, *Annual Report: 1971,* pp. 2–3; *WSJ,* 26 July 1971, p. 19; Arthur E. Rockwell, *WST,* 28 February 1972, p. 27410; *BW,* 11 March 1972, p. 34.

23. *WST,* 25 October 1971, p. 25940; A Richard Immel, *WSJ,* 29 December 1971, p. 20.

24. Daryl Lembke, *Los Angeles Times (LAT),* 8 July 1973, p. VI-3; Immel, *WSJ,* p. 20; *Time,* 12 April 1971, p. 87.

25. Boschken, *Mismarketing,* pp. 53–55; *BW,* 15 May 1971, p. 90.

26. Boschken, *Mismarketing,* p. 54; *Time,* 12 April 1971, p. 87; *BW,* 15 May 1971, p. 90.

27. *WSJ,* 14 October 1971, p. 6; *WSJ,* 26 April 1972. p. 29; Boschken, *Mismarketing,* p. 55. Boschken's work discusses in detail Boise's marketing strategies, the consumer and environmental response, and the resultant litigation surrounding Boise's recreational land development activities in California and Washington state.

28. *BW,* 15 May 1971, p. 90.

29. Harvard Business School Case nos. 9-371-526 and 9-371-527

entitled "Boise Cascade Corporation (A) and (B)," copyrighted in 1971 by President and Fellows of Harvard College and distributed by Intercollegiate Case Clearing House.

30. *WSJ*, 2 March 1972, p. 32; *WSJ*, 6 March 1972, p. 3; *BW*, 11 March 1972, p. 34.

31. *WSJ*, 28 April 1972, p. 10.

32. *WSJ*, 22 June, 1972, p. 22; *WSJ*, 20 June, 1972, p. 32; *WSJ*, 5 June 1972, p. 14.

33. *WSJ*, 14 July 1972, p. 8.

34. *NYT*, 30 July 1972, p. F3.

35. *WSJ*, 19 October 1972, p. 7; Richard Immel, *WSJ*, 1 May 1973, p. 48; *BW*, 10 February 1973, p. 24; Dennis B. Fitzpatrick, "Boise Cascade; Reacquisition of Common Stock as an Internal Investment Decision," Case no. 9-275-685 (1975), distributed by Intercollegiate Case Clearing House; *WST*, 15 May 1972, p. 28394.

36. Fitzpatrick, "Reacquisition," p. 6.

37. Immel, *WSJ*, 1 May 1973, p. 48; Daryl Lembke, *LAT*, July 1973, p. VI-1; *WSJ*, 5 November 1973, p. 20.

38. Immel, *WSJ*, 1 May 1973, p. 48; Fitzpatrick, "Reacquisition," p. 11; *WSJ*, 19 December 1973, p. 19; Harold D. Mayhew, *WST*, 10 November 1973, p. 35046; *WST*, 5 February 1973, pp. 31742-31748. Hansberger remained the largest single Boise stockholder owning 280,000 shares.

39. *WSJ*, 14 March 1973, p. 6; Boise Cascade, *Securities and Exchange Commission: 10-K Report*, December 1973, p. 15; *WSJ*, 7 December 1973, p. 4.

40. *BW*, 1 June 1974, p. 73; *WST*, 15 November 1976, p. 45337; *BW*, 1 June 1974, p. 72; Boise Cascade, *Annual Report: 1973*, p. 2.

41. *BW*, 19 February 1979, pp. 54-55; *BW*, 28 July 1980, p. 102; Pamela G. Hollie, *NYT*, 22 November 1979, p. D1.

42. For examples of the public relations campaign material see *WSJ*, 14 February 1974, p. 18; *BW*, 1 June 1974, p. 72; *Forbes*, 15 May 1975, pp. 80-81; *WST*, 15 November 1976, p. 45336; *Financial World*, 15 March 1977, p. 39; and *Seattle Times (ST)*, 6 December 1978. See Boise Cascade, *Boise Cascade Quarterly (BCQ)* (November 1974):17; idem, *BCQ* (May 1976):25 for examples of informational ads.

43. Boschken, *Mismarketing*, p. 229; *Forbes*, 15 May 1975, p. 81; Boise Cascade, *Report of the Annual Meeting*, 21 April 1981, p. 3; *BW*, 2 June 1980, pp. 98-99.

44. Boise Cascade, *BCQ* (November 1975):8; *WST*, 1 April 1974, p. 36466.

45. Boise Cascade, *BCQ* (November 1978):14. For examples of appropriations-related testimony, see U.S., Congress, Senate, *Department of the*

Interior and Related Agencies Appropriations: FY 1976, pt. 4, 94th Cong., 1st sess., 16–18 April 1975, pp. 1939–1944; U.S., Congress, House, *Implementation of Resources Planning Act of 1974: Oversight Hearings,* 95th Cong., 1st sess., 26 July 1977, pp. 484–505.

46. *BW,* 19 February 1979, p. 55; Boise Cascade, *Annual Report: 1975,* p. 24.

47. Boise Cascade, *BCQ* (August 1978):14; *WSJ,* 14 September 1977, p. 16; *ST,* 6 December 1978.

47. *NYT,* 14 December 1976, p. 3; *WSJ,* 17 February 1978, p. 26; *WSJ,* 14 September 1977, p. 16.

49. *WSJ,* 15 March 1977, p. 2; *WSJ,* 23 March 1977, p. 31; *WSJ,* 24 January 1978, p. 19; *WSJ,* 26 January 1978, p. 3; Jean A. Briggs, *Forbes,* 25 June 1979, pp. 33–36; *WSJ,* 22 March 1977, p. 2; Council on Economic Priorities, "Corporate Payoffs: The Tally So Far," *Business and Society Review* (Fall 1976):55.

50. Council of Economic Advisers, *The Economic Report of the President, Gross National Product in 1972 Dollars, 1929–1980,* no. B-2 (Washington, D.C.: Government Printing Office, January 1981), p. 235.

51. Daryl Lembke, *LAT,* 8 July 1973, p. VI-1; Richard Immel, *WSJ,* 29 December 1971, p. 20.

52. Boise Cascade, *Annual Report: 1980,* p. 30; *BW,* 6 July 1981, p. 74; *BW,* 29 June 1981, pp. 116–117.

53. Boise Cascade, *Report of the Annual Meeting, 21 April 1981, p. 9; BW,* 2 June 1980, p. 98; Boise Cascade, *Annual Report: 1980,* p. 57.

54. Lembke, *LAT,* 8 July 1973, pp. 1, 3.

55. Ibid. For representative statements of Boise's stance on the Wilderness System issue, see Boise Cascade, *BCQ* (August 1973):16; (February 1974):25; (November 1975):13; (May 1976):17–20; (November 1976):11; (August 1977):15; (November 1978):15.

56. For descriptions of Boise's lobbying efforts, see Boise Cascade, *BCQ* (February 1975):13; (November 1975):13; (May 1976):23; (August 1976):11. In addition, see Max Silva, "Lawmakers and Lobbyists," *BCQ* (November 1975):6–8; Alice Dieter, "Doing Something About Government," *BCQ* (May 1976):6–8; Thomas P. Holley, "A View of the 95th Congress," *BCQ* (August 1977):7–8.

6

The Unrelated-Product Firm: Avco Corporation

This chapter describes the management strategy and corporate operations of an unrelated-product firm, the Avco Corporation, during the 1967–1980 period. The case clearly indicates that conglomerate or highly diversified firms have no necessary immunity to the contraction process, despite access to international markets and financial resources. On the basis of consolidated revenues, Avco was ranked as the eighty-fourth largest U.S. industrial in 1967. As a measure of relative decline, Avco had fallen in rank to the nation's 305th largest industrial by 1976. Avco's total employment level dropped from 50,000 to 23,000 during the same period. Avco was no longer considered an industrial firm after 1976, as more than 50 percent of consolidated revenues were generated by nonindustrial operations.[1]

The Delaware Holding Company

Avco was incorporated in Delaware in 1929 to serve as a holding company for American Airways (now American Airlines) and several aviation equipment firms. Fifteen years later, Avco controlled American Airlines, Pan American Airways, Lycoming Manufacturing, New York Shipbuilding, Consolidated Vultee (now the Convair division of General Dynamics), Crosley (electronics, broadcasting, and refrigerators), and New Idea (farm equipment) along with several smaller manufacturing firms. This portfolio of seemingly unrelated businesses resulted from an attempt to garner as many war-related manufacturing contracts as possible. After World War II, government antitrust action was threatened. In response, Avco divested Consolidated Vultee as well as interests in both airlines. Subsequent to divestiture, Avco remained a highly diversified producer of refrigerators, freezers, television and radio sets, kitchen ranges and sinks, radar and fire control systems, aircraft engines, boilers, buses, and farm equipment. The firm also owned and operated several broadcasting companies.

During the early 1950s, Avco acquired the Bendix Corporation. Thereafter the firm suffered such losses that it withdrew from the home appliance business altogether, leaving electronics, and aircraft engines and parts as major business segments. Gradually the firm withdrew from all other consumer product markets with the exception of farm equipment. Subsequent growth strategy was heavily dependent on internal investment in research facilities oriented toward military and space technologies. By 1959 Avco's largest business was contract research for advanced materials, electronics, and missile reentry projects. Ahead of the times, Avco developed the reputation of being a high-technology, science-based conglomerate. The firm's well-financed research groups turned out more ideas and gained more patents than could be utilized by the firm. Consequently, management adopted the policy of selling or licensing new technologies to competitors.[2]

Victor Emanuel, an original Wall Street dealster, was Avco's chief executive during the 1940s and 1950s. He took the firm from a civilian company in the thirties, to a defense company in the forties, and back to a civilian company during the fifties. According to insiders, Emanuel's volatile personality led him to hire and fire important managers almost monthly. Despite Emanuel's financial machinations, his hands-on management style, and his considerable foresight, he was unable to produce steady profits for the firm. Even after Avco became one of the nation's foremost manufacturers of missile nose cones and helicopter engines, management could not dispel the firm's unsteady and uncertain reputation, particularly on Wall Street.[3]

The Acquisitive Conglomerate: 1967–1969

Emanuel's successors, Kendrick Wilson, Jr. (formerly with Lehman Brothers) and James R. Kerr (a former Air Force colonel) set about building a more solid company. From 1960 through 1964, Avco's top management team made few acquisitions and rarely spoke to security analysts. They avoided debt financing and carefully nurtured their businesses in order to build up a strong group of managers to head Avco's divisions. Both men kept themselves busy for four years essentially getting Emanuel's conglomerate in order. At the time it seemed highly improbable that they would repeat Emanuel's pattern of loss of control in the face of financial overextension.

In 1964, Wilson and Kerr began to consider diversification outside of the current product-market scope of the firm. Their goal was to offset the vulnerability experienced by major defense and aerospace contractors dependent on government contracts. Their first diversification acquisition was Delta Acceptance Corporation, a finance company. Next came Bay State Abrasives in 1965. During the late 1960s, Avco became known as an "acquisitive conglomerate" as management moved through acquisition into the operation of life insurance, credit card, land development, motion picture, and specialty steel firms.

High Finance

In February of 1967, the Paul Revere Corporation, a holding company with insurance and finance interests, acquired a 32 percent interest in Avco through a tender offer of $33.00 per share for Avco stock that listed on the New York Stock Exchange at $31.50. The tender offer was unopposed by Avco management. Nine million shares were tendered. One month later, Avco announced merger negotiations with Paul Revere. Avco was designated the surviving corporation. But, the merger got off to a rocky beginning. Former Avco shareholders who had sold their shares to Paul Revere for $33.00 per share appeared at the annual shareholder's meeting in April. At the time, Avco's stock was listed at $42.75 per share. Former shareholders bitterly complained that management had failed to give them adequate information to judge the value of the Paul Revere offer. The annual report had not been mailed until after the closing date for the tender offer. The angry shareholders maintained that had they known about the impending merger with Paul Revere, they would not have tendered their shares. Securities and Exchange Commission records indicated that none of Avco's corporate officers had tendered their shares. Given that information, dissident shareholders claimed that corporate officers had illegally utilized inside information to their own advantage.

When the Avco–Paul Revere merger was finally completed on 24 April 1967, Avco stock listed at $43.50. Disgruntled shareholders brought suit against Avco's management alleging failure to disclose material factors in connection with the tender offer and illegal use of inside information. In addition they complained that the exchange ratio arranged between Paul Revere and Avco in the merger was unfair to Avco shareholders. Out-of-court settlements were eventually negotiated. The merger had such a positive effect on stock values that the New York Stock Exchange acted to curb speculation in Avco shares during December by invoking the 100 percent requirement (no credit purchases). At year-end 1967, Avco common shares had more than doubled their February value.[4]

The man responsible for the Avco–Paul Revere merger was John R. Gosnell, an investment analyst who managed Paul Revere's investment portfolio on behalf of the Harrington family. Harrington family members together owned a controlling interest in Paul Revere. Six Paul Revere directors joined Avco's board, bringing the total number of board members to twenty-two. As a result of the merger, Gosnell's employers ended up with nearly half of the total Avco stock. Since Avco was acquiring a firm that already owned a considerable number of Avco shares, the merger had the effect of shrinking capitalization. Management further shrank capitalization by permitting shareholders to swap half their common shares for convertible preferred shares that offered a higher dividend. In one deal, Avco's common capitalization shrank while Paul Revere assets provided not only cash but a broader, more powerful borrowing base. Gosnell was lauded in the business press for having "pulled off one of the most beautiful pieces of high finance in years." He was rewarded with the chair of Avco's finance committee, where it was expected he would provide "a tremendous help in the area of future acquisitions." Given Avco's new financial structure, Kerr announced plans to acquire an investment company, additional insurance and finance companies, and to "get into industrial electronics and chemicals."[5]

Carte Blanche

During 1968, Avco's sales revenue (constant dollars) increased 15 percent over the 1967 level. In the spring, Kerr announced that Avco was seeking entrance into the "leisure-time field." Avco tried but failed to negotiate the purchase of Twentieth Century-Fox Film Corporation. Instead, Avco acquired Carte Blanche Corporation from First National City Bank of New York for $16 million cash. Kerr announced that Avco would be establishing both franchises and direct subsidiaries of Carte Blanche overseas. He anticipated no major management problems given Avco's prior overseas financial experience. Later in the year Avco acquired Embassy Pictures ($40 million cash) and Huntington Savings and Loan ($22 million). The Huntington purchase brought Avco $120 million in assets. During 1969, Avco acquired the United Bank of Arizona for $12 million; Rancho Bernardo, Inc., a land development company with holdings twenty miles north of San Diego, for $16.4 million; Laguna Niguel, another California land development company, for $10.5 million; and a 92 percent interest in Seaboard Finance Corporation for $171.7 million to complement Avco-Delta, acquired in 1964. Rancho Bernardo and Laguna Niguel became Avco Community Developers; Avco-Delta and Seaboard Finance became Avco Financial Services.[6]

At a time when other conglomerates were receiving critical scrutiny on Wall Street, Avco was cited as one of the few well-managed conglomerates in the country. Investment analysts recommended Avco shares for "good capital gains potential over the near and long term" and lauded Avco for its "effective implementation of the multi-industry approach." Wilson and Kerr restructured the firm into four basic divisions: the government products and services group, the commercial and industrial products group, the financial services group, and the insurance group.[7]

Military Contracts

In terms of Avco's dependence on defense and aerospace contracts, President Kerr predicted at the 1968 annual shareholders' meeting that most of

Avco's military-related operations would become more profitable when hostilities ceased in Southeast Asia. He anticipated continued sales to the armed services plus commercial applications for the Avco gas turbine engine being held in abeyance because of military priority. He also anticipated that domestic space programs would absorb the government funding slack that would result from peace in Vietnam. Regarding Avco's aerospace contracts, the Vietnam-imposed squeeze on the space budget coupled with a sharp drop in ICBM spending and an upsurge in outlays for conventional military weapons again focused attention on the aircraft sector of the aerospace industry. A transition from space projects to the construction of the big, new commercial jets, such as Boeing's 747 and Lockheed's L-1011, was taking place in the aerospace industry. Avco participated in this transition as a major subcontractor for the L-1011. Financial analysts argued that aerospace stocks, depressed by the Paris peace talks and uncertain profit prospects, were still considered to be growth issues and should rebound sharply with production of the new commercial airplanes. In constant dollars, the year-end price close for Avco common shares was $58.86, down from $82.26 in 1967.[8]

In spite of the new commercial aircraft contracts, Avco managed only a 2.9 percent increase in sales revenue (constant dollars) during 1969. While the firm remained the nation's twelfth largest defense contractor, government contracts produced only 44 percent of sales and 15 percent of earnings in 1969 compared to 75 percent of sales and 60 percent of earnings earlier in the decade. Kerr announced that Avco would continue to "trend away" from heavy dependence on defense sales and high-labor content businesses. He expected to see further expansion in the entertainment, financial services, and land development areas.[9]

Money Troubles

Kerr attributed Avco's sluggish growth during 1969 to reduced government business. But that was not the whole story. Avco had moved far enough into the financing business to become a victim of soaring interest rates. Following their long-term diversification strategy, Wilson and Kerr had moved into financial operations as rapidly as possible. But, according to Kerr, "they were all money eaters and we got in just as rates went up and money got tight."[10]

In addition to the dollar squeeze, Kerr noted that the investment portfolios of Avco's financial and insurance operations were negatively influenced by the general stock market decline. Kerr remained optimistic, however, in his belief that consumer finance operations were "recession-proof." He noted that 50 percent of Avco's assets and about 40 percent of its earnings were coming from operations based in California, compared with almost none five years earlier. Kerr envisioned California as the next major U.S. money market. He indicated that Avco would be moving aggressively into land development and housing in California.[11]

Several articles about Avco appeared in the business press in response to falling stock prices in the aerospace industry. Analysts continued to maintain that the market was undervaluing Avco's strength, but common shares fell to $26.52 (constant dollars) at year-end 1969. Kerr blamed the decline on the anticonglomerate climate in Washington, D.C. In December 1969, Kerr was quietly designated president and chief financial officer by Avco's board of directors. Wilson, the financial man, gave up the chief executive spot to become chairman of the board. Wilson was questioned about his continuing role at Avco. He explained that after the Korean War and the space program, he and Kerr had determined that they should shift the company to lessen its dependence on government contracts. He felt that they had successfully followed that strategy to the point that Avco's growth potential had become identified with investments in financial services, land development, civilian aircraft, and the entertainment industry (radio, television, and motion pictures). He maintained that Avco would rely on internal growth rather than acquisition as the firm progressed through the coming period of digestion and consolidation. Wilson emphasized the point that Avco's central management group was first-rate, a fact not reflected by declining stock values. Though authority was necessarily decentralized throughout the firm's far flung operations, Wilson claimed that Avco did not suffer from the management problems generally associated with a conglomerate. Wilson maintained that Avco's managers were experienced and that most control problems were being successfully addressed through the corporate headquarters staff, which had effectively centralized financial controls, budgetary controls, legal activities, labor relations, and overall policy and planning.[12]

The Crisis: 1970–1975

In constant dollars, Avco's sales revenue was 7.2 percent less in 1978 than twelve years earlier in 1967. The number of Avco employees had been cut in half. Year-end stock prices declined from a high of $82.26 to a low of $1.98. Between 1973 and 1974, the firm wrote off $45 million in losses. Consolidated operating statistics for the 1967–1978 period are shown in table 6–1.

Leverage

During 1970, sales revenue declined 11.2 percent in constant dollars. Avco suffered an $8.2 million (constant dollars) operating loss in its commercial

Table 6-1
Avco Corporation's Consolidated Operating Statistics, 1967–1978 in Constant Dollars

Year	Sales and Operating Revenues ($ million)	Percentage Change over Previous Year's Sales	Fortune "500" Ranking	Number of Employees	Common Stock Year-end Price-Close ($)	Earnings per Share Fully Diluted ($)	Net Income ($ million)
1967	1,223.552	—	84	50,000	82.26	n/a[c]	67.793
1968	1,410.516	15.3	78	55,000	58.86	3.43	69.484
1969	1,451.237	2.9	129	55,000	26.52	2.64	59.684
1970	1,288.625	(11.2)[a]	159	50,000	13.57	.44	23.261
1971	1,163.183	(9.7)	184	40,000	16.66	1.78	46.576
1972	1,077.060	(7.4)	226	30,000	15.40	1.91	39.765
1973	1,101.116	2.2	239	30,000	5.86	(2.88)	(21.365)
1974	1,031.945	(6.3)	283	27,000	1.98	(3.29)	(23.692)
1975	976.551	(5.4)	285	23,000	3.54	1.83	39.499
1976	984.505	.8	305	23,000	9.06	2.97	68.195
1977	1,066.889	8.4	b	24,000	12.17	3.49	82.510
1978	1,135.884	6.5	b	25,000	17.42	3.32	80.681

Table 6-1 continued

Year	Long-term Consolidated Debt ($ million)	Interest and Debt Expense ($ million)	Common Dividends ($ million)	Research and Development Expense ($ million)	Capital Expenditures ($ million)	Current Assets ($ million)
1967	n/a	n/a	16.831	n/p[d]	n/a	n/a
1968	n/a	n/a	15.102	n/p	n/a	n/a
1969	1,174.470	85.287	15.789	n/p	58.473	2,875.017
1970	1,454.859	111.071	7.533	n/p	25.598	2,964.712
1971	1,467.876	93.633	none	n/p	17.921	3,770.072
1972	1,636.480	90.473	none	9.150	9.935	3,886.084
1973	1,775.451	113.892	none	9.621	7.865	3,281.200
1974	1,584.724	184.854	none	12.999	11.751	3,089.171
1975	1,308.009	149.308	none	9.472	9.123	3,207.139
1976	1,620.369	132.127	none	9.144	17.615	3,159.053
1977	1,691.189	134.992	none	9.494	19.392	2,910.461
1978	1,736.521	147.704	9.181	n/a	32.455	3,047.030

Source: Compustat.

Note: GNP implicit price deflators were used to convert current dollars to constant 1972 dollars.

[a]Figures in parentheses are negative.

[b]Less than 50 percent of sales revenue derived from manufacturing and thus deleted from *Fortune* listing.

[c]n/a = consolidated data not available.

[d]n/p = data not made public by the firm.

and government aircraft operations. It was offset by earnings in the finance and insurance divisions, but consolidated earnings per common share dropped to $.44. The annual report attributed the loss "in large measure to the generally depressed business climate." Kerr again blamed substantially increased interest rates and reduced procurement by the government, along with the "soft economy," for Avco's poor performance. In order to mitigate the effect of the foregoing factors, Avco's consumer finance operations were redirected to increase the proportion of higher-yielding direct consumer loans. Capital outlays were significantly curtailed, and Kerr intensified Avco's ongoing programs aimed at reducing all controllable expenses. In addition, Kerr announced that he would be divesting business lines that were not compatible with his long-term strategy of moving into "recession-free" service activities and away from cyclical, labor-intensive businesses. In May, dividend payments on common shares were suspended. Subsequently, Kerr announced a plan to substitute additional stock certificates for cash payments to shareholders. He believed that this new policy would be "in the best interests of the stockholders in the present economic environment with extremely high money costs." He also mentioned that the firm's cash requirements were not expected to peak until fiscal 1971.[13]

By August, Kerr was ready to admit to "some sluggishness" in home building, movie making, and life insurance in addition to a large number of delinquent accounts in the Carte Blanche credit card operation, one of the service businesses previously thought to be recession-proof. In fact, the major problem for the highly leveraged firm, one not fully anticipated by management, was higher interest rates. In August of 1970, Avco was carrying approximately $2 billion in debt split equally between long- and short-term instruments. That figure included not only debt resulting from the acquisition program but also reflected the cash needs of recently acquired firms, particularly consumer finance operations. Avco was then ranked as the thirty-ninth most leveraged firm among the *Fortune* "500" industrials.[14]

Kerr announced in August 1970 that Avco would seek to divest its Bay State Abrasives, New Idea Farm Equipment, and Thompson Steel divisions. In addition, the corporation's Lockheed JetStar was put up for sale. Kerr also cut back the government products work force by 13 percent, the commercial and industrial products work force by 21 percent, and the consumer finance operations by 10 percent. He ordered a study of Avco's computer network in the hope of increasing efficiency and establishing more stringent cost controls. The acquisition program had resulted in the need to interface fifteen different computer systems. In the scramble to create new commercial work, the former Avco Ordinance Division was renamed the Precision Products Division and began to manufacture Avco's cartridge color television system for home use. Avco Electronics Division's Tulsa plant began manufacturing motor homes and travel trailers. Avco Systems Division began building sectional housing after aerospace production work ran out. And, Avco Aerostructures began manufacturing modular hospital units.[15]

By September, outside observers were divided in their predictions of Avco's ability to avoid the disaster brought on by the ill-timed use of leverage. Against stockholders' equity of around $420 million, the parent company alone was carrying a debt load of $680 million. Its recently deconsolidated finance subsidiaries (a move made to help keep the parent company solvent) were even more highly leveraged: $1.1 billion debt against $220 million equity. Even worse, Avco and its finance subsidiaries owed over $600 million on commercial paper, which was coming due at an alarming rate. New Avco commercial paper was unsalable. Wilson and Kerr were maneuvered into this corner because common stock values had been so depressed during the early days of the acquisition program. Consequently, they had relied heavily on borrowing for funding expansion. Long-term debt soared from $270 million in 1966 to approximately $965 million in 1969. Wilson and Kerr had gambled on expansion and lost as the cost of money rose even faster than the cost of materials or labor. Kerr acknowledged that they had erred far more on the assumption of the availability of credit. Although they predicted that the economy was headed downward, they incorrectly assumed that interest rates would also decline. Kerr managed to get a group of eighteen banks and insurance companies to recast Avco's short-term debt with an $890 million line of credit and thus was able to buy some valuable time and breathing space. In return, Avco's creditors demanded control over future financial decisions—the price of rescue by the moneylenders. By the end of the year, it appeared that Avco would survive the debt problems, but common stock listed on the New York Stock Exchange at under $9.00 per share ($13.57 in constant dollars) and creditors were demanding further divestiture of assets to reduce outstanding debt.[16]

Cutbacks

During 1971, sales revenues in constant dollars declined another 9.7 percent. The annual report attributed improved performance (that is, no operating loss) to increased earnings from financial services units and increased sales from land development, recreational, and commercial operations. Kerr was able to strengthen Avco's financial position by improving cash flow from operations, decreasing somewhat the need for credit. Because of losses, management discontinued the operation of four television stations and sold a $6.7 million portfolio of financial receivables for $4 million. When the Congress rescued Lockheed and its L-1011 jetliner by guaranteeing $250 million in new bank loans, it also rescued Avco, which had $100 million tied up in plant and inventory for the project (the production of 350 wing sets for Lockheed's giant aircraft). Kerr forced two additional Avco subsidiaries, Cartridge Television, Inc., and Avco Community Developers, to become self-sufficient borrowing entities by refinancing their debt to the parent company through the sale of shares to the public. He also closed a Lycoming Division plant (gas turbine engines for helicopters) in Charleston, South Carolina as the result of decreased sales volume and stopped production at Avco Embassy Pictures. But, Carte Blanche, after fifteen months of losses, was finally able to break even. Financial analysts recommended Avco shares for "high risk accounts" and "possible longer-term appreciation." Common stock values climbed to $16.66 (constant dollars).[17]

Sales revenue declined another 7.4 percent (constant dollars) during 1972 as general economic conditions improved. A further reduction in government business was offset by increased contributions to consolidated earnings from financial services operations. But high debt levels and heavy cash demands continued to preclude the resumption of cash dividends on common stock. Kerr outlined the three major elements of Avco's recovery strategy for stockholders in the annual report:

1. the continued emphasis on the expansion of profitable commercial operations: finance, insurance, broadcasting, reciprocating engine, and laser technology;
2. the consolidation of both production facilities and business units and divestiture of unprofitable units; and
3. the reduction of long- and short-term indebtedness.

He outlined management's general goals as the realization of average annual net earnings of at least 10 percent of stockholders' equity, and average growth in such net earnings of 10 percent or more per year. But, in spite of Kerr's well-publicized recovery plans, common shares traded at $15.40 at year-end (constant dollars).[18]

During 1973, sales revenue in constant dollars increased 2.2 percent over the 1972 level. Avco, however, experienced a $21.4 million (constant dollars) consolidated net loss. Contributing to the 1973 results was a $45.4 million (constant dollars) write-off of investments and costs applicable to Cartridge Television, in which Avco owned a 32 percent interest. Cartridge Television had previously petitioned for arrangement with its creditors under chapter 11 of the Bankruptcy Act. The lowering of inventory values of some of Avco's motion pictures, provisions for anticipated costs of plant closings, losses in the land development subsidiary, and higher interest rates also contributed to the consolidated loss. Four plants were closed during the year: a government ordinance plant in Richmond, Indiana, which had been manufacturing products for Cartridge Television; an electronics plant in Evendale, Ohio; a modular-housing plant in Suncook, New Hampshire; and a printing plant in Boston (a special project, partially funded by the Department of Labor, designed to provide inner-city residents with job experience and management training).[19]

Financial services contributed 47 percent of Avco's consolidated sales revenue, the recreation and land development division contributed 13 percent, and commercial products and research contributed 28 percent during 1973. Government products and research comprised only 12 percent of consolidated sales revenue, a significant reduction. In spite of that figure, when Northrop Corporation lost out to Fairchild in the bidding for an Air Force contract to develop and produce fighter planes, Avco, slated to build engines for the losing Northrop plane, charged that political pressure had unduly influenced the contract award. Avco insisted on a congressional investigation complaining that it stood to lose 4,000 jobs and more than $400 million at its Stratford, Connecticut plant. Avco issued no dividends on common shares during 1973, shares that had dropped in value to $5.86 (constant dollars) by year-end.[20]

Reorganization and Retrenchment

Very quietly, Chairman Wilson who, along with John Gosnell, had been the architect of Avco's disastrous diversification strategy, was demoted to the largely ceremonial title of vice-chairman of the board. He took a substantial cut in pay. Gosnell stepped out of active management altogether. Kerr held on and took full charge of the firm as chief executive officer and chairman of the board. But he too agreed to a reduced salary and benefit package. George L. Hogeman, previously president of the Paul Revere Life Insurance Company, was elected president and chief operating officer of the parent firm. Hogeman took this position essentially to represent and protect the Harrington family investment, which was dwindling daily as stock values plummeted. Three additional Harrington-related directors were appointed to the reconstituted eighteen-man board, giving the Harrington interests effective control.[21]

Nineteen seventy-four proved to be another difficult year for Avco and its management. Consolidated sales revenue declined another 4.2 percent (constant dollars) and the firm registered its second earnings loss in as many years: approximately $23.7 million in constant dollars. During the year, management disposed of its specialty steel division and one of its savings and loan subsidiaries for cash and notes. Radio and television stations in Washington, D.C., and San Antonio, Texas also were sold. The firm wrote off approximately $16 million of Carte Blanche intangible assets in a recapitalization plan designed to strengthen the unit's financial position. In October, cash dividends on preferred stock were deferred until the firm's cash position could be substantially improved. Common share dividends were again deferred and common share prices slipped to $1.98 per share (constant dollars).[22]

In addition, Avco was named in a class action suit brought by the Independent Investors Protective League and seventeen individuals charging fraud. The suit held that the prospectus for the public sale of stock in Cartridge Television, undertaken during 1971, contained misleading and untruthful statements. The suit further claimed that Hornblower and Weeks-Hemphill, Noyes, Inc., touted the stock and agreed to dispose of unwanted shares for Avco's management and majority stockholders. The suit sought $20 million in damages.[23]

Kerr described Avco's problems from management's point of view in the annual report to shareholders. He explained that extremely tight money-market conditions and high interest rates were the principal factors adversely affecting Avco's performance. At year-end 1974, Avco and its subsidiaries had close to a billion dollars of outstanding debt on which the interest varied with current market rates. Consequently, higher interest rates had a delayed but significant effect on earnings and cash flow. Interest paid by Avco on parent-company debt rose 16.5 percent during 1974. At Avco Financial Services, interest expense as a percent of gross income rose to 31.2 percent from 26.4 percent a year earlier. In addition, high money-market yields led to a sustained outflow of deposits from savings and loan institutions affecting their performance and draining the supply of funds traditionally earmarked for home mortgages. The limited availability of mortgage money had an adverse impact on the housing market throughout the country and on Avco Community Development in particular. Sales of residential and industrial property declined by one-third, net losses doubled, and financing requirements (for unsold properties) rose sharply.[24]

Higher interest rates and the developing recession had a similar but less severe impact on Carte Blanche. The combined effects of increased costs, recession, and the high costs of money also led to the cancellation of the HS-146 airliner program by Hawker-Siddeley Aviation, Ltd. Avco Lycoming-Stratford had previously agreed to produce the turbofan engines required for the airliner. In response to all of this bad news, Kerr warned that Avco would have to continue to divest assets—despite his failure to obtain full market value during the recession.[25]

This unusually candid explanation of Avco's financial troubles may well have been a rebuttal to a critical article that appeared in the business press during April of 1974. *Forbes* editors complained that Avco's officers flatly refused to discuss any of the firm's problems with the press. They criticized that in less than six years, Avco had "deteriorated from a highly promising conglomerate into a series of probably avoidable disasters." They blamed management for investing in all of the "fad" businesses of the 1960s: land development, leisure activities, and consumer financial services. They took Wilson and Kerr to task for exposing shareholders to excessive risk as they moved into movie production, credit cards, land development, and the television cassette and record businesses. They claimed that Avco lacked the appropriate management expertise for these new businesses, which were worlds removed from aerospace and farm machinery. They charged that the biggest mistake made by Avco managers was in building too large a stake in the consumer lending and savings and loan businesses, which left the firm's total earnings far too interest-rate sensitive.[26]

Although sales revenues declined another 5.4 percent in constant dollars during 1975, Kerr was able to avoid another consolidated loss. According to the annual report, consumer finance subsidiaries maintained earnings despite the effect of the recession on collections. The commercial products and research divisions turned in a strong performance. Earnings continued to decline, however, in Avco's insurance subsidiaries because of increased accident and health claims. Losses were posted by the motion picture subsidiary and the recreation and land development group, which was still suffering from a severe housing slump.

Avco was able to reduce the parent company debt by $106 million in part through the sale of three radio stations, two television stations, and Avco Records Corporation for $33.7 million in cash. Sale of Avco Savings and Loan Association was also completed and netted approximately $20.1 million in cash and a $1 million note. After the fiscal year ended, management completed the sale of three more television stations for $29 million in cash. Dividends were withheld on both common and preferred shares. On a more positive note, accumulated tax credits from previous years' losses reduced Avco's federal tax rate from the statutory 48 percent to annual rates ranging from 33 to 33.9 percent between 1975 and 1980.[27]

Stabilization: 1976–1980

Nineteen seventy-six was a year of stabilization for Avco, although sales revenue increased less than 1 percent in constant dollars. Preferred dividends were resumed but arrearages remained unpaid. Losses at Avco Community Development were cut in half, and Avco Financial Services, the Paul Revere companies, and the Lycoming divisions were profitable. Avco was able to refinance the parent company debt. The firm picked up three major contracts with long-term significance: XM-1 battle tank engines for

NATO, a Rockwell International contract for wing sets for B-1 bombers (a fleet of 244), and reentry systems for the ICBM missile program. Because Avco was unable to unload either Avco Embassy Pictures or Carte Blanche, management completed the sale of Avco Broadcasting, one of its more profitable businesses.[28]

In an interview in November of 1976, Kerr explained that Avco still had "two turkeys left." One was Avco Community Development (ACD) where Kerr, stuck with a huge inventory of finished houses, was forced to cut prices and sell before taxes and interest costs put the entire operation under. In addition, after Avco had invested $7.5 million in its Laguna Niguel community in Orange County, the California Coastal Zone Conservation Act (enacted in 1972) restricted further development. ACD lost its argument to be allowed to continue development of the land before the California Supreme Court. Kerr stated his willingness to take the case to the U.S. Supreme Court if necessary. The remaining problem, according to Kerr, was Avco Embassy Pictures. Production had stopped entirely and the subsidiary was attempting to syndicate its film library in order to decrease its cash drain on the parent firm. By late 1976, Kerr was identifying Avco's strength and growth potential with financial services, farm equipment, and helicopter engines.[29]

The Mop-up Campaign

Sales revenue and earnings began to improve during the 1977–1978 period. Common share dividends were resumed for the first time since suspension in mid-1970. Preferred stock arrearages were eliminated. Common shares were valued at $17.42 (constant dollars) at year-end 1978, an appreciable increase from the 1974 low of $1.98, but still a 79 percent decline from the 1967 value.

Management was finally able to sell Carte Blanche back to Citicorp for a price "roughly the same as the price it had been carried on the books." Even ACD was back in the black with the recovery of the California housing market and the sale of $17 million of Rancho Bernardo land, which significantly reduced both debt and carrying costs. Kerr was congratulated in the business press for his "mop-up campaign" and for Avco's successful "turnaround." However, Avco's total consolidated debt load remained enormous, totaling nearly $2.5 billion in May of 1978 compared with only $684 million of stockholders' equity.[30]

In the 1978 annual report, Kerr described Avco's principal lines of business as financial services and aerospace. Though he complained that expectations for future growth were tempered by the "great economic uncertainty" of the times, he was encouraged by the "conservative shift in public and political sentiments.'' He predicted that as long as the general economy remained reasonably stable, Avco's two principal lines of business would prosper. The post–World War II baby-boom population would increase the demand for insurance, real estate, and financing. And the steady growth pattern in military and commercial aviation markets would stabilize those markets leaving them "relatively insensitive to changes in the economy." Kerr did not mention the competitive threat of the Europeans and the Japanese who were fostering the development of their own civilian aircraft production with one eye set on eroding the U.S. share of the world market for aircraft.[31]

Turnaround?

Avco generated nearly $2 billion in net revenues during 1979 and then again in 1980 while common stock values averaged $27.00 per share. Avco picked up a major contract for 200 center wing and keel beam sections for Boeing's new 757 medium-range jetliners. Only Avco Embassy Pictures remained in the red. The firm even managed to avoid losses on its Iranian management services and aircraft parts contracts when the Shah's government collapsed because of prepayment requirements for work in progress.[32]

The California Coastal Commission granted approval for Avco to develop 580 oceanfront acres at Laguna Niguel, though the development of the remaining 820 acres in that parcel remained contingent on obtaining further coastal development permits. ACD signed an agreement with Twentieth Century-Fox Film Corporation to study the feasibility of forming a joint venture to develop a resort hotel, an eighteen-hole golf course, and a conference/recreational center on a portion of the Laguna Niguel development. ACD adopted a new policy of improving its commercial and industrial properties for use as income producing facilities rather than simply selling the undeveloped land. In the long-term, this policy was expected to supply ACD with a more predictable cash flow and earnings rate in addition to providing some insulation from the cyclical nature of the land development business. By 1980, ACD owned 15,000 acres in southern California and planned to develop six new communities including 100,000 new residences during the 1980s.[33]

Though Kerr appears to have accomplished a dramatic turnaround, Avco's financial structure remains problematic. Kerr was able to reduce parent company obligations as a percentage of total capitalization between 1974 and 1980. But, while assets exceeded $5.8 billion at year-end 1980, consolidated total indebtedness exceeded $3.3 billion. Kerr was more successful in reviving the Paul Revere investment portfolio, which originally had reflected heavy speculation in new equity issues and common stocks. After the general stock market declines of 1970 and 1974, portfolio earnings had slumped. Kerr's direct supervision of consequent portfolio investment toward the more conservative A-rated bonds, commercial mortgages, and federal government agency obligations resulted in an 11 percent annual increase in portfolio earnings from 1974. Avco's common shares, on the other hand, continued their dismal market showing in large part because of the dilution threat posed by the conversion rights of two huge issues of convertible bonds and convertible preferred stock sold to finance earlier acquisitions. If all issues were converted, Avco's common capitalization would double. This, of course, would improve the balance sheet, but greatly reduce earnings per share. With its common shares undervalued by the market, Avco qualifies as a prime target for takeover as profitable divisions or subsidiaries could readily be sold off by new management in order to reduce debt. Any successful takeover organization would then have full control of Avco's remaining assets—assets obtained at a very modest cost.[34]

In Avco's 1980 annual report, Kerr described Avco's continuing objectives as twofold: first, to expand its profitable business lines and develop new opportunities in keeping with the firm's desire to maintain a balance between service and manufacturing businesses and between private and governmental customers; and second, to create an overall corporate climate that encourages consistent earnings growth for its investors, quality service for its customers, and satisfying career opportunities for its employees. During the year, the finance and insurance group contributed 55 percent to Avco's total revenues and 62 percent to its operating profit. The products and services group contributed 45 percent and 38 percent, respectively. Kerr's announced strategy for the products and services group was to concentrate on special markets where the firm could develop leadership positions and to again emphasize government defense contracting.[35]

During 1980, only 27 percent of Avco's revenues were generated by government defense contracts, although 51 percent of backlog related to such contracts. Kerr anticipated a significant increase in government defense expenditures through 1985. His strategy for the finance and insurance group was to continue to reduce the interest-sensitive short-term portion of debt financing. He worried that inflation might further reduce profits in financial services, land development, farm equipment, and executive aircraft engines as such items are normally purchased with discretionary income. Altogether, Kerr characterized his future strategy as "balanced diversity." Whether or not his turnaround will endure remains highly dependent on his ability to steer Avco through the turbulent economy of the 1980s.[36]

In 1980, Avco business units were composed of the following divisions and subsidiaries:

Finance and Insurance

Financial Services	Avco Financial Services Group, and Cartan Travel Bureau, Inc.
Credit life, disability, and casualty insurance	Avco Financial Insurance Group
Life insurance, annuities and other	The Paul Revere Life Insurance Group
Accident and health insurance	The Paul Revere Life Insurance Group

Products and Services

Transportation structures and engines	Avco Aerostructures Division, Avco Lycoming-Stratford Division, and Avco Lycoming-Williamsport Division
Management services	Avco International Services Division (engineering and marketing consulting services)
Land development	Avco Community Developers, Inc.
Other	Avco Embassy Pictures Corp., Avco New Idea Farm Equipment Division, Avco Medical Products Division (mechanical support systems used in treatment of cardiovascular disease), Avco Electronics Division (commercial electronic equipment, computer-based control systems), Avco Everett Research Laboratory, Inc. (high-technology research and development primarily for defense and energy research), Avco Specialty Materials Division (advanced composite materials for aerospace and sporting goods), and Avco Systems Division (high-technology products and services primarily for Defense Department).

Evaluating Avco's Response Pattern

Although it is difficult to present a coherent picture of an organization as varied and complex as Avco, the firm's experience with contraction indicates the extent to which a slow-growth domestic economy can negatively influence even a highly diversified, multinational conglomerate. The primary interdependent factors that contributed to Avco's contraction episode include:

1. the slowdown in real growth of the domestic economy in conjunction with rising interest rates and a tight money market that resulted in depressed revenues and increased operational costs for Avco's community development and consumer finance operations;
2. fluctuating government expenditures for defense and aerospace projects that resulted in cutbacks in government products and research divisions;
3. the general stock market decline that reduced the value of Avco's insurance portfolio investments;
4. management's overly ambitious diversification program that led not only to some marginal investments (Carte Blanche, Avco Embassy) but also ultimately overstressed Avco's management resources;
5. management's reliance on debt financing (notes and bonds) first for acquisition, and then to forestall creditors;
6. management's belief that certain segments of the domestic economy (consumer finance, the California land market) were recession-proof; and
7. the inability of management to parlay past government-financed research projects into commercially successful products. This failure was at least partly the result of the drain on the firm's capital expenditure and product development budgets caused by debt-leverage strategies.

Internal Rationalization

The Avco story indicates that the multinational conglomerate structure does not necessarily protect corporate resources from the negative impact of a declining national economy. Access to international financial markets, gains on foreign currency exchanges, and the ability of management to assign costs and prices to foreign divisions and subsidiaries in a manner that is most profitable to the firm failed to alleviate Avco's money troubles. Approximately one-fifth of Avco's assets are located outside of the United States: primarily in Canada and Australia, but also in Europe, South America, and the Middle East. During the three-year period from 1978 to 1980, foreign operations (including exports) contributed 39 percent of Avco's consolidated profits and 22 percent of consolidated revenues.[37]

Despite the fact that Avco's corporate management and control system was built specifically to operate a highly diversified group of manufacturing businesses, when management sought expansion through merger with the Paul Revere financial enterprises, that system failed to provide profitability beyond the first year. Consequent forays into savings and loan, credit card, movie making, television cassette, and land development operations proved even more disappointing. Management's diversification strategy, based on a "trending away" from defense sales and high labor-content businesses, did little to increase profitability. Avco's new businesses all succumbed to problems related to a period of economic slowdown with concurrent inflation. As interest rates climbed, Avco suffered from high levels of interest-sensitive short-term debt as well as contracting revenues in the financial and insurance divisions.

Money troubles in 1969 and 1970 led to companywide efficiency and cost-cutting programs: an increased emphasis on high-yield consumer loans; divestiture of business out of line with the service-sector growth strategy ("recession-free"); attempts to tighten financial controls and better integrate management information systems; curtailed expenditures for capital outlays and research and development projects; layoffs; cutbacks in executive compensation programs; and sale of the firm's jet airplane. Management scrambled to create new commercial work by converting manufacturing facilities from defense-related work to the production of television cassettes, travel trailers, sectional housing, and modular hospital units. Efforts were undertaken to obtain contracts with foreign companies to utilize Avco's manufacturing facilities for the production of goods for the U.S. market. (As the relative value of the U.S. dollar declined, this strategy gained appeal for manufacturers based in countries with stronger currencies.) Finally, common stock dividends and eventually preferred dividends were eliminated.[38]

By late 1970, pressure from Avco's creditors and Harrington-family representatives on the board resulted in a major divestiture and financial restructuring plan aimed at improving cash flow and raising the funds needed to cover short-term notes and interest payments on long-term debt (bank loans and bonds). The financial restructuring program separated the financial services and land development businesses into unrestricted subsidiaries. This left the parent company and the unrestricted subsidiaries as separate borrowing entities dependent on different groups of creditors. The future borrowing power of the parent company was then greatly restricted and sources of cash flow for the parent company were reduced to cash generated from the restricted subsidiaries and a share of earnings paid as dividends from the unrestricted subsidiaries.

By 1973 not only had professional management relinquished control of Avco's financial structure to creditors, but the firm's daily operations were overseen by owner representatives. Avco's board of directors was reconstituted with nine of the eighteen members representing Harrington-family interests. Wilson and Gosnell, the architects of Avco's diversification strategy, were forced out of active management. Hogeman was moved from his Paul Revere post to oversee consolidated operations as president and chief operating officer. Kerr, as Avco's new chief executive officer, was directed to undertake an organizational restructuring and consolidation program that would return Avco to financial health and halt the rapidly declining market value of Avco shares. He immediately began the process of switching Paul Revere's insurance-related investment portfolios from common stocks to fixed income securities. By 1978, these represented 94 percent of the total portfolio.

Kerr's retrenchment program necessitated a reformulated corporate strategy of heavy divestiture and efforts to consolidated remaining facilities and business units. To maintain cash flow, Kerr was forced to divest both profitable and unprofitable businesses even though he was unable to obtain full market value for assets. He closed down production facilities, stopped production at Avco Embassy, and sold off broadcasting, recording, steel, land development, savings and loan, and eventually credit card operations. During 1973 and 1974 he wrote off approximately $55 million in losses for Carte Blanche and cartridge television operations. He restructured the firm into two major groups, financial services and aerospace-related products and services. He also began to redevelop Avco's role as a major defense contractor. Avco's government products and research revenues had gone from 75 percent of the total in 1959 to 44 percent in 1969, and then decreased to a mere 12 percent of total revenues by 1973. Kerr succeeded in increasing Avco's government products and research revenues to 27 percent of the consolidated total by 1980, with 51 percent of the firm's record backlog related to U.S. government contracts. Government research and development monies prevented Kerr from having to curtail basic research efforts during the most difficult years of Avco's contraction episode. Avco expended 14 percent of Products and Services Group revenues for research and development activities during 1980—a figure that compares favorably with the aerospace industry average.[39]

Kerr's retrenchment program once again placed Avco in the vanguard of the late 1970s trend for conglomerate firms to move toward a high technology renaissance in operations after years of emphasis on financial performance. ITT and General Electric have recently followed this pattern. Kerr's reformulated growth strategy seeks balanced diversity (between service and manufacturing businesses and between private and governmental customers) and an annual return of at least 10 percent of stockholders' equity whereas previous growth strategies focused on increasing the total size of assets and revenues.[40]

External Rationalization

Irrespective of management's general policy of restricting public scrutiny by avoiding interviews with the business press and limiting information flow, a partial picture of managerial efforts to rationalize the firm's turbulent external environment can be drawn. The influence gained by creditors and major investors during the crisis period severely encroached upon management's discretionary decision-making authority. Court actions brought against Avco's management by small investors (Paul Revere merger and Cartridge Television offerings) no doubt played a role in Avco's plummeting common stock values. Of course, the fact that management exposed shareholders to excessive risk with the diversification-acquisition program, the fact that Avco retained a high stake in interest-sensitive businesses, and the failure of managerial control also had a substantial impact on stock values. After 1976, Kerr tried to reverse the negative public image of Avco's growth and dividend potential by what seems to have been Avco's first systematic public relations effort aimed at the investment community. Nevertheless, management's inability to balance the divergent interests and competing claims of various classes of shareholders and creditors resulted in basic strategy constraints.

The impact of consumer and environmental interest groups on the firm is unclear from the information at hand, but ACD was forced into lengthy delays and costly revisions of plans to develop 1,400 acres of coastal land in southern California. Consumer resistance to ACD housing may well have increased after development projects became the target of environmental concern. In any event, ACD operations failed to pick up even after the general economy recovered from the 1974–1975 recession. The Avco story presents no direct evidence that the activist role assumed by consumers and environmentalists in California during the early 1970s over the land development issue contributed to Avco's decision to withdraw from various land development efforts. But it seems fair to assume that Avco's management would have recognized the external constraints represented by environmentalist pressures and further would have associated some share of ACD losses, either directly or indirectly, to such pressures. With the exception of aerospace contracting, the Avco material does not provide sufficient information to comment on management activities designed to rationalize markets via arrangements with competitors to divide markets or fix prices. Likewise, public information relating to corporate involvement in activities designed to influence state and local regulatory commissions is sparse.

Avco's finance and insurance businesses are state regulated for the most part.

A more complete picture evolves regarding Avco's efforts to influence the federal budgeting process as it relates to the aerospace industry. Kerr testified before Senate hearings in 1971 on behalf of an emergency loan guarantee for Lockheed Aircraft Corporation. He blamed Lockheed's near bankruptcy on general economic conditions and Department of Defense red tape rather than any management error. Kerr publicly demanded an investigation into Department of Defense contracting procedures in 1973 when Avco lost out as a subcontractor to Northrop on an Air Force fighter plane contract. Management actively supported the point of view that the defense budget should be doled out equally among competing aerospace firms unencumbered by the political patronage system that has come to control the granting of defense-related contracts by the Congress. Avco representatives repeatedly testified before Congress regarding the need for an Office of Technological Assessment, the need for higher NASA appropriations, and the increased need for government supported research and development in the aerospace industry where historically federal monies have supported the development of both product and process technology. Government, of course, has also been the primary consumer of related output.[41]

Avco representatives testified on behalf of and lobbied for research and demonstration projects that would utilize Avco-developed technologies, including appropriations for an Office of Coal Research. Avco was seeking further support for the development of its magnetohydrodynamic process initiated under previous government contracts. Management also actively sought a long-range research planning program and the development of a systematic communications network between the Department of Defense and the various aerospace contractors in an attempt to further rationalize the U.S. defense and aerospace industries. Avco supported efforts to relax antitrust constraints against competing U.S. aerospace firms who desired to share technology under joint-venture arrangements. All this lobbying activity was presumably directed at making Avco's external environment and the U.S. aerospace market more predictable, stable, and secure. Not unlike Boise's efforts to stabilize the government-controlled supply of needed raw materials, Avco representatives attempted to stabilize the supply and conditions of government-controlled defense contracts.[42]

In summary, Avco's contraction experience resulted in a financially restructured firm that remains a multinational conglomerate. The new management team has eschewed rapid growth through acquisition and adopted more conservative internal growth strategies. Growth in the Financial Services Group is now primarily dependent on demographic variables, general economic conditions, and continued speculative growth in the California housing market. Growth in the Products and Services Group is primarily dependent on escalating government defense expenditures and a stable market (or contracting environment). Kerr believes that both commercial and military aerospace demand will stabilize and become increasingly insensitive to changes in the general economy.

There is significant evidence that Avco's internal operations are now more closely managed. Although debt-leveraging practices have been curtailed, debt management remains a major problem for Avco, affecting management discretion and flexibility, stock values, and even long-term viability. Management's somewhat belated attempts to influence the investment community and further stabilize the federal contracting process can be interpreted as efforts to reduce the level of risk and uncertainty in Avco's external environment which, for the reasons discussed above, accelerated as revenues contracted during the period under study.

Notes

1. *Fortune,* 15 June 1968, p. 200; *Fortune,* May 1977, p. 378.

2. *Wall Street Journal (WSJ),* 18 February 1976, p. 1.

3. *Forbes,* 1 February 1968, pp. 24–25.

4. *WSJ,* 20 February 1967, p. 8; *Forbes,* 1 February 1968, p. 25; *WSJ,* 14 April 1967, p. 18; *New York Times (NYT),* 14 April 1967, p. 55.

5. *Forbes,* 1 February 1968, pp. 20, 26.

6. *WSJ,* 27 March 1968, p. 10; *WSJ,* 1 April 1968, p. 5; *WSJ,* 9 April 1968, p. 14; *WSJ,* 21 May 1968, p. 10; *WSJ,* 11 December 1968, p. 38; *WSJ,* 23 January 1969, p. 4; *WSJ,* 11 April 1969, p. 12; *WSJ,* 8 August 1969, p. 21; *WSJ,* 14 October 1969, p. 17; *WSJ,* 28 November 1969, p. 2.

7. *Financial World (FW),* 18 September 1968, pp. 11–12; Salah El-Shahawy, *Wall Street Transcript (WST),* 28 October 1968, p. 14746.

8. *WSJ,* 12 April 1968, p. 7; *FW,* 9 October 1968, p. 12.

9. *Fortune,* 1 August 1969, p. 74; *Business Week (BW),* 29 August 1970, p. 78.

10. Robert A. Wright, *NYT,* 12 February 1970, p. 51.

11. Ibid.

12. *WST,* 6 January 1969, p. 15404; *NYT,* 26 June 1969, p. 61; *FW,* 30 July 1969, p. 5; *FW,* 15 October 1969, p. 8; *WSJ,* 11 April 1969, p. 12; *BW,* 29 August 1970, p. 78; *Nation's Business,* April 1970, pp. 62–68.

13. *WSJ,* 12 February 1971, p. 6; Avco, *Annual Report: 1970,* pp. 14, 17, 4; *WSJ,* 27 April 1970, p. 23; Avco, *Annual Report: 1970,* pp. 4–5.

14. *BW,* 29 August 1970, pp. 78–79; *Fortune,* May 1970, p. 222.

15. *BW,* 29 August 1970, p. 82.

16. *Forbes,* 1 September 1970, pp. 17–18.

17. Avco, *Annual Report: 1971,* p. 4; *WSJ,* 31 August 1971, p. 4;

WSJ, 9 November 1971, p. 19; *BW,* 9 October 1971, pp. 40, 42; *WST,* 21 July 1971, p. 24812.

18. Avco, *Annual Report: 1972,* pp. 1–2.

19. Avco, *Annual Report: 1973,* p. 2; Gene Smith, *NYT,* 30 June 1973, p. 43; Avco, *Annual Report: 1973,* pp. 3, 14.

20. Avco, *Annual Report: 1973,* p. 10; *BW,* 27 January 1973, p. 22.

21. *Forbes,* 1 April 1974, pp. 23–24; *Forbes,* 1 November 1976, p. 63.

22. Avco, *Annual Report: 1974,* pp. 10–11; *WSJ,* 23 December 1974, p. 12; *NYT,* 1 October 1974, p. 54; *Forbes,* 1 November 1976, p. 64.

23. *WSJ,* 15 February 1974, p. 24.

24. Avco, *Annual Report: 1974,* pp. 3–4.

25. Ibid.

26. *Forbes,* 1 April 1974, p. 24.

27. Avco, *Annual Report: 1975,* pp. 1–14; idem, *Annual Report: 1976,* p. 31; idem, *Annual Report: 1978,* p. 23; idem, *Annual Report: 1980,* p. 35.

28. Avco, *Annual Report: 1976,* pp. 2–3; *FW,* 1 November 1978, p. 38.

29. *Forbes,* 1 November 1976, p. 64.

30. *WSJ,* 25 September 1978, p. 16; *WSJ,* 22 September 1977, p. 28; *Barron's,* 19 June 1978, pp. 31–33; *FW,* 1 November 1978, pp. 38–39.

31. Avco, *Annual Report: 1978,* p. 2.

32. Avco, *Annual Report: 1980,* pp. 35–36, 49.

33. Paul Gibson, *Forbes,* 2 April 1979, pp. 58, 62; Avco, *Annual Report: 1979,* p. 16; idem, *Annual Report: 1980,* p. 19.

34. Gibson, *Forbes,* pp. 58, 62; Avco, *Annual Report: 1980, pp. 49, 44, 33.*

35. Avco, *Annual Report: 1980,* pp. 1–24.

36. Ibid.

37. Avco, *Annual Report: 1980,* p. 44. Foreign operations data were previously not made public by the firm.

38. Avco, *Annual Report: 1979,* p. 17.

39. Avco, *Annual Report: 1980,* pp. 3, 11.

40. See *BW,* 6 July 1981, p. 63; *BW,* 15 December 1980, pp. 66–80; *BW,* 16 March 1981, pp. 110–118.

41. U.S. Congress, Senate, *Emergency Loan Guarantee Legislation Hearings,* 92d Cong., 1st sess., 14 June 1971, S. Rept. 1981, pp. 323–335; *BW,* 27 January 1973, p. 23; U.S., Congress, House, *Hearings on Military Posture,* Pt. 2. 92d Cong., 2d sess., 29 March 1972, H. Rept. 12604, pp. 10461–10546; U.S., Congress, Senate, *Office of Technological Assessment for the Congress,* 92d Cong., 2d sess., 2 March 1972, S. Rept. 2302 and H. Rept. 10243, pp. 84–86; U.S., Congress, Senate, *NASA Authorization for Fy75,* Pt. 1, 93d Cong., 2d sess., 21 March 1974, pp. 75–87 and Pt. 2, 13 March 1974, pp. 537–570; U.S., Congress, House, *Aeronautical Research and Development,* 92d Cong., 2d sess., 20 January 1972, pp. 938–945.

42. U.S., Congress, House, *Department of Interior and Related Agencies Appropriations for FY75*, Pt. 5, 93d Cong., 2d sess., 8–11 April 1974, pp. 755–770; U.S., Congress, Senate, *FY78 Authorization for Military Procurement, Research, and Development*, Pt. 7, 95th Cong., 1st sess., 16 March 1977, pp. 5139–5251; U.S., Congress, House, *Hearings on Military Posture*, Pt. 2, 92d Cong., 2d sess., 29 March 1972, H. Rept. 12604, pp. 10461–10546; and U.S., Congress, Senate, *Role of Aviation*, 91st Cong., 1st. sess., 2 May 1969, pp. 166–177.

Part III
Context for Policy

Part III summarizes the material presented in the corporate studies in terms of implications for corporate managers and public policymakers. This final chapter suggests the need for a broad public debate of the industrial-policy issue as a means of elevating discussion above ideological rhetoric and developing the public understanding and support necessary for the implementation of comprehensive policies.

7

Lessons from the Studies

The discussion of the growth debate in chapter 1 reveals the extent of the slow-growth problem in the U.S. economy, the concern for the overall competitive strength of U.S. industry, and the lack of consensus surrounding national industrial policy issues. The review of the theoretical literature related to the behavior of the firm in chapter 2 demonstrates pervasive assumptions of growth and a propensity to treat the corporate decision maker faced with contracting revenues as a special case, a short-term phenomenon, unlikely to warrant further investigation. The study of sales-revenue contraction among 600 major U.S. corporations in chapter 3, however, indicates that over 12 percent of those firms experienced six or more consecutive years of contracting revenues during the 1967–1977 period (constant dollars). And, of the total, 10 percent experienced absolute contraction, reporting a smaller revenue base in 1977 than eleven years earlier. Finally, the corporate studies set forth in chapters 4 through 6 describe and analyze the contraction process for three firms with contrasting levels of diversification from dominant-product Zenith Corporation to unrelated-product Avco Corporation. Generalizations drawn from those studies provide several lessons for corporate managers and those involved in the process of shaping national industrial policy alternatives. Caution must be exercised in generalizing from a small number of cases to the larger corporate world, but tentative conclusions can be drawn. The following discussion responds to the issues set forth at the conclusion of chapter 2.

Implications for Managers

Internal Resource Allocation

What do the studies reveal about strategic response and dominant patterns of internal resource allocation during the contraction process? Predictably, managers acted to enhance technical rationality or utilize more efficiently available corporate resources. Low-productivity plants were closed, surplus workers were laid off, and major long-range planning programs were undertaken. Capital expenditures were deferred and inventory control sys-

185

tems were instigated. All three firms switched to the last-in, first-out (LIFO) method of inventory accounting in order to be able to rapidly correct for the impact of inflating costs.[1] Stringent financial control systems were also instigated to monitor operating budgets, working capital levels, and debt accrual. In the Boise and Avco cases, major creditors and stockholders forced financial controls on management in order to protect loans and limit risk exposure, as losses threatened liquidity.

Simultaneously, managers acted to enhance the level of organizational rationality by reorganizing executive-level management (changing personnel) and restructuring the firm. In all three firms decision making was recentralized in response to the contraction process. Planning, budgeting, and strategy formulation activities were controlled and carefully monitored by executives at the corporate headquarters level. Boise and Avco have retained their more centralized decision structures. Zenith's second attempt to diversify, however, led to a third restructuring effort that decentralized decision making among new product-line division heads. It is noteworthy that in each case reorganization and restructuring followed intense criticism of management by outsiders, including directors, major shareholders, creditors, the investment community, and the press. Nevertheless, in all cases management responded to increasing environmental uncertainty and forced divestiture by adapting structure to new circumstances within a relatively short period of time.

Given the widely held view that highly diversified firms operating in international markets have the most rational structure for maintaining growth and ensuring stability, the retreat from foreign markets and the patterns of divestiture described in the corporate studies could not have been easily predicted. Regardless of the differing 1967 diversification levels, the contraction process resulted in less diversification and a return to the basic industries in which management was most experienced. Although Zenith attempted to correct declining revenues with diversification into international markets by acquiring Swiss watch operations, the firm was forced to retreat from its new-product markets because of cash-flow and debt-management problems. Clearly, diversification did not automatically solve growth problems nor define appropriate strategy during the contraction process.

In all cases, cash flow and debt management dictated a short-term turnaround outlook and considerably reduced decision flexibility and discretionary behavior among executives. Managers were forced to sell off profitable corporate divisions and subsidiaries in order to keep their firms viable. Divestiture strategies were governed more by the need to cut losses than by rational plans to divest low-productivity operations or redeploy resources toward more profitable investments. Fighting to maintain domestic market share and profit margins, the then less-diversified and smaller-sized firms drew back from higher-risk foreign markets. During the contraction period, even if managers had wanted to extend foreign operations, they were restrained from doing so by creditors and shareholders who pressed for stabilization within the domestic framework. With recovery, however, management at all three firms began to consider foreign markets once again.

Other responses included reductions in research and development budgets. Zenith cut out basic research altogether, increasing its reliance on partnerships with past rivals for the development of new products. It is more difficult to assess the long-term impact of cutbacks at the other two firms. Avco's basic reliance on government-funded research for its manufacturing operations kept management from having to ravage basic research budgets. Boise's competitors remain considerably more research-intensive than Boise, which may mean trouble for new-product and process innovation in the future.

Capital expenditure budgets were reduced at all three firms while revenues were contracting. Previous diversification allowed managers at Boise and Avco to curtail operations in their more capital- and labor-intensive businesses, although, as mentioned above, cash-flow problems forced divestiture of the most profitable businesses as well. At Avco, not only did capital expenditures decline, but the firm moved away from capital- and labor-intensive manufacturing businesses toward insurance and consumer finance activities, which by 1978 generated more than half of total revenues. Managers at Boise continually referred to their long-term strategy of withdrawal from labor-intensive production processes. The movement away from capital- and labor-intensive businesses should reduce costs for the firms in question; over the long-term, however, the curtailment of capital expenditures could render the firms less competitive. It is difficult to assess how long it will take Zenith, Boise, and Avco to recover fully from contraction-related cutbacks in capital and research and devlopment budgets. On the whole, it appears that firms experiencing contraction for a prolonged period can regain profitability and even shareholder confidence, but production capability, technological stance, and market position may be severely eroded for much longer periods of time.

Patterns of internal resource allocation highlighted the basic conflict between management, creditor, and shareholder interests that occurs when growth is temporarily halted. Creditor interests prevailed. Managers relinquished a considerable degree of control over corporate strategy decisions. Shareholders lost dividends, saw the value of their shares decline, and the long-term growth potential of their investment diminish as earnings from profitable businesses were applied against debt rather than plowed back into operations. From the shareholder point of view, Boise's and Avco's early growth through acquisition strategies produced no real value (other than short-term gains in stock prices) and led to expensive damage suits on behalf of disgruntled shareholders from acquired firms or divested subsidiaries. The issuance of convertible debentures and other relatively imaginative securities to finance early acquisitions (in lieu of borrowing money or handing over cash) eventually depressed the value of Boise and Avco shares. After Boise's forced divestiture program, the value of outstanding shares increasingly became a function of management's ability to influence public policies regarding public lands. Each of the corporate studies indicate that debt-management problems inhibit not only market value but overall decision flexibility, the ability to diversify, penetrate foreign markets, and carry out research and development activities during and after a contraction episode.

In a very real sense, the firms described in the corporate studies both contributed to and suffered from the trend toward slower economic growth. Zenith, Boise, and Avco lost competitive strength in the marketplace and were left more dependent on government subsidies, regulation, or contracts than before the contraction episodes. In all three cases, a short-term perspective and defensive mode characterized internal managerial responses. Although internal structure was adapted to new strategy, the studies suggest that the long-term ability of the corporation (the preeminently adaptive organizational form) to adjust to curtailed revenues is diminished in a highly interdependent environment. The evidence also suggests that internal morale and turnover problems hampered adjustment. Although there is not enough evidence to speculate about whether or not the degree of political rationality increased or decreased with the contraction threat, intense politicking did surround resource allocation decisions during the divestiture phase at all three firms studied. Resource allocation decisions were predictably governed by efficiency as opposed to equity criteria.

The Demand for Government Intervention

How did the decline in government fortunes affect the demand for government intervention in the marketplace? Clearly, in the face of declining corporate revenues, executive-level managers attempted to increase their control over their firms' external environment. The ability to influence government officials to safeguard corporate interests became central to recovery efforts. For the most part, corporate interests, and in the broader sense a profitable industrial sector, were identified with a strong national economy. Managers at Zenith were involved in a ten-year effort to persuade the government to intervene on behalf of the consumer electronics industry to restrict imports. After divesting nonforest product businesses, Boise undertook a major campaign to influence Forest Service cutting and land-use policies in an effort to reassert control over its major source of supply. The thrust of Boise's extensive lobbying effort was for increased governmental intervention insofar as it is thought to enlarge the Forest Service's historical role of managing natural resources to include responsibility for protecting the forest products industry and the jobs it creates. At Avco, management became involved in lobbying efforts to rationalize the government contracting process so that the defense and aerospace firms involved in research and development for government-sponsored projects could more readily plan for their own operations.

Despite the free-market rhetoric that characterized annual reports and public statements during the period under study, corporate officials at Zenith, Boise, and Avco consistently sought government aid in various forms. This ambivalence illustrates three basic and contradictory assumptions prevalent in the business community. The first assumption is that free markets, despite the externalities imposed on third parties, are preferable to government intervention in the marketplace. The second is that government is *responsible* for providing social overhead capital and for managing the economy in a manner that will provide favorable conditions for business growth and stability. The third assumption is that managers are *responsible* for shaping the government policies and regulations that affect the businesses they manage.

The corollary of these assumptions is that business should be able to externalize some of the costs of economic decline to the government or the public at large. Consumers are asked to bear the higher cost of goods protected by tariffs and quotas. Shareholders are asked to accept a lower rate of return on their investment. Taxpayers are asked to pick up the tab for indirect subsidies, secured loans, extended unemployment insurance, and retraining programs for laid-off workers. And tax laws protect future corporate profits from the statutory level of taxation in direct proportion to the size of actual losses.

Although chief executives at Zenith, Boise, and Avco publicly argued for free markets, they also bitterly complained about the government's inability to keep the economy on a growth trajectory. Their failure to anticipate and correct for changing market conditions, financial overextension, and unprofitable investment decisions was not caused but only exacerbated by the slow-growth economy (inflation, high interest rates, foreign competition, and changing national priorities). In addition, their ability to shape government policy was constrained by the activities of competing interest groups and the complexities of economic interdependence.

Dependence on Exchange Relationships

How do corporate executives handle their dependence on exchange relationships during the contraction process? The corporate studies support the conclusions of sociologist Tom Burns who has persuasively argued that the totality of circumstances (economic, political, sociological, and technological) external to the corporation have a more powerful effect on its growth and survival than do factors that are internal, more visible, and more susceptible to understanding and some form of control or controlled response. The ascendance of the impact of these external forces on the behavior of the firm comes during a period when the economic web of interdependence among interest groups in our society is rapidly increasing in scope and complexity. According to Burns,

> We have reached a fundamentally different situation from that obtaining when piecemeal change could be made in social, economic, or political institutions and organizations, as and when it seemed best, and when organizational policies could be changed, discarded, or created without much regard being paid to the social fabric of which they formed a part. Decisions, planning, and action in science, educational, economic, and social affairs, no less than in corporations, must take cognizance of an ever-increasing span of considerations if they are to be effective and if they are not to produce as many adverse effects as profitable ones.[2]

This interdependence, intensified by the new players who seek to broaden participation in the economic maximization game, restricts corporate strategy alternatives. Interest groups with goals and demands counter to business interests can now force a hearing of those views in the courts if they do not receive satisfaction in the public policymaking process. The intrusion of new players into the traditional business-government economic policymaking relationship represents a transformation of that relationship. To the extent that the new players inhibit rather than encourage compromise based on mutual need for stability and economic growth, they represent a fundamental change. Because the new players have the power to force the decision process from the offices of government officials and corporate executives into the courts, their mere presence significantly curtails the ability of corporate managers to reduce environmental uncertainty via their exchange relationship with government. The result is an increasingly antagonistic, litigious, and therefore costly external environment for the firm.

The corporate studies indicate an increased need for the firm to rationalize its exchange relationships with creditors, shareholders, competitors, consumers, and regulators during the contraction process. They also indicate reduced ability to control those relationships. The extent to which

litigation or the threat of litigation constrained corporate decision flexibility
was an unexpected finding. Suits brought by shareholder, consumer and
environmental activist groups undoubtedly had a lasting impact on managers at Boise and Avco. Neither management group is likely to treat the land
development business or consumer advocacy groups in quite the same manner again. There is little question that litigation exacerbated the loss of control experienced by corporate managers during the various contraction
episodes. Activist suits tended to make past managerial strategies and decisions appear not only ill-conceived by frequently illegal. Boise's chief executive now defines his role as one of balancing divergent claims against corporate resources. Boise's experience with contraction clearly sensitized executive-level management to the potential impact of outside claimants.

Zenith also suffered negative effects from the consumer movement during a period when management was under fire from every direction. The increasing interdependence of competing interests involved in the imports
debate forced Zenith into the courts to protect its own interests when the exchange relationship with government failed to produce favorable results.
The interests of government officials were divided between those carrying
the free-trade banner and those supporting Zenith's protectionist position.
In all three cases however, the firms' exchange relationships with government regulators became increasingly complex and eventually more antagonistic in tenor. In each instance, management attitudes toward regulators
during the contraction process became increasingly defensive, suggesting
that managers felt themselves to be losing rather than gaining ground in
terms of their ability to influence government officials. This diminished
ability to influence may indicate that the transformation process described
by Schumpeter and later by Heilbroner, where privileges of the business
class decline as the industrial sector loses centrality in the economy, is
underway.

The Vocabulary of Decline

Another issue raised during the preparation of the corporate studies is the
extent to which the descriptive vocabulary of corporate decline retains
assumptions of the neoclassical growth synthesis. This is important
because, as Robert K. Merton (1967) has pointed out, our conceptual language tends to fix our perceptions, and, derivatively, our thoughts and
behavior.[3]

In reviewing the materials related to the twenty-one-firm population
that experienced absolute contraction during the 1967–1977 period, the
refusal of corporate spokesmen to publicly acknowledge impending crisis
and their vigor in maintaining a deceptively optimistic stance was notable.
Failure to adopt corporate outlooks to guide decision processes reflective of

changing cultural values and the changing economy was frequent. The tendency to discuss macroeconomic conditions and corporate contraction episodes in terms of restoration to a previous state of normality or the status quo was common. In addition, the descriptive vocabulary of decline is not only negative but imprecise, beginning with the term *decline* itself. (Appendix C presents a listing of code words and phrases for economic decline and the contraction process extracted from the corporate annual reports of the twenty-one-firm population that experienced contraction during the 1967–1977 period.)

The above observations suggest that we lack positive cultural sanctions to encourage clear thinking about the implications or ramifications of declining rates of growth. If the status quo is in fact fundamentally changing in response to the conjoined and simultaneous impact of slower economic growth, increasing economic interdependence, and the ethos of entitlement, it would seem that our current descriptive vocabulary inhibits rather than enhances our ability to cope with such change. The need to adapt effectively to a less abundant American dream demands the ability to reevaluate the premises of our dominant value system. The discussion of decline-related issues clearly would be aided by the development of a more precise and less negative descriptive vocabulary. Specifically, we need to be able to discuss economic units that contract in size but remain viable, as well as the contraction process itself, free from the constraints of a value-laden vocabulary that assumes contraction, steady state, or slow-growth conditions to be deviant cases.

Implications for Policy

There are three major industrial policy alternatives in the United States today. The first is the preservation of the present form of managerial capitalism with its emphasis on growth through merger, nonprice competition among the few, indirect subsidy, and government protection meted out in response to political clout. The second is further movement along the road to democratic socialism, as envisioned by Schumpeter, where economic planning and the pattern of investment in the economy reflect a stronger interventionist role for government. The third choice is a shift toward a more decentralized industrial structure composed of smaller, export-competitive economic units brought about through the breakup of large corporations, restriction on mergers and some forms of nonprice competition, and perhaps even some form of worker control over the investment process. As Marris and Mueller (1980) have pointed out, the choice is not obvious and cannot be left to the evolutionary process of managerial capitalism on the grounds that whatever organizational and industrial structure emerges must be assumed to be the most efficient simply because it is the one process "selected." The choice must reflect an understanding of the corporation and of its actual modes of competition. Those who support a given scenario are entitled to their preference, but they are almost certainly wrong to claim that a particular approach is the most productive or efficient. In any case, efficiency will depend to an increasing degree upon the *fit* between domestic policy and the evolving world economy.[4]

In defining the most appropriate role for government in creating a favorable environment for business in the next decade, conservative proposals for national industrial policy differ little from the national policies promulgated during the last decade. With the locus of investment decision making firmly within the private sector, the three firms considered survived and recovered (at least for the moment) from their bouts with contracting revenues. They survived, however, as weaker competitors, with their near-term strategies constrained by the exacting demands of debt management. Market forces that theoretically would have encouraged the less-competitive corporate entities to phase out production or transfer resources to more profitable investments were mitigated by creditor and management interests and the reliance on political clout to restabilize environmental conditions. Avco was able to transfer some military production to civilian goods, but the efficiency of that strategy was severely curtailed by debt-management considerations that forced selloffs and closures in a less than rational pattern, given the firm's long-term outlook. The extent to which Avco, Boise, and Zenith were forced into the courts as a final decision arena contributed to the loss of managerial control over recovery strategies.

Tax subsidies and credits helped all three firms to survive during the most difficult periods, and Zenith was able to garner additional consideration under trade readjustment provisions of the Trade Expansion Act. Conservative proposals aimed at increasing tax subsidies and credits would no doubt further aid contracting firms, but such firms are rarely in a position to fund capital expenditures, so that liberalized depreciation schedules, for example, would be of limited value. The question also arises as to whether it is in the national interest to grant tax subsidies indiscriminately to firms that are unprofitable regardless of causal factors. If tax subsidies and credits are not large enough to fund the transfer of corporate resources to high-productivity operations, then they will act to slow disinvestment and in effect contribute to slower economic growth.

In the Zenith study, tax subsidies and credits eased the transition to offshore sourcing. When market conditions changed, they also helped ease the firm back into a disastrous extension of production capacity aimed at markets in which Zenith was losing its competitive edge. The inordinate pressure of foreign competition may argue against the representativeness of the Zenith case, but if approximately 10 percent of major American corporations suffer from absolute contraction during periods of slow economic growth, as did Zenith, then we have to ask whether the laissez faire attitude embodied in conservative proposals may actually work to hinder overall economic efficiency. Reliance on the search for the highest rate of return simply may not be sufficient to revitalize firms or to phase out those suffering from prolonged episodes of contraction.

Liberal and Conservative approaches to national industrial policy share an overriding concern for economic growth. Liberal approaches, however, go on to outline some level of government control over the capital formation and deployment process in order to achieve alterations in traditional patterns of investment. The concern is for the velocity and the rationality of capital mobility rather than the overall level of investment in the economy. Liberal approaches generally seek to restructure the American economy by phasing out its least-productive elements with a minimum deflection of economic resources to aid that transition. Liberals envision an industrial policy that is capable of setting up criteria against which claims for government aid and subsidies can be measured, as opposed to the current dominance of entrenched and politically powerful interests. Such a policy may have guided decision makers at Zenith into moving their considerable resources into new businesses. It certainly would have cut short the firm's costly legal battles. An industrial policy that would provide incentives for transition would very likely decrease reliance on the courts as the final arbiter in the marketplace. No doubt such changes would increase economic efficiency throughout the economy given its highly interdependent nature.

Although the difficulties involved in developing a national policy designed to encourage investment in high-growth potential markets should not be underestimated, government-based incentives for firms to move investment toward those markets would have benefited decision makers in all three firms. Incentives to encourage exports would strengthen the competitive capabilities of all three firms: Zenith with home entertainment products for western European markets; Boise with wood and paper products for Pacific Rim markets; and Avco with finance, insurance, and management services throughout the world. Avco's basic research and development capability could easily be directed toward domestic-growth markets such as energy development if appropriate incentives were in place. Such policies would, of course, require a major national commitment to change. Short of that commitment, targeted corporate tax cuts rather than across the board cuts would at least act to discourage firms from hanging on to low-productivity units because of the tax advantages that accrue with losses.

Approaches to national industrial policy that call for broad participation and the development of public support would also alter the patterns of response illustrated in the studies. Inclusion of the new players at the inception of the public policymaking process should act to reduce the level of disruption caused when their interests are excluded. If differences can be compromised outside the advisory legal system, the entire policymaking process becomes less costly. Without broad participation in what will inevitably be our major economic policy of the next decade, we cannot expect to maintain the public support needed to implement policies that will demand some sacrifice and result in changes in the status quo of an increasingly interdependent and politicized economy.

Radical approaches to a national industrial policy are more difficult to analyze in terms of the corporate studies. Radical approaches are in fact more accurately categorized as critiques than specific proposals. These critiques call for the democratization of the investment process and generally focus on the social fallout associated with conservative and liberal proposals for disinvestment. They maintain that the new players can effectively participate in the formulation of a national industrial policy, categorically denying the conservative position that the market would work if it were not for pressures brought to bear by marginal groups. They further maintain that government revitalization programs should be directed at workers rather than failing firms.

Proposals for the democratic control of economic decisions concerning investment, organization of the work place, plant location, technology, and employment strategy run contrary to the demands of technical rationality that governed managerial decisions at Zenith, Boise, and Avco during their contraction episodes. In each instance, managers acted to cut losses as quickly as possible as they lost decision discretion to creditors, shareholders, and the demands of the equity market. The studies indicate a great hesitancy on the part of corporate decision makers to allow any of the new players to make inroads on their decision-making prerogatives. It seems unlikely that they would have been able to cope with the inclusion of worker representatives in corporate decision processes, particularly if that involvement included demands for maintaining a firm of constant size with acceptable but nonaccelerating returns for the good of the community. Corporate managers are psychologically geared to and financially rewarded for growth and a specified return on investment. If the corporate studies are indicative, it would take strong public demands and the development of internal organizational incentives to sanction acceptance of worker involvement in corporate decisions.

The corporate contraction process is varied and complex, but the findings discussed in this book suggest that a clearer understanding of the process and the changing economic environment should be of benefit to corporate managers. The larger public policy issues also present considerable difficulties. Resolution of the fundamental question of whether or not the capital allocation process is best left unfettered (free to follow rate of return) and firmly within the private sector will present many problems given our historical commitment to free enterprise—or at least to the persuasive rhetoric of market ideology. For the second time in this century, economic decline is forcing us to reexamine the basic premises of our domestic economy in terms of our evolving national interests.

Notes

1. The switch from first-in, first-out (FIFO) to last-in, first-out (LIFO) formulas for inventory accounting deflates a firm's reported profits as the cost of goods sold is reported at the price of the last item added to inventory. This method substantially eliminates profits gained between the time inventory is originally purchased and when it is sold. LIFO accounting essentially corrects for inflation in favor of the firm.

2. Tom Burns, "On the Rationale of the Corporate System," *The Corporate Society,* ed. Robin Marris (New York: John Wiley and Sons, 1974), p. 42.

3. Robert K. Merton, *On Theoretical Sociology* (New York: Macmillan Co., The Free Press, 1967), p. 145.

4. Robin Marris and Dennis C. Mueller, "The Corporation, Competition, and the Invisible Hand," *Journal of Economic Literature* (March 1980):59.

Appendix A
Original Population

1967 *Fortune* Group Including 500 Industrials, 50 Merchandising Firms, and 50 Transporation Firms

ACF Industries
AMP
Abbott Laboratories
Abex
Addressograph-Multigraph
Admiral
Agway
Air Products and Chemicals
Air Reduction
Albertson's
Allegheny Ludlum Steel
Allied Chemical
Allied Mills
Allied Stores
Allied Supermarkets
Allis-Chalmers
Aluminum Co. of America
Amerada Petroleum
American Airlines
American Bakeries
American Biltrite Rubber
American Can
American Chain and Cable
American Commercial Lines
American Cyanamid
American Enka
American Export Industries
American Home Products
American Machine and Foundry
American Metal Climax
American Motors
American Optical
American Petrofina
American President Lines
American Radiator and Std Sanitary
American Smelting and Refining
American Sugar

American Tobacco
Ampex
Amphenol
Amsted Industries
Anaconda
Anchor Hocking Glass
Anheuser-Busch
Archer Daniels Midland
Areden Mayfair
Armco Steel
Armour
Armstrong Cork
Armstrong Rubber
Arvin Industries
Ashland Oil and Refining
Associated Dry Goods
Associated Transport
Atchison, Topeka and Sante Fe Ry
Atlantic Coast Line RR
Atlantic Richfield
Automatic Retailers of America
Avco
Avon Products

B.V.D.
Babcock and Wilcox
Bangor Punta Alegre Sugar
Beatrice Foods
Beunit
Becton, Dickinson
Beech Aircraft
Beech Nut Life Savers
Bell and Howell
Bemis
Bendix
Bethlehem Steel
Black and Decker Manufacturing

Blaw Knox
Bliss (E.W.)
Blue Bell
Boeing
Boise Cascade
Borden
Borg-Warner
Borman Food Stores
Braniff International
Bristol Myers
Brown
Brown Shoe
Brunswick
Bucyrus Erie
Budd
Burlington Industries
Burroughs

C F and I Steel
Cabot
California Packing
Calumet and Hecla
Campbell Soup
Campbell Taggart Assoc Bakeries
Canada Dry
Cannon Mills
Canteen
Carborundum
Carnation
Carpenter Steel
Carrier
Case (J.I.)
Castle and Cooke
Caterpillar Tractor
Ceco
Celanese
Central Soya
Cerro
Certain-teed Products
Cessna Aircraft
Champion Spark Plug
Chemetron
Chesapeake and Ohio Ry
Chesebrough Pond's
Chicago Bridge and Iron
Chicago, Burl and Quincy RR
Chicago, Mil, St Paul and Pac RR

Chicago and North Western Ry
Chicago Pneumatic Tool
Chicago, Rock Island and Pac RR
Chrysler
Cincinnati Milling Machine
Cities Service
City Stores
Clark Equipment
Clark Oil and Refining
Cluett, Peabody
Coastal States Gas Producing
Coca Cola
Colgate Palmolive
Collins and Aikman
Collins Radio
Colonial Stores
Colt Industries
Commonwealth Oil Refining
Cone Mills
Consolidated Cigar
Cons Electronics Industries
Consolidated Freightways
Container Corp. of America
Continental Airlines
Continental Baking
Continental Can
Continental Oil
Control Data
Cook Coffee
Cooper Industries
Corn Products
Corning Glass Works
Cotton Producers Association
Cowles Communications
Crane
Crowell, Collier and Macmillan
Crown Cork and Seal
Crown Zellerbach
Crucible Steel
Cudahy
Cummins Engine
Curtis Publishing
Curtiss-Wright
Culter-Hammer
Cyclops

Dan River Mills
Dana

Dean Foods
Deere
Delta Air Lines
Di Giorgio
Diamond Alkali
Diamond International
Donnelley (R.R.) and Sons
Douglas Aircraft
Dow Chemical
Dresser Industries
Du Pont (E.I.) de Nemours

Eagle-Picher Industries
Eastern Air Lines
Eastern Gas and Fuel Associates
Eastman Kodak
Eaton Yale and Towne
Electric Storage Battery
Eltra
Emerson Electric
Emhart
Endicott Johnson
Englehard Industries
Erie-Lackawanna RR
Essex Wire
Ethyl
Evans Products
Ex-Cell-O

FMC
Fairchild Camera and Instrument
Fairchild Hiller
Fairmont Foods
Falstaff Brewing
Farmers Union Central Exch
Farmland Industries
Federal Mogul
Federal Pacific Electric
Federated Department Stores
Fibreboard
Fieldcrest Mills
Firestone Tire and Rubber
Flintkote
Food Fair Stores
Food Giant Markets
Ford Motor
Foremost Dairies
Foster Wheller

Freeport Sulphur
Fruehauf

Gamble-Skogmo
Gardner-Denver
General American Transportation
General Aniline and Film
General Baking
General Cable
General Dynamics
General Electric
General Foods
General Mills
General Motors
General Precision Equipment
General Telephone and Electronics
General Tire and Rubber
Genesco
Georgia Pacific
Gerber Products
Gillette
Gimbel Brothers
Glidden
Goodrich (B.F.)
Goodyear Tire and Rubber
Grace (W.R.)
Grand Union
Granite City Steel
Grant (W.T.)
Great Atlantic and Pacific Tea
Great Northern Ry
Green Giant
Greyhound
Grinnell
Grolier
Grumman Aircraft Engineering
Gulf Oil
Gulf and Western Industries

Hammermill Paper
Handy and Harman
Hanna Mining
Harbison-Walker Refractories
Harnischfeger
Harris Intertype
Harsco
Hart Schaffner and Marx
Heinz (H.J.)

Hercules
Hershey Chocolate
Hess Oil and Chemical
Heublein
Hewlett-Packard
Hobart Manufacturing
Hoerner Waldorf
Honeywell
Hooker Chemical
Hoover
Hoover Ball and Bearing
Hormel (Geo. A.)
Houdaille Industries
Howmet
Hunt Foods and Industries
Hupp
Hygrade Food Products

I T E Circuit Breaker
Ideal Cement
Illinois Central Industries
Indian Head
Ingersoll-Rand
Inland Container
Inland Steel
Interchemical
Interco
Interlake Steel
International Business Machines
International Harvester
International Milling
International Minerals and Chemical
International Packers
International Paper
International Silver
International Tel and Tel
Interstate Bakeries
Interstate Department Stores
Iowa Beef Packers
Island Creek Coal

Jewel Companies
Johns-Manville
Johnson and Johnson
Jonathan Logan
Jones and Laughlin Steel
Joy Manufacturing

Kaiser Aluminum and Chemical
Kaiser Industries
Kaiser Steel
Kayser-Roth
Keebler
Kellogg
Kellwood
Kelsy-Hayes
Kendall
Kennecott Copper
Kern County Land
Kerr McGee
Keystone Steel and Wire
Kidde (Walter)
Kimberly Clark
Koerhring
Koppers
Kresege (S.S.)
Kroger

Land O'Lakes Creameries
Lear Siegler
Leaseway Transportation
Lever Brothers
Libbey-Owens-Ford Glass
Libby, McNeil and Libby
Liggett and Myers Tobacco
Lilly (Eli)
Ling Temco Vought
Link Belt
Lipton (Thomas J.)
Litton Industries
Lockheed Aircraft
Lone Star Cement
Lorillard (P.)
Louisville and Nashville RR
Lowenstein (M.) and Sons
Lucky Stores
Lukens Steel

Mack Trucks
Macy (R.H.)
Magnavox
Mallory (P.R.)
Marathon Oil
Maremont
Marshall Field

Martin Marietta
Matson Navigation
May Department Stores
Mayer (Oscar)
Maytag
McCall
McDonnell
McGraw-Edison
McGraw-Hill
McLean Industries
McLouth Steel
Mead
Mead Johnson
Merck
Midland-Ross
Miles Laboratories
Minnesota Mining and Mfg
Missouri Pacific RR
Mobil Oil
Mohasco Industries
Monsanto
Montgomery Ward
Moore and McCormack
Morrell (John)
Morton International
Motorola
Murphy (G.C.)
Murphy Oil

National Airlines
National Biscuit
National Can
National Cash Register
National Dairy Products
National Distillers and Chemical
National Gypsum
National Lead
National Steel
National Tea
Needham Packing
New York Central RR
N.Y., N.H. and Hartford RR
New York Times
Newberry (J.J.)
Newport News Shipbuilding
Norfolk and Western Ry
North American Aviation

Northern Pacific Ry
Northrop
Northwest Airlines
Norton

Ogden
Olin Mathieson Chemical
Olivetti Underwood
Otis Elevator
Outboard Marine
Owens-Corning Fiberglas

Pabst Brewing
Pacific Car and Foundry
Pacific Intermountain Express
Pacolet Industries
Pan American World Airways
Parke-Davis
Parker-Hannifin
Peabody Coal
Penney (J.C.)
Pennsalt Chemicals
Pennsylvania RR
PepsiCo
Pet
Pfizer (Chas.)
Phelps Dodge
Philadelphia and Reading
Philip Morris
Phillips Petroleum
Phillips Van Heusen
Pillsbury
Pittsburgh Plate Glass
Polaroid
Porter (H.K.)
Potlatch Forests
Procter and Gamble
Pullman
Purex

Quaker Oats

Radio Corp of America
Ralston Purina
Rapid-American
Rath Packing
Rayonier

Raytheon
Reading
Red Owl Stores
Reichhold Chemicals
Republic Steel
Revere Copper and Brass
Revlon
Rex Chainbelt
Rexall Drug and Chemical
Reynolds Metals
Reynolds (R.J.) Tobacco
Rheem Manufacturing
Rheingold
Richardson Merrell
Riegel Paper
Riegel Textile
Ritter Pfaudler
Roadway Express
Robertson (H.H.)
Rockwell Manufacturing
Rockwell Standard
Rohm and Haas
Rohr
Roper (Geo. D.)
Ruberoid
Ryan Aeronautical

SCM
Safeway Stores
St. Joseph Lead
St. Louis-San Francisco Ry
St. Regis Paper
Schenley Industries
Schering
Schlitz (Jos.) Brewing
Scott Paper
Scovill Manufacturing
Seaboard Air Line RR
Seagram (Joseph E.) and Sons
Sears, Roebuck
Sharon Steel
Shell Oil
Sheller-Globe
Sherwin-Williams
Signal Oil and Gas
Signode
Simmons

Sinclair Oil
Singer
Skelly Oil
Smith (A.O.)
Smith Kline and French Laboratories
Soo Line RR
Southern Pacific
Southern Ry
Southland
Spartans Industries
Sperry Rand
Spiegel
Sprague Electric
Springs Mills
Square D
Staley (A.E.) Manufacturing
Standard Brands
Standard Oil of California
Standard Oil (Ind.)
Standard Oil (N.J.)
Standard Oil (Ohio)
Standard Packaging
Standard Pressed Steel
Stanley Warner
Stanley Works
Stauffer Chemical
Sterling Drug
Stevens (J.P.)
Stewart-Warner
Stokely Van Camp
Stop and Shop
Studebaker
Sun Oil
Sunbeam
Sunray DX Oil
Supermarkets General
Swift

TRW
Tecumseh Products
Teledyne
Tenneco
Texaco
Texas Gulf Sulphur
Texas Instruments
Textron
Thiokol Chemical

Tidewater Oil
Time Inc.
Times Mirror
Timken Roller Bearing
Todd Shipywards
Trane
Trans World Airlines
Transcontinental Bus System

Union Camp
Union Carbide
Union Oil of California
Union Pacific RR
Union Tank Car
Uniroyal
United Airlines
United Aircraft
United Merchants and Mfrs
United Shoe Machinery
U.S. Gypsum
U.S. Industries
U.S. Lines
U.S. Pipe and Foundry
U.S. Plywood-Champion Papers
U.S. Shoe
U.S. Smelting Refining and Mining
U.S. Steel
Universal American
Upjohn

Varian Associates
Von's Grocery
Vornado
Vulcan Materials

Walgreen
Wallace-Murray

Walter (Jim)
Ward Foods
Warner Brothers
Warner-Lambert Pharmaceutical
Warner and Swasey
Warwick Electronics
West Point Pepperell
West Virginia Pulp and Paper
Western Air Lines
Western Electric
Western Publishing
Westinghouse Air Brake
Westinghouse Electric
Weyerhaeuser
Wheeling Steel
Whirlpool
White Consolidated Industries
White Motor
Wickles
Wilson
Winn-Dixie Stores
Witco Chemical
Woodward Iron
Woolworth (F.W.)
Worthington
Wrigley (Wm.) Jr.

Xerox

Yellow Transit Freight Lines
Youngstown Sheet and Tube

Zayre
Zenith Radio

Appendix B
Research Population

Including 403 Industrials, 6 Nonindustrials, 37 Merchandising Firms, and 29 Transportation Firms

SIC	Firm Name
1000	Amax
	Asarco
	Hanna Mining
	Texasgulf
1211	Eastern Gas and Fuel
	St. Joe Minerals
1311	American Petrofina
	Getty Oil
	Natomas
	Occidental Petroleum
1499	Freeport Minerals
1600	McDermott (J.R.) and Co.
	Pullman
2000	General Foods
	General Mills
	Gerber Products
	Kellogg
	Norton Simon
	Pillsbury
	Quaker Oats
	Standard Brands
	Ward Foods
2010	Esmark
	General Host
	Greyhound
	Hormel
	Iowa Beef Processors
	Mayer (Oscar) and Co.

SIC	Firm Name
	Rath Packing
	United Brands
2020	Beatrice Foods
	Borden
	Fairmont Foods
	Kraft
	Pet
2030	Campbell Soup
	Castle and Cooke
	Del Monte
	Green Giant
	Heinz (H.J.)
	Stokley-Van Camp
2041	International Multifoods Corp.
2046	CPC International
	Staley (A.E.) Manufacturing Co.
2048	Ralston Purina
2050	American Bakeries
	Campbell Taggart
	Nabisco
2062	Amstar
2065	Hershey Foods
	Wrigley (Wm.) Jr.

SIC	Firm Name	SIC	Firm Name
2070	Archer-Daniels-Midland Central Soya Cook Industries	2510	Mohasco Simmons
2082	Anheuser-Busch Pabst Brewing Schlitz (Jo.) Brewing	2600	Brown Company Crown Zellerbach Hammermill Paper Co. International Paper Kimberly-Clark
2085	Heublein National Distillers and Chem. Seagram		Mead Potlach St. Regis Paper Scott Paper
2086	Coca Cola PepsiCo		Union Camp Westvaco
2111	American Brands Liggett Group Philip Morris Reynolds (R.J.) Inds.	2649	Bemis
		2650	Diamond International Federal Paper Board Fibreboard Inland Container
2200	Burlington Inds. Collins and Airman Cone Mills Dan River Fieldcrest Lowenstein (M.) and Sons Riegel Textile Springs Mills Stevens (J.P.) West Point-Pepperell	2700	Western Publishing
		2711	New York Times Co. Times Mirror
		2721	Cadence Industries Time, Inc.
2270	Armstrong Cork	2731	Grolier Macmillan McGraw-Hill
2300	Blue Bell Cluett, Peabody Hart, Schaffner and Marx Jonathan Logan Kellwood Phillips-Van Heusen U.S. Industries	2750	Donnelley (R.R.) and Sons
		2800	Allied Chemical American Cyanamid Celanese Diamond Shamrock Dow Chemical
2400	Boise Cascade Champion International Evans Products Georgia-Pacific Weyerhaeuser		Du Pont (E.I.) de Nemours Ethyl Corp. Grace (W.R.) and Co. Hercules Koppers

SIC	Firm Name	SIC	Firm Name
	Monsanto	2911	Amerada Hess
	Morton-Norwich Products		Ashland Oil
	Olin		Atlantic Richfield
	Pennwalt		Cities Service
	Rohm and Haas		Clark Oil and Refining
	Union Carbide		Continental Oil
			Exxon
2810	Air Products and Chemicals		Gulf Oil
	NL Industries		Kerr-McGee
	PPG Industries		Marathon Oil
	Stauffer Chemical		Mobil
			Murphy Oil
2820	Akzona		Phillips Petroleum
	Reichhold Chemicals		Shell Oil
			Standard Oil Co. (California)
2830	Abbott Laboratories		Standard Oil Co. (Indiana)
	American Home Products		Standard Oil Co. (Ohio)
	Lilly (Eli) and Co.		Sun
	Merck and Co.		Texaco
	Pfizer		Union Oil Co. of California
	Richardson-Merrell		Witco Chemical
	Schering-Plough		
	Smithkline Corp	2950	Certain-teed
	Squibb		Flintkote
	Sterling Drug		GAF
	Upjohn		Johns-Manville
	Warner-Lambert		National Gypsum
			Robertson (H.H.)
2841	Colgate-Palmolive		Walter (Jim)
	Procter and Gamble		
	Purex	3000	Armstrong Rubber
			Firestone Tire and Rubber
2844	Avon		General Tire and Rubber
	Bristol-Myers		Goodrich (B.F.)
	Chesebrough-Pond's		Goodyear Tire and Rubber
	Gillette		Uniroyal
	Revlon		
		3069	American Biltrite
2850	Insilco		
	SCM	3140	Brown Group
	Sherwin-Williams		Genesco
			Interco
2870	International Minerals and		U.S. Shoe
	Chemical		
		3210	Corning Glass
2890	Cabot		Libbey-Owens-Ford

SIC	Firm Name	SIC	Firm Name
3221	American Can Anchor Hocking Continental Group Crown Cork and Seal National Can Owens-Illinois		Reading Industries Revere Copper and Brass UOP
		3429	Stanley Works
3241	Ideal Basic Industries Lone Star Industries	3430	American Standard Wallace-Murray
3270	U.S. Gypsum	3449	Ceco Chicago Bridge and Iron Hoover Universal
3290	Norton Owens-Corning Fiberglass Vulcan	3494	Crane Keystone Cons. Industries
3310	Allegheny Ludlum Industries Armco Bethlehem Steel Bliss and Laughlin Industries Carpenter Technology Cyclops Inland Steel Interlake Kaiser Steel Lukens Steel Lykes McLouth Steel National Steel Porter (H.K.) Republic Steel Sharon Steel U.S. Steel Wheeling-Pittsburgh Steel	3498	Signode
		3510	Combustion Engineering Foster Wheeler Outboard Marine Roper
		3520	Allis-Chalmers Deere
		3531	Bucyrus-Erie Caterpillar Tractor Clark Equipment FMC Koehring
		3533	Dresser Industries
3330	Aluminum Co. of America Kaiser Aluminum and Chemical Kennecott Phelps Dodge Reynolds Metals	3536	Harnischfeger
		3540	Cincinnati Milacron Warner and Swasey
3341	Harsco	3550	Black and Decker Mfg Emhart Ex-Cell-O Joy Mfg Midland-Ross
3350	General Cable Handy and Harman		

SIC	Firm Name	SIC	Firm Name
3560	Cooper Industries Curtiss-Wright Gardner-Denver Hobart Ingersoll-Rand Parker-Hannifin Stewart-Warner	3651	RCA Zenith Radio
		3652	Warner Communications
3568	Wheelabrator-Frye	3662	Harris Motorola Raytheon
3570	Addressograph-Multigraph Burroughs Control Data Corp IBM NCR Xerox	3670	AMP Fairchild Camera and Instrument Texas Instruments Varian Associates
		3679	Ampex Lear Siegler Mallory (P.R.) and Co.
3573	Honeywell Sperry Rand	3711	American Motors Chrysler Ford Motors General Motors
3580	Carrier Corp Tecumseh Products Trane		
3600	Emerson Electric General Electric North American Philips Westinghouse Electric	3713	Cummins Engine International Harvester White Motor
3610	Bunker-Ramo Eltra Gould McGraw-Edison UV Industries	3714	Arvin Industries Bendix Borg-Warner Champion Spark Plug Dana Eagle-Picher Eaton Federal-Mogul Fruehauf Houdaille Industries Maremont Sheller-Globe Smith (A.O.) TRW Timken
3622	Cutler-Hammer Square D		
3630	Hoover Maytag Scovill Mfg Singer Sunbeam Whirlpool White Consolidated Industries	3720	Cessna Aircraft Lockheed

SIC	Firm Name
	Northrop
3721	Beech Aircraft
	Boeing
	McDonnell Douglas
3728	Rohr Industries
	United Aircraft Products
	United Techologies
3730	Bangor Punta
	General Dynamics
	Todd Shipyards
3740	AFC
	Amsted
	GATX
3760	Grumman
	Martin Marietta
	Rockwell International
	Thiokol
3823	Hewlett-Packard
3841	Becton, Dickinson and Co.
	Johnson and Johnson
	Sybron
3861	Bell and Howell
	Eastman Kodak
	Minnesota Mining and Manufacturing
	Polaroid
3940	AMF
	Brunswick
4011	Burlington Northern
	Chessie System
	IC Industries
	Norfolk and Western Ry
	St. Louis-San Francisco Ry
	Santa Fe Industries
	Seaboard Coast Line Industries

SIC	Firm Name
	Soo Line RR
	Southern Pacific
	Southern Ry
	Union Pacific
4210	Consolidated Freightways
	Leaseway Trans. Corp
	Roadway Express
	Yellow Freight System
4400	Moore McCormack Resources
	Tidewater
4511	American Airlines
	Braniff International
	Continental Air Lines
	Delta Air Lines
	Eastern Air Lines
	National Airlines
	Northwest Airlines
	Pan American World Airways
	Seaboard World Airlines
	Trans World Airlines
	UAL, Inc.
	Western Airlines
4811	American Tel and Tel
	General Tel and Electronics
4830	Cowles Communications
4922	Coastal States Gas
	El Paso
	Texas Gas Transmission
5050	Engelhard Minerals and Chem.
5093	Ogden
5120	Foremost-McKesson
5140	Di Giorgio
5199	Saxon Industries

SIC	Firm Name	SIC	Firm Name
5211	Matwickes		Stop and Shop
			Supermarkets General
5311	Allied Stores		Winn-Dixie Stores
	Arlen Realty and	5912	Walgreen
	Development		
	Assd Dry Goods	5990	ARA Services
	Federated Department Stores		
	Gamble-Skogmo	5992	Dart Industries
	Hess's		
	Macy (R.H.)	6145	Beneficial
	Marshall Field		Household Finance
	May Department Stores		
	Penney (J.C.)	6199	Loews
	Vornado		
	Zayre	7011	Holiday Inns
5331	K-Mart	7213	Sears Industries
	Murphy (G.C.)		
	Rapid-American	7394	DPF
	Woolworth (F.W.)		
		9997	Avco
5411	Albertson's		Colt Industries
	Allied Supermarkets		Gulf and Western Industries
	American Stores		IU International
	Borman's		International Tel and Tel
	Colonial Stores		Kaiser Industries
	First National Stores		Kidde (Walter)
	Food Fair		LTV
	Great Atlantic and Pacific		Litton
	Tea		Northwest Industries
	Jewel Cos		Signal Cos
	Kroger		Studebaker-Worthington
	Lucky Stores		Teledyne
	National Tea		Tenneco
	Safeway Stores		Textron
	Southland		Trans Union

Appendix C
Code Words for Decline

Descriptive Vocabulary from Annual Reports

Words
captive
consolidation
contain
contraction
cure
curtail
cutbacks
degradation
deterioration
deviation
diminution
discontinue
disengage
dissolved
erosion
erratic
marginal
modernize
realignment
rearrange
rebound
rebuild
recoup
recover
rectify
redeem
redeploy
redirection
redouble
reduce
reemploy
reevaluation
refine
regain

regenerate
regroup
reindustrialize
remedy
renew
renovate
reorganize
repair
reposition
restore
restructure
rethink
retire
retrench
return
revaluation
revamp
reverse
revive
stamina
streamline
tighten
transition
turnaround
uncertain
vulnerable

Phrases
curtailed employment
decreased commitment to
deemphasizing certain areas
diminished market
disengage from markets
divestiture and retrenchment
    program

economic losers
extended contraction
failed and has been dissolved
financial restructuring
handicap of the . . . division
hone down
infusion of new blood
leadership maturity
marginal units
mature product line
meager margins
more capable of acting aggressively
new American ideology of
  retrenchment
overextended
pattern of accommodation
period of consolidation and
  assimilation

price degradation
pruning process
recovery program
reemploy the proceeds
retarded growth
return to
revaluation of assets
reverse the downward trend
reverse the economic and social
  attitudes that have generated
  industrial decline
severe erosion of prices
stringent cost reduction
substantial rearrangement
test stamina of
weeding out unprofitable
  operations

Index

Index

About the Author

Katherine Hughes received the Ph.D. in business administration in 1979 from the University of Washington, where she was a recipient of the Newcomen Award in business history. Dr. Hughes now works as a free-lance writer. Her research interests include business strategy and industrial policy.